Virtual Models in Theatre, Art and Architecture

Performance + Design is a series of monographs and essay collections that explore understandings of performance design and scenography, examining the potential of the visual, spatial, material and environmental to shape performative encounters and to offer sites for imaginative exchange. This series focuses on design both for and as performance in a variety of contexts, including theatre, art installations, museum displays, mega-events, site-specific and community-based performance, street theatre, design of public space, festivals, protests and state-sanctioned spectacle.

Performance + Design takes as its starting point the growth of scenography and the expansion from theatre or stage design to a wider notion of scenography as a spatial practice. As such, it recognizes the recent accompanying interest from a number of converging scholarly disciplines (theatre, performance, art, architecture, design) and examines twenty-first-century practices of performance design in the context of debates about postdramatic theatre, aesthetic representation, visual and material culture, spectatorship, participation and co-authorship.

Series Editors

Stephen Di Benedetto, Joslin McKinney and Scott Palmer

Scenography Expanded: An Introduction to Contemporary Performance Design
Edited by Joslin McKinney and Scott Palmer
978-1-4742-4439-8

The Model as Performance: Staging Space in Theatre and Architecture
Thea Brejzek and Lawrence Wallen
978-1-350-09590-8

The History and Theory of Environmental Scenography: Second Edition
Arnold Aronson
978-1-4742-8396-0

Contemporary Scenography: Practices and Aesthetics in German Theatre, Arts and Design
Edited by Birgit Wiens
978-1-3500-6447-8

Sound Effect: The Theatre We Hear
Ross Brown
978-1-3500-4590-3

Immersion and Participation in Punchdrunk's Theatrical Worlds
Carina E. I. Westling
978-1-3501-0195-1

Consuming Scenography: The Shopping Mall as a Theatrical Experience
Nebojša Tabački
978-1-3501-1089-2

Digital Scenography: 30 Years of Experimentation and Innovation in Performance and Interactive Media
Néill O'Dwyer
978-1-3501-0731-1

Sites of Transformation: Applied and Socially Engaged Scenography in Rural Landscapes
Louise Ann Wilson
978-1-3501-9516-5

Contemporary Performance Lighting: Experience, Creativity and Meaning
Edited by Katherine Graham, Scott Palmer and Kelli Zezulka
978-1-3501-9516-5

Extended Reality Performance: Scenographic Practice in Virtual and Augmented Reality Technologies
Edited by Néill O'Dwyer, Joanne Scott and Gareth W. Young
978-1-3505-0743-2

Virtual Models in Theatre, Art and Architecture

Making Worlds

THEA BREJZEK AND LAWRENCE WALLEN

methuen | drama
LONDON • NEW YORK • OXFORD • NEW DELHI • SYDNEY

METHUEN DRAMA
Bloomsbury Publishing Plc, 50 Bedford Square, London, WC1B 3DP, UK
Bloomsbury Publishing Inc, 1385 Broadway, New York, NY 10018, USA
Bloomsbury Publishing Ireland, 29 Earlsfort Terrace, Dublin 2, D02 AY28, Ireland

BLOOMSBURY, METHUEN DRAMA and the Methuen Drama logo are trademarks of Bloomsbury Publishing Plc

First published in Great Britain 2026

Series design: Burge Agency
Cover image: 60th International Art Exhibition – La Biennale di Venezia
Yael Bartana: Light To The Nations – Generation Ship, 2024
3D Model. Installation View.
Courtesy the Artist and LAS Art Foundation
Photo: Andrea Rossetti

A catalogue record for this book is available from the British Library.

Library of Congress Cataloging-in-Publication Data

Names: Brejzek, Thea author | Wallen, Lawrence author
Title: Virtual models in theatre, art and architecture : making worlds / Thea Brejzek and Lawrence Wallen. Other titles: Performance + design
Description: London ; New York : Methuen Drama, 2026. | Series: Performance + design | Includes bibliographical references and index.
Identifiers: LCCN 2025007738 | ISBN 9781350449800 hardback | ISBN 9781350449848 paperback | ISBN 9781350449817 epub | ISBN 9781350449824 pdf
Subjects: LCSH: Technology and the arts | Virtual reality–Philosophy
Classification: LCC NX180.T4 B74 2026 | DDC 701/.05--dc23/eng/20250519
LC record available at https://lccn.loc.gov/2025007738

Series: Performance and Design

Typeset by Deanta Global Publishing Services, Chennai, India

For product safety related questions contact productsafety@bloomsbury.com.

To find out more about our authors and books visit www.bloomsbury.com and sign up for our newsletters.

Dedicated to

Emer. Prof Dr Wolfgang Greisenegger,

University of Vienna

Contents

Figures

Acknowledgements

Thank you for your support; Morehshin Allahyari, Arisa@teamLab, Arnold Aronson, Yael Bartana, Gerhard Blechinger, Caspar Maria, Jane Collins, Darat al Funun, Char Davies, Cristina D'Alessandro, Silvia De Toffoli, Stephen di Benedetto, Mark Dudgeon, Greg@Bernard Tschumi Architects, Hamidah, Helmut, IFA Stuttgart, Isabella@Forensic Architecture, Jiang@LuYang Studio, Kelly@Oxman, Brigitte Marschall, Julie Martin, Joslin McKinney, Marina Merli, Wolfgang Muench, Haytham Nawar, Scott Palmer, Published by, Rashad, Andrea Rossetti, Hans Peter Schwarz, Jeffrey Shaw, Socìetas Raffaello Sanzio, Tanya@immersence, Teddy@Studio Olafur, Ursula, University of Technology Sydney, Apichatpong Weerasethakul, Ella Wilson, Diana Wood Conroy and Yoko@Dumbtype.

Introduction

The border between the virtual and the real has become increasingly porous and fragmented, with virtual models being made *real* and real objects being made *virtual* in an ongoing mirroring and entanglement between virtual and physical artefacts. Defined as a digital representation of an object, idea, concept or theory that oscillates between representations and/or constructions of past, present and future, it is argued that the virtual model has its own reality and *locus*. Following exploratively the groundbreaking works of artists who use the virtual model to propose counterpositions to dominant anthropocentric narratives of control, gender, race, nation and identity, this project unfolds the territory of the virtual model in the expanded practices of theatre, art and architecture, emphasizing its performative, epistemic and worldmaking capacity.[1] Posited as *dispositif*, the virtual model enables the articulation and transportation of propositions through fiction and science fiction through digital transformation and configuration, resulting in processes of re-territorializations, new imaginaries, utopias and dystopias.

The key discursive companions to this volume are Rosi Braidotti's writings (2017 and 2018), whose feminist critical transhumanist philosophy addresses defamiliarization as a tactical strategy resulting in reimaginations of social, cultural and political narratives that are traced in many of the artistic works discussed, and Gilles Deleuze and Felix Guattari with their project on nomadology (1987). Impulses come from the social and political sciences with Bruno Latour, especially in his new media and curatorial collaborations with curator Peter Weibel and relentless critique of the Cartesian body-mind split, Carlos Castoriadis' concept of the *social imaginary* and Greg Bird's investigations into the dispositif. Donna Haraway remains an influential figure in feminist artistic and theoretical discourse and is heard in the context of the virtual model in relationship to her work on the subversive capacity of science fiction, the cyborg and the significance of *other voices* and *other stories*. The artists' own voices and texts remain central, stemming from interviews and written formats that are paramount in this project, as is the need to contextualize their verbatim statements into the why's and how's regarding their engagement with the virtual model. Key case studies result from first-hand observation as audience members across the performing arts and as visitors to diverse biennales, international exhibitions, galleries and museums to sense curatorial trends and concerns and to *find* the works that reflect upon a culture tendentially willing to silence the other stories and the other voices, to evoke Donna Haraway. Additional sites of observation deepened our knowledge about works and artists through conversations, interviews and artists' websites, which gave context to specific works and documented whole bodies of work. Reviews, lectures, performances and other forms of communication were invaluable in forming a detailed, fluid and expandable archive. First-hand knowledge of the institutions introduced and some of the artists discussed was an additional impulse to gather thoughts and materials from research institutions such as the Centre for Art and Media Karlsruhe (ZKM) that foregrounds advocacy for the Digital Society, Extended Reality and the New Media Arts in research, production and exhibition. International festival and conference engagements offered collegial encounters and critical feedback, including the Prague Quadriennale for Performance Design and Space (PQ), Cairotronica, Ars Electronica and the Venice Biennale (Art, Architecture and Theatre).

The first chapter, 'On the virtual model', describes this project's site as a *thin sliver of the porous border separating the virtual and the real.* Arguing that the expanded practices of theatre, art and architecture are inherently immersive, interactive and worldmaking, this chapter proposes a definition of the virtual model as not only a digital representation of an object, idea, concept or theory but further defines it as *dispositif.* Its capacity to put forward counter positions that transgress existing social, cultural and political imaginaries is posited and contrasted with the role of fiction. The realm of fiction, introduced as the third realm between the real and the virtual, manifesting as science fiction scenarios in several works discussed, allows for other narratives and other voices to be devised (see Haraway 2019). The section 'Model, Doppelgänger and Digital Twins' reflects on differences and similarities between the physical and virtual model and proposes the authors' previously articulated concept of the *architectural doppelgänger* as a precursor to its twenty-first-century manifestation, the digital twin (DT). Constructed to comprehend phenomena in the physical world, digital twins can be described as real-time simulations of dynamic physical assets. The terms AI (artificial intelligence), ubiquitous computing and the Internet of Things (IoT) are briefly explained in the context of the central technologies used to construct digital twins and virtual models. Overall, digital infrastructure and the digital society develop in a close synergistic discourse where virtual models extend and communicate between the physical and virtual realms. Distinctions between the physical and virtual models, however, are not absolute, and it is posited that both exist and are produced on a continuum of modelling practices and methods.[1] Their epistemic and performative capacity in producing and communicating knowledge affirms their central role in the understanding of space. Their incomplete and necessarily fragmentary character and mirroring between material and immaterial realms opens the discussion to what Deleuze terms 'doing cartography' (Deleuze 2023: 231), referring to the work necessary to make visible the structure of the social apparatus. The cartography between the map and the territory, model and reality is explored through the performance and exhibition of the virtual model, which only ever represents a fragment in an infinite realm. Briefly outlining the works discussed in the following chapters, the fragmentary territory between the real and the virtual that these works sit on is outlined and, through Deleuze, the artistic propositions affirmed as processes of deterritorializations (see van Houtoum 2010: 377–8) resulting in reterritorializations, new imaginaries, utopias and dystopias. This first chapter aims to unfold this project's territory by focusing on demarcations, similarities and uncertainties between the virtual and the real as these relate to the realities of the expanded practices between theatre, art and architecture in the emergence of a digital society.

Chapter 2, titled 'Art, science and engineering – imagining the digital', introduces a pre-digital period of cultural production that pivotally underpins the artists introduced in Chapters 3 and 4. This chapter traces the resurgence of unique art and science collaborations during the 1960s and outlines the intertwined histories of the emergence of media art and propositional or radical architecture as counter-narratives to an existing social and architectural imaginary and the adoption of performative and ephemeral dimensions of the theatre.

Commencing with the collaboration between engineers from AT&T's research department, Bell Labs and New York visual artists, dancers and choreographers, composers and performance artists that led to the performance series *9 Evenings: Theatre and Engineering in 1966*, the wholly experimental character of the initiative, which involved artists such as John Cage, Lucinda Childs, Steve Paxton and Robert Rauschenberg, is explored. Articulate and ambitious in what they wanted to investigate, the artists were supported by Bell engineers who were provoked to design new or modify existing technologies outside the pragmatic constraints of commercial usefulness. At the same time, the artists fully exploited the capacities and expressive potentialities of technology and live performance at a time when the miniaturization of technology and computer-controlled cueing, developed among other technological innovations for *9 Evenings,* were very much at their beginning. Bell electrical engineer Billy Klüver, together with Rauschenberg, instrumental in the realization of *9 Evenings*, expressed the explicit aim for this singular initiative to act as the first step towards an organization dedicated to future collaborations between artists and engineers, realized with the forming of Experiments in Art and Technology (EAT) in 1966. Simultaneously, on the other side of the Atlantic, the emergence of utopic architecture, exemplified by the Italian Radicals, separated the act of building from the concept of architecture. In their utopic counterpositions to the ideals of functionality proclaimed by modernism, they put forward propositional and visionary concepts of the city as a machine and society as nomadic. Their collages, films, manifestos and exhibitions demonstrate the beginning of architecture's adoption of the performative and ephemeral dimensions of the theatre, art and media that remain applicable today. The chapter concludes with the research agency Forensic Architecture (FA)'s work and their use of virtual models to dispel dominant narratives and acts of political violence and genocide constructed and performed by state actors. Overall, this chapter draws an arc from the experimental use and expansion of digital technologies in live performance and, thus, a re-articulation of all theatrical elements to the ironic articulation of what architecture is and what future living might be and, finally, moving to the present, introduces the central use of the virtual model in political advocacy practice highlighting and emphasizing, as in the previous chapter, the capability of the virtual model to call out existing imaginaries and articulate counterpositions.

Chapter 3, 'Performing the virtual model in the material world', investigates the virtual model's performative dimensions and its potential to construct and deconstruct site, nation, gender, class and culture through close readings of selected works by four artists from Asia and the Middle East. Focusing on performative and mediated critiques of dominant political and cultural narratives, their articulations of possible other futures and positioned in blurred genres between performance, installation and exhibition, these artists are engaged with pressing cultural, social and environmental issues. They hold a critical position in reframing the use of technology in artistic contexts through their work with extended reality technologies (XR) and digital performance, installation, modelling, additive printing and video. As central technologies in their works, they carry and communicate new articulations of narrative, subject and society from the perspective of the *other*. It is posited that the virtual model as dispositif operates between the material and the immaterial body – in a mediatized environment as in the works of Japanese performance collective Dumb Type or entirely dematerialized as an ungendered avatar trapped in a virtual posthuman techno world in the works of LuYang. Morehshin Allyahari's reimaginations of Islamic mythology and cultural history and Yael Bartana's sci-fi reimaginations of Jewish mythology expand an artistic vocabulary that embraces the virtual body in the material world. Curator Çağla Ilk's question, 'Is abandoning the earth the ultimate consequence of the failure of humanity as a collective?' (*Thresholds* 2024: 24), articulates what Rosie Braidotti describes as the 'tactical method of defamiliarization, that is to say, disconnection of the subject from familiar and habitual patterns of identity' (Braidotti in Alemani 2022: 220). The artists and artist groups are contemporaries in deterritorializing the political imaginary as an artistic strategy from their respective conceptual perspectives and distinct aesthetics. In the works discussed in this chapter, humans and machines enter diverse and different, often symbiotic relationships, marred by interferences and uncertainties propelling the audience on journeys that are urgent and relentless, frequently overwhelming in their visual or acoustic elements, and overall, affording critical agency through the human-machine interface. Artists and artists groups create other spaces and other worlds through digital technologies from the threshold position of being *other* and act as observers of the contemporary; as collectors and translators of histories and stories, they imagine the future through the virtual model.

Chapter 4, titled 'Immersion, animism and technology', addresses virtuality as a methodological, dramaturgical and aesthetic strategy capable of depicting, expressing and communicating transformative processes, individual journeys and communal experiences from a posthumanist and postphenomenological standpoint, where technology, nature and culture interrelate and inspire rather than *other* one another. With a focus on perception, participation and interactivity, the artists' use of technology does not define their overall oeuvres but points to specific concepts and reasonings that lead to mechanistic and virtual configurations. In this, animism and techno-animism are a testament to that porous border between the virtual and the real that this project aims to articulate. In the highlighted work by Romeo Castellucci, *The Rite of Spring* (2014), mechanistic technology operates as a performative, deconstructive, scenographic actor, while digital technology acts as an immersive and animistic agent imbued with sentience. Immersion and techno-animism permeate the works of Icelandic artist and singer Björk through her symbiotic relationship with digital and virtual technologies in creating her fluid persona, whereas the Thai filmmaker Apichatpong Weerasethakul's scenic installations and projection performances oscillate between dreams and wakefulness utilizing and queering the vocabulary of virtual reality. Transformations between human and animal, animate and inanimate, are central to Björks's 'post-optimistic animism' (Björk in Molinari 2024), while Danish Icelandic visual artist Olafur Eliasson embraces virtual reality in a continuation of his aim to create atmospheres and enable individual experiences and journeys within a virtual world that allows for discovery and wonder. However, whereas Eliasson offers an open invitation into his skilfully researched and realized *friendly* virtual creations, Weerasethakul's biography, cultural beliefs and eclectic cinematic influences are shown to shape his approach to *nature-culture* as a single mysterious entity in continuous metamorphosis. To Weerasethakul, the seamless transformations that the virtual model offers are of a similar fluid quality as one's drifting thoughts in meditative practice or in that transitional state between wakefulness and sleep that psychology calls hypnagogia, in which intense sensory perceptions can be experienced. The roles of experience and memory in virtual environments and live performance are revealed at the intersection of physicality and virtuality. In this chapter, animism and techno-animism are shown to be ways to perform technology as a co-actor and co-producer of constructed worlds. Fluid personas and continuous transformations between human, nonhuman, animal and plant and the dissolution of a Cartesian subject-object split and the dogma of Euclidian geometry dissolve in these works, giving way to new perceptions and a critique of binary positions.

In the final chapter of this project, 'Researching the virtual', the artworks of several pioneering virtual reality artists from the 1990s are discussed, providing a foundational artistic context or grammar for future artists' engagement with VR. Thirty years later, opera projects augmented by XR in the 2010s were explored for their technical and dramaturgical innovation, establishing a similar context for future performances. Simultaneously, a typology and theoretical contextualization were developed, acknowledging XR's complexities, limitations and possibilities for theatre makers previously unfamiliar with the complexity of the parallel and competing narratives that the introduction of such technologies imposes. While tracing the development of twentieth-century exploration into the integration of interactive and virtual technologies into the live performance event through individuals and institutions, the question posed at the end of the chapter, 'Where do we go if we stop going to the theatre as a physical location?' remains virulent as the central provocation for the performing arts' new engagement with virtual technologies and their dissemination. The chapter outlines recent interdisciplinary labs situated in institutional research museum contexts and embedded in performing arts companies. For artists, access to emerging and state-of-the-art hardware and software through residency programmes and project-based collaborations is crucial to developing virtual components and their dialogical integration into live events. Introducing seminal institutions such as the Centre of Art and Media (ZKM) in Germany (since 1989) through several key works that emerged directly from artists associated with this institution outlines a foundational typology of artistic engagement with the virtual. Such investment continues into the twenty-first century through interdisciplinary XR labs that operate across theatre, art and architecture, exemplified by MIT's (Massachusetts Institute of Technology) Media Sense Lab and the Royal Opera House's Audience Lab, where new formats of the integration between the real and the virtual are explored and tested resulting in their presentation to the (participating) public. National and European-funded institutions aligned with European-wide performing art institutions are introduced, and their collaborative networking activities that bring together computer scientists, engineers, scenographers, dramaturgs, directors and performers as early steps in exploring digital and virtual technologies are outlined. Already leading to performances with international teams in several European state theatre companies, these long-term-funded initiatives aim to find new performance formats by integrating virtual technologies into the live event.

Through close readings of artists' works created in the 2020s and brief introductions of seminal prescient works from the 1960s and 1990s in performance, new media and utopic architecture, this project traces radical concepts, collaborations and practices. The urgency of re-imagining the political, social and cultural imaginaries through the virtual model as dispositif pervades the works discussed and affirms the power of creative thought across and between the disciplines of theatre, art and architecture.

Thea Brejzek and Lawrence Wallen, Venice/Sydney 2025

1

On the Virtual Model

The Site

This chapter lays out the site on which this project lies, a thin sliver of porous border between the virtual and the real. It argues for the fundamental immersive, interactive and worldmaking quality of expanded practices in art, architecture and theatre (performance). It puts forward a working definition of the virtual model as a digital representation of an object, idea, concept or theory that oscillates between representations and/or constructions of past, present and future. Posited in this chapter as *dispositif*, or critical instrument, the virtual model is able to reveal and uncover the power relations, hierarchies and dependencies of the algorithms that define the contemporary social imaginary as the set of rules that capitalist society lives by and regards as true. The capacity of the virtual model, as dispositif, to transcend anthropocentric and binary positions and to reimagine and create new imaginaries of difference and multiplicity is outlined. Brief entry points into the artists and artist collectives' artworks are collated, previewing the primary case studies discussed in detail in the following chapters. Critical posthumanist and feminist positions with recourse to Deleuze and Guattari's project on nomadology accompany and enrich this discussion. In charting the history of the virtual in Western thought, which has been primarily linked to its relationship with the real, this project further aligns the virtual model with the notion of the *doppelgänger* and the digital twin (DT) and concludes that the virtual possesses its own locus and its own reality. In the artistic practices discussed here, the virtual model is positioned as cosmopoietic and an instrument of inquiry into knowledge itself.

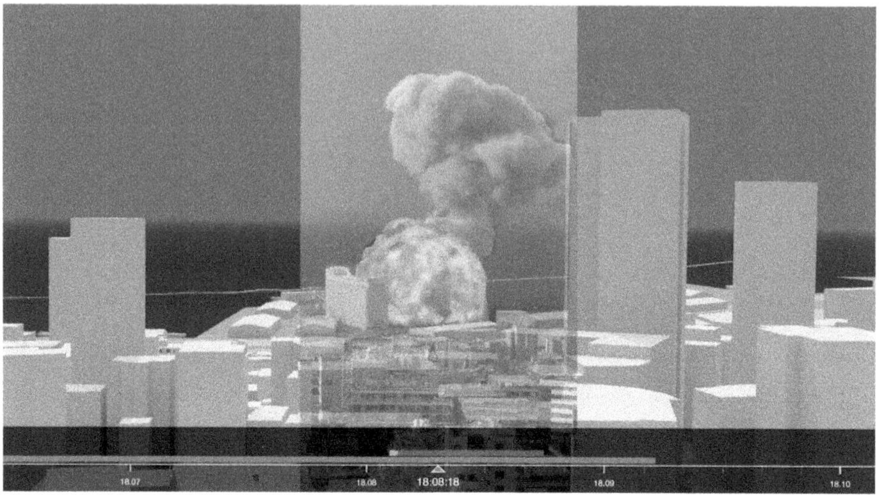

FIGURE 1.1 *Animation still from a virtual simulation of the Beirut Port Explosion 2020 produced by UK research agency Forensic Architects as part of an investigation by independent newspaper* Mada Masr *into the causes and aftermath of the explosion. Image © Forensic Architecture 2020.*

The virtual model – dispositif and critical instrument

The border between the virtual and the real has become increasingly porous and fragmented, with virtual models being made *real* and real objects being made *virtual* in an ongoing mirroring and entanglement between virtual and physical artefacts. It is on this porous and interstitial border, occupied by artistic production, where the focus of this project lies, acknowledging that art, architecture and theatre have always been immersive, interactive and inherently worldmaking in the myths, narratives and immaterial and ephemeral spaces that they reveal. The contemporary realities of theatre, architecture and art inhabit a territory where the border, the map and the territory are continually redrawn as objects take on dynamic qualities, where they fragment, double and multiply with an emphasis on the non-hierarchical relationality between the virtual and the real while continually co-producing reality, imagination and representation. In technical terms, the virtual model is understood as a networked, interactive and modifiable digital artefact stored as data within a computer environment representing an object, idea, behaviour or set of relations. The transition from physical to virtual models signifies a shift in how models are perceived and utilized. Building on François Lyotard's call for 'an energetic intensification of the theatre dispositive' (Lyotard 1976: 107) against dominant hierarchies and structures in its artistic and spatial organization, this project extends Pavis' concept of the theatre as dispositif (Pavis 2012) and scenography as dispositif (Wiens 2014 and 2019: 6) to the virtual model as dispositif. The virtual model occupies a critical site of negotiation between the real and the virtual. Not a closed system but rather a 'heterogenous ensemble' as Foucault describes the dispositif (1977), the virtual model as dispositif is positioned as the central disruptive and critical transmission instrument specialized in the conduction and critique of stimuli between the virtual, the real and, as is elaborated in the following, the imagined. In this, the definition and context of the virtual model in this project are less related to concepts and analyses of the reorganization of the institution or the system of theatre or the spatial reorganization of the (system of) scenography but are rather engaged with a re-articulation of the dispositif as a critical instrument or apparatus between the virtual and the real that can unpack and interrogate the structural conditions and power relations that lie beneath the digital platforms and data organizations that increasingly regulate all aspects of society in the twenty-first century. With this re-articulation of the dispositif in mind, the virtual model operates as a tool for critically investigating the social, political and cultural systems of inclusion and exclusion underlying today's data collections and algorithms. Largely invisible, these systems create and affirm dominant narratives that the virtual model as a networked, interactive and modifiable digital artefact is able to reveal, subvert and redirect. The virtual model as dispositif reflects the structural qualities of Michel Foucault's seminal definition,[1] especially in his recognition of the dispositif or apparatus as having 'a dominant strategic function' (Foucault 1977: 151–2), yet its emphasis in the artistic practices discussed in this project is directed towards the dissolution of that dominant narrative through and towards what the dispositif does. What the virtual model does is one of the primary questions posed, and Giorgio Agamben's expansion or *spelling out* of Foucault's term assists in an understanding of the dispositif or apparatus as an entity that exists in the present and can *action* 'literally anything that has in some way the capacity to capture orient, determine, intercept, model, control, or secure the gestures, behaviours, opinions, or discourses of living beings' (Agamben 2009: 14). Following Agamben yet shifting his definition of dispositif to a system or machine or instrument, Greg Bird writes that '*Dispositifs* disassemble and reassemble things, unfolding them and taking them apart *to* reconfigure and redistribute them' (Bird 2023: 01). Bird's definition is compelling for this project as the dispositif is understood as a performative entity that actively does, undoes and does differently. In looking at virtual models in the works by artists and artist collectives, we deduce that they do exactly that: as active instruments, the virtual models (dispositifs) reveal systems of relations, organizations and hierarchies and propose alternatives, dystopian and utopian scenarios, possible futures and persistent desires through the utilization of a third realm beside the real and the virtual, namely that of fiction. Fiction, that which is imagined but not constructed, shares the immateriality of the virtual and the familiarity of the real and comprises one of the 'lines' of the dispositif or 'apparatus' that, so Deleuze, makes up its composition, 'lines, each having a different nature [. . .] each line is broken and subject to *changes in direction*, bifurcating and forked and subject to *drifting*' (2023: 231). However, as Bird notes in his discussion on the definition and operations of the dispositif, 'Agamben, Deleuze, Foucault, as well as Michael Hardt and Antonio Negri, all point out that dispositifs produce their subjects' (2018: 36). The virtual model thus carries the disturbing narratives of power relations and binaries of exploitation and extraction. It redirects these to artistic processes of transgressing borders, nations, genders and identities towards a territory of differences and multiplicities. With an acute understanding of the impending ecological catastrophe the Earth is hurtling towards, the multidisciplinary artists and collectives represented here devise new visions and imaginaries of the political, social and cultural. Çağla Ilk, in her curatorial text accompanying the German contribution to the 2024 Venice Biennale, *Thresholds,* describes its title as 'the awakening of a longing for the deterritorialization of the political imaginary' (Thresholds 2024: 24). It is avail, in the context of artistic inquiries into the political imaginary introduced in this project (see Chapters 3 and 4), to briefly relate Ilk's intricate phrasing to Deleuze and Guattari's political-philosophical thinking where the term describes foremost a movement or 'line of flight' (Deleuze and Guattari 1987), a freeing or escape from repressive systems. Not an end unto itself, however, the term

> deterritorialization is not necessarily spatial and, what is more, emphasizes instead the freeing of a certain fixation and order and nomadically moving *towards* different (territorial) reconfigurations and assemblages and new reterritorializations, provoking or inducing new deterritorializing desires.
>
> (HOUTUM 2010: 377–8)

The possibility for transformation lies in the movement away and the (nomadic) movement towards. Deterritorialization, as desire and process, thus, relates to the freeing or rethinking of political and social imaginaries from conventional notions of nation-state, gender and identity and a movement towards new ways of thinking and representing the future.

The imaginary and the imagined

The social imaginary, so philosopher and political theorist Cornelius Castoriadis (1984), does not present as an ahistorical fixture but is instead redefined by each historical epoch and each society as a set of values and institutions through which individuals imagine the whole (of a nation, for instance) to be real. Thus, the social imaginary is not individual, so Castoriadis further, 'This element, which endows the functionality of each institutional system with its specific orientation, which overdetermines the choice and connections of symbolic networks' (Castoriadis as cited in Thompson 1982: 664). In this, the imaginary takes on agency, manifesting as it examines, proposes and visualizes 'how society constitutes itself' (Browne and Diehl 2019: 394). It is characterized by a collective vision of a future where the imagined may become actualized. Re-examining the social imaginary, Canadian philosopher Charles Taylor argues that 'The social imaginary is not a set of ideas; rather it is what enables, through making sense of, the practices of a society' (Taylor 2002: 91), and he explains in a later passage, 'I speak of *imaginary* because I'm talking about the way ordinary people "imagine" their social surroundings, and this is often not expressed in theoretical terms; it is carried in images, stories, and legends' (Taylor 2002: 106). Thus, the process of the deterritorialization (and re-territorialization) of the social, cultural and political imaginary as a creative and symbolic act through and with the virtual model emphasizes the model's cosmopoietic (worldmaking) and epistemological capacity. Contending not only the virtual model's epistemic capacity but also critically questioning knowledge itself as a system of power, Rosi Braidotti's differentiation between the speed of the de-territorialization of 'minor subjects of knowledge', namely queer, feminist, diasporic, poor and de-colonial, and what she calls the 'majority-driven epistemic acceleration' (Braidotti 2018: 45) is significant. Not only is the speed of these *minor* subjects much slower, but their investment is into a different kind of knowledge, a posthuman, rhizomatic knowledge grounded in the experience of being or *becoming* the *minor*. Braidotti argues further that, following on from feminists' perspectives as outsiders in the 1970s,

> an imaginary political alliance with the 'techno-teratological' world (Braidotti 2002) of the science fiction horror genre [has been formed]. This alliance promotes the insurrection of women – as the others of 'Man' – and other 'others', like LBGT+, non-whites (postcolonial, black, Jewish, Indigenous and native subjects) and non-humans (animals, insects, plants, trees, viruses, fungi, bacteria and technological automata).
>
> (BRAIDOTTI 2018: 39)

They, 'the others of "Man"', human and non-humans, are the authors and subjects of the diverse configurations and manifestations of the virtual in the multidisciplinary works of the artists and artist collectives discussed in this project. By extension from Braidotti's theoretical framing of the posthuman critical humanities, this project observes and follows the artistic processes of the deterritorialization of an existing social and political imaginary towards an imaginary of difference. The imaginary, or fiction, thought of as the third realm next to the real and the virtual, manifests in many different formats, stories and concepts. Having introduced the term socio-technical imaginaries with Sang-Hyun Kim, social scientist Jasanoff reiterates the truism that 'Technological innovation often follows on the heels of science fiction' (Jasanoff 2015a: 11) as the crucial opening statement in her seminal 2015 book and concludes that

> Science fiction [. . .] is a repository of sociotechnical imaginaries, visions that integrate futures of growing knowledge and technological mastery with normative assessments of what such futures could and should mean for present-day societies. Utopic or dystopic, these fictions underscore the self-evident truth that technologically enabled futures are also value-laden futures.
>
> (JASANOFF 2015B: 352)

Jasanoff integrates the imagined within a (science) fiction framework into the concept of socio-technical imaginaries, allowing for the term to transcend its pragmatic technical focus and become a useful instrument in collectively projecting and imagining the sliver of *other territories* that the artists in this monograph inhabit. Donna Haraway writes in her foreword to writer Ursula Le Guin's iconic essay, *The Carrier Bag Theory of Fiction* from 1988, 'It matters what stories we tell to tell other stories with; it matters what concepts we think to think other concepts with' (Le Guin 2019: 10).

It also matters who tells the other stories, the other concepts and why. The *other* stories and *other* concepts discussed in this project emerge from artists' deep discontent with dominant stories, with contemporary dominant concepts of hierarchies and binaries between humankind, nature and technology. Their artistic responses – through processes of deterritorialization, re-territorialization and the creation of new epistemes, form the centre of the following chapters, of which a kind of distillation is offered here, highlighting the criticality and diversity of their approaches. Discontent in the case of filmmaker Achitpong Weerasethakul with the destruction of the natural environment of his native Thailand and Southeast Asia more widely, discontent also with the straight stories, the daylight stories, discontent that results in the choice for slowness and stillness in his films and to portray and hold on to the liminal state between waking and dreaming, this fragile and singularly erotic state. Rage in the case of iconoclastic stage director and scenographer Romeo Castellucci and Societas Raffaele Sanzio (SRS), rage against the civilizational camouflage of primal fears and desires, rage that results in the pictorial and scenic dissection of myths, norms and conventions on his stage where animism operates as a shocking presence and symbol or metaphor for technology. Animistic configurations return in Weerasethakul's moody Southeast Asian landscapes and narratives of Shamans and transformations of humans and animals into mythical creatures and in Icelandic singer Björk's relentless digital transformation between humans and nonhumans, humans and wilderness, on stage and in virtual reality (VR). Rage also in the case of feminist, multidisciplinary artist Morehshin Allahyari, rage against Western colonialism and its digital products, rage against the destruction of cultural artefacts by ISIS, rage that results in her virtual re-imagining of the mythical figures of the Middle East and their queering. Fields of difference open in Israeli artist Yael Bartana's installation, *Light to the Nations* (2024), where new histories are imagined, citing and transgressing contested aesthetics and tropes of nationalism and patriotism, suprematism and colonialism and presented as uncertainties in the face of a global catastrophe. In this, Bartana's work belongs to what critical posthumanist Rosi Braidotti calls the 'imaginary political alliance' (Braidotti 2018: 39) of the *other of man* in the territory of science fiction as a propositional vehicle for possible futures. Several of the digital counterpositions to nation, state, identity, race and gender by artists in this project play out through science fiction scenarios as these offer the articulation of other worlds, other societies and other desires in the form of utopian and dystopian imaginaries. Presenting a radical post-gender, post-identity and post-nation state digital techno world, LuYang shows the solitary subject immersed and trapped in a reimagined dystopian Buddhist wheel of reincarnation. In the relentless transformation that the *saṃsāra* (the cyclic realm of endless rebirth) demands, humans, nonhumans and animals are unified in their eternal struggle, personified by the artists' ungendered avatar called DOKU. In contrast to the virtual, mythological journeys of LuYang's protagonist, the singer and artist Björk's virtual world is determined by subjectivity, a sense of darkness and melancholy juxtaposed with an optimism she finds in the landscapes of her native Iceland. Björk's world transcends the dominant anthropocentric imaginary and the artist reimagines herself through continuous digital transformations as a creature living in symbiosis with all living and non-living entities. In a live context, digital masks created from moulds of Björk's face with human-animal features communicate different personas of the singer throughout the performance. Björk's private world of transformation and optimism is inspired by Timothy Morton's object-oriented ontology that sees hope where the collapse of the Earth has already occurred (see Morton 2013). Visual artist Olafur Eliasson also derives a certain smiling optimism from Morton's writings, and his reimaginations counteract, as do Björk's, the dominant imaginary built on the subordination of all nonhuman entities. Eliasson's installations, public artworks, sculptures and VR projects all aim to expand the senses and the visitors' or users' exploration of worlds and spaces of geometry and physics. Equally, the research agency Forensic Architecture (FA) utilizes digital technologies to visualize what is not or only partially visible. FA occupies a site in our discussion that harnesses the format of the exhibition to reveal, counteract and evidence acts of state violence in current political imaginaries worldwide by employing digital architectural tools and methods. In their exhibition, *The Nebelivka Hypothesis* (2023), discussed in this project, FA proposes, supported by scientific archaeological findings and subsequent visualizations, the deterritorialization of dominant ideologies of urbanism and power and the re-territorialization of notions of urban settlements as uncentred and devoid of hierarchies. Overall and significantly, the new imaginaries in the works discussed articulate cultural transformation and exchange and possible futures based on multiplicity in a clear departure from binary and anthropocentric positions. The virtual model as dispositif is evident in the works discussed, that is to say, its potential to reveal and uncover power structures of data and organization that shape social and political lives and affirm dominant imaginaries. As a critical instrument, the virtual model's capacity to transgress, reimagine and redirect these is equally evident. In this, the virtual model enables the presentation of artistic positions of a cosmopoiesis allowing for multiple forms of knowledge and difference.

Model, Doppelgänger and the digital twin

The model's primary task, so American model theorist Marx W. Wartofsky is to enable the future, a concept that aligns with the future-focused characteristics of the imaginary. For Wartofsky, models are purposeful 'modes of action' and 'experimental probes' that require being 'performed' rather than merely devised (Wartofsky 1979: 148). As teleological instruments, they are creative rather than conservative and can communicate far beyond what they comprise. In parallel, German philosopher and model theorist Herbert Stachowiak argues in his classic study *Basic Model Theory* that the model is necessarily an abstract representation of reality (Stachowiak 1973: 131–3), with the primary intention of reducing complexity and focusing on specific attributes to be visualized and analysed to comprehend distinct phenomena. The authors' earlier monograph, *The Model as Performance: Staging Space in Theatre and Architecture* (Wallen and Brejzek 2018), investigated the history and development of the physical scale model from a performative paradigm that explored its cosmopoietic (worldmaking) and epistemic qualities to analyse what the physical model is and what the model does from a scenographic perspective. The physical model was argued as an active agent in the making of space within an extended art, theatre and architectural discourse, defying its historical second-order status of merely facilitating the construction of future *real* buildings or *real* set designs. In this second volume, reflection is undertaken on the similarities and differences between physical and virtual models. It is focused on the entanglement between the two, evoking arguments around the authors' previously articulated notions and identification of the autonomous model, the spatial *doppelgänger* (double), and the fragment and its inference of the whole while making the role of fiction explicit as the third realm. From a scenographic perspective, in coalescence with a performative paradigm that looks upon cultural practice as performance, all models are considered cosmopoietic and worldmaking in that they are components of or create entire worlds.

Overall, what, in the previous volume, was proposed was a new reading of the model's history as a history of agency and performativity that frees the model from its professional pragmatism yet acknowledges its central importance in the design process. What the model constitutes is less relevant than its performative and discursive potential in architectural, theatrical and curatorial practice, as well as in conceptualizing and leading design studios where virtual and analogue models continue to be a core discursive component. A close look at the model reveals instances across the disciplines that move beyond the purely iterative and representational towards gaining an autonomous status. These models constitute their end-product, and no further artefact is produced from them. Such models are highly referential and lie outside the traditional taxonomy of the iterative and the representative model. In rethinking and expanding the model's traditional taxonomy, these models are defined as autonomous. The autonomous model is neither process-driven nor representational but conceptualized as an independent object. Such a model is framed in this project against the background of expanded practices, along with the disciplines' desires to reflect on conventional modes of making and representation. In the history of theatre, this development is linked to the interpretive mirroring of the world in the confined space of the stage. From a scenographic perspective, virtual models, like their physical counterparts, have worldmaking capacities that are central to creating entire virtual worlds and are active agents in the making of space. The journey towards theoretical engagement with the model began with an exploration and definition of the architectural *doppelgänger*: spaces and architectures in the physical realm that exist more than once and are positioned opposite each other, a category of spaces that are both *the same* and *other*. The idea of the model as a double or doppelgänger is analogous to its literary twin first defined by nineteenth-century German linguists, the brothers Grimm, in their 1838 *German Dictionary* as a double walker, or somebody who is thought to show himself at the same time at two different locations.

Here, *double subject* and *architectural doppelgänger* are inscribed into the mythical, romantic *double walker*. Further reflection on the concept of the architectural doppelgänger suggests that the dual space is rarely an identical twin but is more likely to present itself across several sites in diverse scales and temporalities. Critical is that the initial definition of the architectural doppelgänger is extended beyond the physical realm into the realms of the virtual and the fictional. Two parameters characterize the architectural doppelgänger. The first is theatricality, in that only the spectator gaze can confirm the doppelgänger's existence and establish a heightened presence or perception. The second comprises the emergence of a performative space between site, spectator and doppelgänger(s) for the duration of the gaze, or 'performance'. Notably, the doppelgänger might not exclusively be a mythical twin, existing side by side or as a ghosting presence or digital twin but instead could have been constructed in another place at another time in a different medium. Such an *architectural doppelgänger* performance may no longer be a simultaneous or unified occurrence but somewhat fragmented and defined by complex relationships between the two subjects, including original and copy, idea and representation, model and object.

As a prime example of an architectural doppelgänger, the Parthenon Gallery in Bernard Tschumi's Acropolis Museum (2009) and the building of the Acropolis (447 BCE) exemplify a *double* relationship. The museum comprises three volumes or floors in a layered system of ground, middle and upper glass pavilions. The ground floor floats above the archaeological ruins that predate the museum, and the centre comprises the primary archaeological galleries. Both are aligned with the existing urban grid. By contrast, the glass pavilion at the top of the museum is shifted and brought into exact parallel alignment with the Parthenon. At this level, the exhibit is a 1:1 scale model of the Parthenon's frieze, lowered to eye height. The floor-to-ceiling windows facilitate a direct visual connection between the 1:1 model and the Parthenon, allowing both to be viewed simultaneously. Fragments of the remaining frieze and darkened

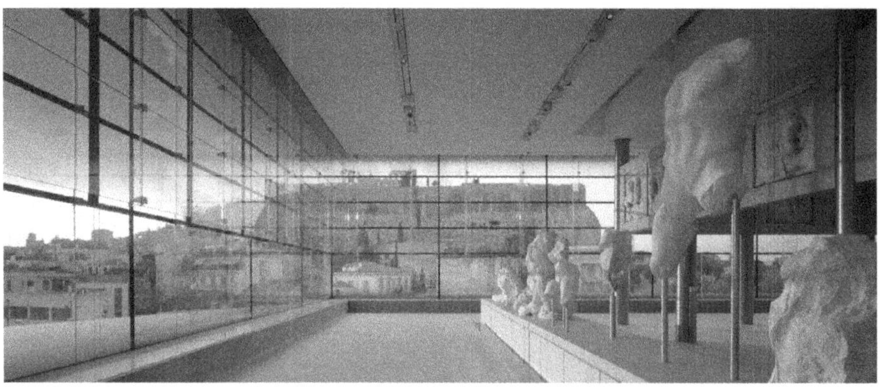

FIGURE 1.2 *The Parthenon Gallery in Bernard Tschumi's* Acropolis Museum *from 2009. Photo: © Christian Richters. Courtesy of Bernard Tschumi Architects.*

plaster copies that indicate the form and positioning of the original pieces are mounted on large reflective stainless-steel pipes, symbolizing the columns of the Parthenon. Visually and metaphorically interrupting this axis of history are the remnants of the Dionysian Theatre, located between the Acropolis and the Acropolis Museum. The museum appears behind the theatre's proscenium (stage), revealing itself as the other self: the site that houses both the actual and missing relics that justify its existence. The museum that is looked at and, in turn, observes the Parthenon is a double space, a space that speaks, in negation, of the potentiality of a whole while presenting as a full-scale model, both autonomous of and referential to the Parthenon (Brejzek and Wallen 2022). In the twenty-first century, the doppelgänger, rather than an exception, has become ubiquitous with the implementation of the digital large-scale digital twins. Digital Twins (DT) are a subset of virtual models in that all DTs are virtual models, but not all virtual models are DTs. The virtual model, as an intrinsic component of a DT, has the primary function of creating new knowledge and insights based on incomprehensible amounts of real-time and historical data, emphasizing their epistemic functions. As the essential functions of the virtual model, both within and beyond the fields of art, architecture and theatre, have significant and increasing correlations with their analogue counterpart, the digital twin also has a critical capacity. Defined as 'an executable virtual model of a physical thing or system' (Wright and Davidson 2020), the digital twin of a physical object requires 'a model of the object, an evolving set of data relating to the object, and a means of dynamically updating or adjusting the model in accordance with the data' (Wright and Davidson 2020). The primary difference between a virtual model and a digital twin is encapsulated in the term *executable*; thus, not all virtual models are digital twins, as many are non-executable; however, all digital twins can be classified as virtual models. Further, most non-executable virtual models have visual similarities to their analogue counterparts. In contrast, a digital twin may remain an abstract representation of a complex interactive system, retaining its primary and original function as a real-time digital simulation of a dynamic physical asset. Thus, digital twins are designed to mirror the physical world in the virtual world to understand certain phenomena, test and develop strategies for optimization and intervention.[2] Such developments have been facilitated by two critical advanced technologies: artificial intelligence (AI) for the analysis of data and the Internet of Things (IoT) for data collection. In its most general definition, artificial intelligence 'is a technology that enables computers and machines to simulate human learning, comprehension, problem-solving, decision making, creativity and autonomy' (Stryker and Kavlakoglu 2024). The Internet of Things (IoT) denotes 'a network of physical devices, vehicles, appliances, and other physical objects that are embedded with sensors, software, and network connectivity, allowing them to collect and share data' (IBM 2024).

Both technologies, AI and IoT, are foundational in expanding and interfacing virtual worlds while being critical in current and future scientific and artistic interventions in this realm. The rise of these technologies has rapidly expanded the possibility of nearly infinite virtual realms impacting and re-imagining the digital society. The establishment of the terminology and reality of the digital society in the late-twentieth century, enabled by the universal uptake of the internet, ubiquitous computing, AI and IoT, has been outlined within the *EU Digital Strategy* (2022–2030) and the Japanese government's 2017 term *Society 5.0*, which characterizes the Digital Society as 'a super-smart society [. . .] which envisions a transformation to a sustainable, inclusive socio-economic system enabled by digital technologies, including AI and robotics' (UNESCO 2021: 42). In parallel to the general uptake of digital tools, a string of conceptual terms and cultural keywords have entered common usage to make sense of and define the digital society; researchers from the Alexander von Humboldt Institute for Internet and Society in Berlin affirm the truism that 'Terminology defines Reality' (Katzenbach and Bächle 2019: 2) and classify relevant terms such as datafication, platformization and algorithmic governance, while actively acknowledging that the meaning of these terms is evolving rapidly. To address this issue, the Institute hosts a publicly accessible, continuously updated database of definitions for 'extending, opposing or updating the concepts, their premises or consequences' (Katzenbach and Bächle 2019), based on the understanding that the terminology of a fast-evolving digital society is constantly being re-evaluated and redefined by the media, policymakers and the public. Thus, digital infrastructures and the priorities of a digital society exploit each other in a continuous synergistic discourse, with virtual models crucially extending and communicating between the real and the virtual realms.

The map and the territory

However, the distinctions between physical and virtual models are not absolute; they represent different points on a continuum of modelling practices, each with strengths and limitations. Models serve a dual epistemic function: they produce knowledge through distinct modelling processes, and they communicate knowledge through their final form. Recognizing models' performative and epistemic dimensions allows for the appreciation and use of their full potential as tools for creating and understanding space. Models, whether physical or virtual, play a crucial role in shaping a critical understanding of the world, acting as both representations and agents of change or, in the case of the autonomous model, transcending the model's traditional representational function, collapsing the categories of original and copy or past and present. The model as object and idea is discussed here as an epistemic tool or instrument that consistently produces and communicates knowledge as concept and form progress and converge in the final product. Model-making and modelling processes comprise fundamental research practices to explore form, extend material properties or speculate on future developments and uses in the disciplines. But there is also another dimension to the model, linked to invention and imagination more than to the pragmatic needs of the scenographer and architect in that models are physical and conceptual instruments of the cosmopoietic act – they can create and comprise entire worlds. Alongside plans and drawings, models are principal instruments in the design and communication processes of theatre and architecture. Design models clarify and explain spatial configurations and relations, placing the building or set design in its scalar and topographical context. The positioning of artistic expanded practices in and between theatre, art and architecture at the border between the real and virtual allows for a discussion on the territories that they inhabit, the fragmentation (in that only ever a fragment of a virtual world can be shown) that is inferred and the material and immaterial spatial doubling that is inherent in the continuous mirroring between worlds. It is on this territory's porous border between material and immaterial worlds where our writings and case studies collide through theoretical proximity and diverse geographic and gender identities, clustered only momentarily within this monograph as a conduit to other worlds both created and yet to come. Foucault, so Deleuze,

> talked of lines of sedimentation but also lines of 'breakage' and of 'fracture.' Untangling these lines within a social apparatus [dispositif] is, in each case, like drawing up a map, doing cartography, surveying unknown landscapes, and this is what he calls 'working on the ground'. One has to position oneself on these lines themselves, these lines which do not make up the social apparatus but run through it and pull at it from North to South, from East to West, or diagonally.
>
> (DELEUZE 2023: 231)

Cartography, as a practice of orientation and disruption, was referred to by Polish American scientist and linguist Alfred Korzybski, who wrote that 'The map is not the territory it represents', arguing that in order for the map to be useful, it must have 'a similar structure to the territory' (Korzybski 1948: 33). He continues to say that if 'the map could ideally be correct, it would include, in a reduced scale, the map of the map; the map of the map of the map; and so on endlessly' (Korzybski 1948). Argentine writer Jorge Luis Borges' (1899–1986) 1946 short story *On Exactitude in Science* from 1946 echoes Korzybski's ideas yet fictionalizes the relationship between the map and the territory to the level of (tragic) absurdity. Borges proposes in a single-paragraph short story the fabrication of a perfect 1:1 map that 'is so detailed and precise that it becomes a perfect replica of the territory, with the result that it becomes useless for practical purposes because it replaces the very thing that it is intended to represent' (Mindrup 2022) thus rendering traditional cartography obsolete. Borges' provocation against the perceived exactitude of science between reality and its (virtual) representation parallels spatial and artistic practice, articulating the relationship between 'that which is' and 'that which is seen' as mediated through representation. On the border between the virtual and the real, the focus shifts to incomplete structures representing realities as fragments, striving for completeness yet denying it to the viewer. The fragment, derived from the verb 'to fracture', is seen as an active method of making sense of the world. A post-representational approach suggests that reality and representation, or the map and the territory, do not precede each other but are relationally co-produced, moving beyond Baudrillard's notion of simulacra, where the map precedes the territory and the hyperreal replaces the real. The relational co-production of map and territory, original and copy, model and reality infers that only ever a fragment of what is produced can be perceived. The virtual model realized, performed and exhibited on the fragment of a territory of the (near) infinite provides a case in which material elements or fragments infer a vast immaterial world that parallels fiction in its lack of materiality. As Deleuze argues, the possible and the virtual are not directly equitable because the virtual 'possesses a full reality by itself' (Deleuze 2014: 275) while 'the process undergone by the possible is [. . .] a "realization"' (Deleuze 2014). Nevertheless, the territory that this project demarcates comprises cultural interventions and interstitial borders embracing spatial elements of the physical, the virtual and the fictional in a continual play between the material and the immaterial. The occupation of the border between the virtual and the physical for artistic purposes is a mere sliver of a greater territory, designated as a cultural landscape for theatre art and utopic architecture to deploy concepts between the virtual, the physical and the possible. The fictional supposition of a fragment of the territory dedicated to the sources, concepts and artists of this project allows for selected material from biennales, theatres and museums referred to here as *sites* to be located within the confines of the project that use curatorial clustering to sharpen the notional framework, albeit with the inherent risk of exclusion. The fragment and the double are characteristics of the territory's topography and its virtual, worldmaking qualities by virtue that the fragment can hold the memory of and infer the whole and the double acts as a virtual reflection or shadow of the real. Cartography, the art of representing the physical through the abstract art of map making, assumes that objects are locational and fixed. However, the new territory is in constant flux, dynamically reconfiguring the parts or fragments of an ever-evolving interconnected realm. Comprising material and immaterial components, a digital map of this territory evolves as fast as the territory transitions while invariably and constantly retaining a memory of each operation.

In *The Mapping Journey Project* (2008–11) Moroccan French artist Bouchra Khalili (born 1975 in Casablanca) interrogates the map and the territory in a multi-screen projected video installation. The hands of migrants are seen as they draw their personal routes across the main Mediterranean migration routes and narrate their perilous journeys in pragmatic terms of '. . .from. . .to. . .back. . .to. . .onwards to. . .arrived at. . .left. . ..', etc. The diasporic movement of migrants across North Africa and Europe highlights the impenetrability of nation-state borders, and by simply documenting their journeys through storytelling and the redrawing of the territory into their map, cartography and political hegemony are revealed as controlling instruments. The installation opens a virtual world of possible other maps, routes, journeys and territories, supported by Khalili's parallel hanging of the related artwork, *Constellations* (2011), eight silk screens that translate the descriptions of the journeys into astronomical constellations and networks of stars. These stars carry the names of the cities of departure, transition and arrival, Annaba, Marseille, Milan . . . Each migrant journey, each fragment of desire, contains a material reality embedded with an immaterial memory while simultaneously inferring the forms and spaces for its completion, both material and otherwise. Khalili's maps or models are instruments that reveal hegemonic control with its implied technologies of surveillance and punishment. In the act of narrating the journey and drawing upon the maps, the refugee narrator draws one world and imagines another. The work seen as dispositif is tied to iteration, ideation and a continuous process of modelling and imaging, akin to how theatre assembles and portrays imagined worlds. The maps serve as a platform or stage for the creation of worlds. In this cosmopoetic act, the journey becomes a recollected world for the protagonist and evokes a desire for worldmaking in the audience that underpins the long history of making models in all their varying forms, and the seldom realized imagined promise.

The real and the virtual

While frameworks to understand and describe the virtual have evolved and shifted over the centuries and continue, in dialogue with technological innovations, to transcend static assignations and definitions, the discourse surrounding both terms and concepts is still primarily concerned with the relationship between the real and the virtual. In interrogating this history, Wolfgang Welsch claims that the virtual cannot be understood as a static and univocal concept but that a significant shift in its understanding has occurred since Aristoteles' 'first philosophy' of being, the *Metaphysics* (around 350 BCE), and his discussion of the distinction and relatedness between the *virtual*, the *actual* and the *potential* as linked to matter and time are useful (Welsch n.d.). This shift, so Welsch, has seen the 'virtual' departing from its origin as a dualistic ontological concept in Aristotelian thought towards diverse metaphysical positions by metaphysical idealist philosopher Gottfried Wilhelm Leibniz, by Immanuel Kant, a guiding intellectual force for the Enlightenment and by transcendental empiricist Deleuze who all see the virtual as belonging to cognition and epistemology. This transference presents a complex endeavour that moves from asking the question of what the nature of the virtual is (ontology) to interrogating its role in the production of knowledge through experience, the senses, and thought (epistemology). The consequence of such a shift towards cognitive and epistemological questions regarding the virtual implies an understanding of the virtual as a separate entity from the real. It allows for the virtual to possess a degree of autonomy from the real while, at the same time, both its relatedness is affirmed and its otherness defined (Welsch n.d.: 6). Looking back, however, the early history of the philosophical engagement with the virtual is closely linked to dualistic ontological frameworks, and its conceptual origin lies in Aristotle's concept of 'being' set out in Book VII (Z) of his *Metaphysics*. Here, Aristotle differentiates between the contrasting forces of *energeia* (actuality) and *dynamis* (potentiality) as the dual elements that comprise the virtual (being). He coined the term *energeia* to describe an innate possibility for change that any existing thing or material can have through motion (gr *kinesis*) or activity. *Energeia*, or reality, thus denotes the inherent capacity or power that is related to an existing 'thing'. By contrast, *dynamis* (potentiality) is not the 'real existing' thing but the capacity of something to transition into a different state towards a state of fulfilment (Aristotle, *Metaphysics*, Book 9, [1045b], [27]). Aristotle explains that

> the actuality resides in the thing produced; e.g. the act of building in the thing built, the act of weaving in the thing woven, and so on; and in general the motion resides in the thing moved. But where there is no other result besides the actualization, the actualization resides in the subject; e.g. seeing in the seer, and speculation in the speculator, and life in the soul.
>
> (ARISTOTLE, *METAPHYSICS*, BOOK 9, 1050A [22])

The terms *energeia* and *dynamis* thus cannot be defined separately but are ontologically dependent on each other, as something that acts and something that is acted upon, and that may not change but is different from before. Aristotle's position is supported by Thomas of Aquinas, who introduces the term 'virtual' for 'potential' in *Summa Theologica*, Question 76, Article 8, Objection 5. Aquinas' use of 'virtual' originates in the Latin *vir* (man) and *virtus* (virtue), thus both in the gendered, male and the concept of virtue. His concept of the virtual correlates with *dynamis* or 'potentiality' as it presents as a realm of (teleological) transformation. Aquinas' position is mentioned here as Deleuze influentially will again embrace the metaphysical dimension of the virtual. It is Leibniz, as empiricist and mathematician, who moves the historical project of the 'virtual' away from the limits of ontology (that which is real) and towards epistemology and the question of how we know what we know, thus affording a more active and dynamic view of the virtual as an inner drive towards actualization or, cognition. In a much-quoted passage, Leibniz suggests that our ideas and truths exist innately in us as 'inclinations, dispositions, tendencies or virtualities' (Leibniz as cited in Cottingham 1988: 63), thus linking the concept of the virtual explicitly to cognition and hence to epistemology. Innate, so Leibniz, is therefore solely the virtual cognition of certain ideas whose actualization occurs through perception. Leibniz's position is a significant departure from Aristotle's dualistic concept towards an intellectualization concerned with the workings of the production and acquisition of knowledge. Furthering the shift of the 'virtual' towards not only dynamism but also autonomy, Kant declares the location of the soul 'virtual' rather than 'spatial' (Kant 2014: A 25, § 19) and, as Welsch points out, articulates the 'virtual' not as an 'antecedent version of the real' as in the Aristotelian tradition but as its 'counterpoint' (Welsch 2024). In contrast to Aristotle, Kant's ontological dualistic system does not inscribe a sequential character or temporality to the virtual. For Kant, there is the real world on the one hand, and virtual 'thought objects', the so-called *Gedankendinge*, are understood to be virtual reality on the other. According to Kant, these thought objects are the soul, God and the world, entities with no corresponding objects in the real world (see Kant 2014: 492). Deleuze counters Kant's notion of ideas as unifying, totalizing and conditioning with the concept of the virtual field in that 'the virtual is actualized by differentiating itself in variable directions' (Smith 2009: 41). Deleuze *differentiates* the concept of the virtual towards a concept of multiplicities of both real and virtual elements while affirming the autonomy of the virtual and emphasizing its embeddedness in reality (see Bergson 1991 [1896] and Deleuze 1991 [1966]). Ansell-Pearson writes that 'for Bergson, it is the *part* that is virtual and the *whole* that is real (2005:1112). Deleuze affirms Bergson's notion of the virtual as 'opposed not to the real but to the actual' (Deleuze 1991: 272) and clearly distinguishes the virtual from the possible. He says

> The only danger in all this is that the virtual could be confused with the possible. The possible is opposed to the real; the process undergone by the possible is, therefore, a 'realization.' By contrast, the virtual is not opposed to the real; it possesses a full reality by itself. The process it undergoes is that of actualisation. It would be wrong to see only a verbal dispute here: it is a question of existence itself.
>
> (DELEUZE 2014: 275)

The oscillating exchange between the virtual and the actual (Deleuze 1989: 81, 108–9) occurs in the 'crystal image' in a simultaneity of time past and time present as, by example, in Deleuze's concept of the cinema image. The notion of time 'splitting', as he says, into past and present ('the virtual image of the past and the actual image of the present', Ansell-Pearson 2005: 1124) yet united in the image of the crystal, manifests in virtual reality environments that without exception are constructed from numerous 'planes' of temporalities. In a broader interpretation, one might look upon the virtual model as corresponding to Deleuze's crystal and posit that the crystal (image) holds within it the cosmopoietic act of blurring the real and the virtual in an intensity of temporalities – an act of worldmaking that remains forever unfinished and infinite. The virtual model's potential (virtual) transformations constitute a transgression of both conceptual and temporal aspects of making compared to the physical model. The model's past, present and future are inscribed in its programming and lie dormant until actualized. Each actualization remains stored in the model's memory, extant and unlike the physical model's material traces of making and remaking, the virtual model transforms seamlessly and without an outward trace. Worlds conceptualized and constructed virtually thus transcend the limitation of a fixed and singular locus by the virtual model's transformative and network capacity – virtual worlds can be authored, designed and shared across networks in real-time. In the virtual world, location, time and memory appear newly defined yet analogous to the cognitive processes of human memory that operate with the sequential operations of encoding, storage and retrieval or recall (Melton 1963). Historically, virtual worldbuilding as a teleological technique for effective encoding and successful recall occupies a central position in the mnemonic tradition of classical rhetoric concerned with 'artificial' or constructed memory rather than the 'natural' memory of everyday life. The oldest extant rhetorical treatise and mnemonic system, *Ad C. Herennium de ratione dicendi (Rhetorica ad Herennium*, Anon. 1954) from around 80 BCE demonstrates the importance of the *locus* (location) and sequential *loci* (plural of *locus*) for the encoding and retrieving of objects to be remembered. To this effect, the treatise describes in detail the construction of a world of architecturally distinct scenes that hold the items to be remembered. Bergson, on whose concepts of time and memory Deleuze's ontology of the virtual builds, points out the simultaneity of perception and memory: 'Step by step, as perception is created, the memory of it is projected beside it, as the shadow falls beside the body' (Bergson 1975: 157). In contrast to Bergson's conception of (natural) memory, the mnemonic memory of the orator is artificial. While also linked to perception originally, the orator adds to the constructed memory systems of spatial organization and recall. The unknown author of *Ad C. Herrenium*, wrongly thought to have been Cicero, distinguishes between natural and artificial memory. 'The natural memory is that which is embedded in our minds, born simultaneously with thought. The artificial memory is that memory which is strengthened by a kind of training and system of discipline' (*Ad C. Herrenium*, Anon. 1954: 207). The treatise systematically introduces the future orator to the mental operations necessary to master the art of memory. As in any mnemonic system, great emphasis is given to the sequential or chronological way in which memory items can be retrieved in the correct order. Precisely imagined backgrounds and scenes ('locis et imaginibus' *Ad C. Herrenium*, Anon. 1954: 208) in which the mnemonic objects or figures are placed are paramount to their successful recall. The treatise's instructions deliver a blueprint for a virtual model and the building of a virtual world by a single author for the distinct purpose of efficient memory and recall during the real-time event of a speech given. Backgrounds must be composed with a view for the entire scene to be remembered easily in its entirety and in detail. For this reason, the author recommends that each scene should be separated from the next one by 'approximately thirty feet' in their spatial sequencing and encourages his readers to create their own virtual backgrounds should they so wish (*Ad C. Herrenium*, Anon. 1954). Taken together, imagination and the virtual create a past that connects memories with the world. In her discussion of the real and the virtual in Bergson and Deleuze, Silvia Capodivacca points out that 'Like imagination, the virtual is also a producer of memories-images, whose degree of past contraction varies according to circumstances. Imagination and the virtual operate by images rather than concepts, by figures of time rather than through lines of reasoning' (Capodivacca 2022: 48). Constructed in time, memory images in a mnemonic system are sequenced into memory scenes, distinct from each other and based on perception as much as on imagination, reinforcing the fact that imagination and memory offer the raw material for the design of virtual worlds. The mnemotechnical techniques of the antique *ars memoriae* were revived by Renaissance scholar and orator Giulio Camillo. Set down in written form in Camillo's manuscript *L'Idea del Theatro* from 1550, and, according to sources of the time, built at half scale as an enterable wooden construction first in Venice, then in Paris, the *Theatro* operated both as a representative model of a theatre and as an autonomous model for the storage and production of knowledge through a performative act. The theatre aimed to represent all external and internal knowledge accessible to man through text and images. In the tradition of antique mnemonic systems such as *Ad C. Herrenium*, the *Theatro's* operation was based on linking images and words in specific locations within an overall physical environment, such as a room, a house or even an entire city. The orator placed the words and phrases to be remembered into exact locations, as well as choosing and delivering imagery that would evoke a specific term. During the mental operation of navigating the complete spatial narrative from object to object and between words and imagery, the speech in its totality would be retrieved from the loci. It could thus be remembered chronologically, linked and enriched with the orator's subjective associations, ensuring a masterful delivery. Lina Bolzoni points out the theatrical dimension of these antique mnemotechnical spatial constructions, and particularly of the images, the so-called *imagines agentes* (agent images) themselves.

> Animated by mnemonic images, they [the locations] became scenes in a theatre where every element was disguised and transformed so that it could be used in a performance of *ars memoriae.*
>
> (BOLZONI 1999: 13)

Following the antique rhetorical tradition, Camillo's memory theatre offered an abundance of mythological, magical and historical *imagines agentes.* These would provide a single verbal association to the orator and written material. Written and visual materials were stored in the theatre's tiered seating areas, leaving no space for a potential audience to sit. Camillo based the spatial organization of his theatre of memory on Vitruvius' model of the Roman amphitheatre but intriguingly reversed the audience-stage relationship. Instead of the action occurring on the stage with the audience positioned in the orchestra and tiered ascending seating, the single orator-protagonist situated himself on the stage facing the semi-circular tiered seating area where the eternal knowledge, in images and written documents, was deposited for his retrieval. Camillo's reversed theatre for one operated as an analogous yet interactive scenography and required to be accessed and activated both mentally and physically. The individual act of linking the exhibited knowledge together to compose the perfect speech carried explicit performative character. There are no extant models or illustrations, and Camillo's fragmentary text does not fully explicate the design and workings of his theatre. Yet there is an identifiable order to his memory system that Francis A. Yates has meticulously reconstructed in her 1966 classic study, *The Art of Memory* on the Hebrew *Sephiroth* (the ten divine emanations or spheres in the Cabbalistic Tree of Life), as locations of eternity and on the seven columns of the Temple of Salomon. The ambassador Viglius Zuichemus' vivid description of his visit to the theatre confirms that this was not a passive construction but one in which the orator on the stage must choose and link imagery and texts to their fullest potential.

> The work is of wood [. . .] marked with many images, and full of little boxes; there are various orders and grades in it. He gives a place to each individual figure and ornament, and he showed me such a mass of papers, that though I always heard that Cicero was the fountain of richest eloquence, scarcely would I have thought that one author could contain so much or that so many volumes could be pieced together out of his writings.
>
> (ERASMUS, *EPISTOLAE*, ED P.S. ALLEN AND OTHERS, IX, P. 479, AS CITED IN YATES 1996: 136)

In his letter to Erasmus, Viglius describes Camillo's operation of the many little boxes containing excerpts from famous speeches (mostly Cicero's, it can be assumed). This implies that for the orator to access the collected knowledge, he would need either an assistant to move between the tiered segments to open boxes and select excerpts to hand to the orator or the actor-orator himself would be moving on and off the stage to do so. The orator's need to physically and mentally activate the repository to create new and different productions of knowledge through the live linking of concept, image and word shows Camillo's model theatre to be a highly performative and immersive space. The scaled-down memory theatre comprises a model that enables the intimate performance of scenes of knowledge by and for the orator, whose stage extends to the auditorium, thereby performing the theatre's entire interior. In sum, Camillo presents a theatre that is able to produce all of man's present and future knowledge: a creative, teleological, physical and conceptual model operating in the present but directed to the future. Similar to the mnemonic techniques articulated in *Ad C.Herrenium*, the orator designs a virtual architecture whose scenes are retrieved sequentially together with the objects, numbers or figures to be verbally recalled without fail. While not influential at its time, Camillo's strategies for ordering knowledge and the theatricalization of its production saw a resurgence from the 1990s onwards. Artists and scholars, analogizing the World Wide Web and its locational, associative and near-infinite network structure, in effect, digitally reinterpreted his memory theatre. Departing from Yates' earlier focus on the theatre's cabbalistic and hermetic symbolism, these new works sought to distil a kind of embryonic, iconographic *programming* language from Camillo's sixteenth-century model. Media theorist Peter Matussek argues for a contemporary resurgence of the theatre of memory, stating recent neuropsychological findings in relation to the organization, storage and retrieval of memory.

> Memories no longer seem to us to constitute a passive inventory for deposit and withdrawal; rather, they seem far more like actors in a succession of changing stage settings. A telling metaphor shift in the neuro-sciences goes hand in hand with corresponding changes in the ways we speak about computers. In the wake of advances in interactive applications, the function of digital technology is no longer described merely in terms of 'storage and retrieval', but rather in terms of the performativeness of images in motion.
>
> (MATUSSEK 2001: 3)

Camillo's virtual reality counterparts, exemplified here by an early interactive work, Hegedues' *Memory Theatre VR* from 1997 can create intermedial dynamic images and linguistic connections visualized in the virtual world. Hegedues, by example, entices the viewer/participant to actively and seamlessly transverse diverse landscapes of knowledge by tapping into subjective and fictitious virtual worlds and finally constructing one's inner virtual world as a result of the performative experience. 'Real' and 'virtual' exist in parallel in this installation in the form of a VR theatre in the round. Hegedues' *Memory Theatre VR* presents an enterable model as epistemic in that the installation produces endless combinations from four virtual worlds into ever-new and different knowledge sets for the viewer and is performative in its spatial layout and usability. Yet, *Memory Theatre VR* is not based on a claim of a universal knowledge or complete history of VR but emphasizes subjectivity and deconstruction as curatorial strategies for virtual worldmaking. 'World-making', so philosopher Nelson Goodman is always a 'remaking' of other worlds or elements thereof already in existence (Goodman 1978: 6). Underlying Goodman's study into worldmaking is his view of the arts as a 'mode[s] of discovery, creation and enlargement of knowledge', therefore constituting an 'integral part of metaphysics and epistemology' (Goodman 1978:102). Linking worldmaking directly with the production of knowledge as Goodman does implies that this act is not to be (mis)understood as copying of 'what is' but that its central, creative strategies perform processes of 'composition', 'deformation' and 'weighting', among others (Goodman 1978:101), that are related to reality but must reach beyond its immediate confines. In this understanding, and extrapolating from Goodman, worldmaking, as shown in the virtual and augmented reality artworks and performances introduced in this project, encompasses construction and reconstruction, invention and assemblage, fact and fiction and manifest translated into nonverbal symbolic systems of representation.

The locus of the virtual

Virtual worlds, as examined in this project through a brief, critical history of the 'virtual' in philosophy, have come to be understood as products of strategies that construct loci autonomous from the 'actual' or the 'real', but that own their, distinct reality or realness. Philosopher Olaf Wallenstein and visual artist Koo Jeong confirm in a discussion on Koo's recent augmented reality works, titled *Ontologies of the Virtual,* that 'the virtual does not make place and physical location irrelevant' but asks for it to be 'conceived [. . .] differently' (Wallenstein and Koo Jeong n.d.). The act of cosmopoiesis, encompassing the performative capacity to envision and construct worlds, begins in the studio and continues through representation beyond its confines. The map, the model and the world are created and imagined at the same time. On the fractured border between the physical and virtual territories, artistic practices embrace the digital and virtual model as a departure from physical limitations, able to inscribe conceptual, performative and ephemeral qualities into their stories. The virtual and the real thus occupy different spaces, yet the virtual model's critical capacity lies in the interaction between physical and virtual space. Unique to the virtual realm is that a virtual locus carries infinite numbers of further or other loci within itself. Thus, it presents as unstable and rhizomatic rather than a stable and linear body (entity). Any single virtual model is to be understood as one of the innumerable worlds perpetually in a fluid motion. The process of worldmaking through the virtual model remains forever unfinished and forever marked by potentiality. Its faculty, as dispositif to expose and bring to light concealed mechanisms of power, of data organization and hierarchies, manifests in the works by artists and artist collectives in this project as deliberate processes of what Deleuze and later Braidotti call processes of deterritorialization and reterritorialization. As articulated in the scenographies of performance, installation and film, these are the primary and fundamental aspects of new, propositional imaginaries that reimagine, redirect and transgress contemporary dominant imaginaries of the binary, the hierarchical and the exploitative.

2

Art, science and engineering – imagining the virtual

Media art, visionary and virtual architecture

The emergence of new media art and the rise of technology-fuelled imaginary architecture converged and intertwined in the 1960s. Focusing on New York and Northern Italy, this chapter maps key movements in the foundational period of pre-digital electronic technology adoption as a conceptual and critical component in the arts, underpinning the aesthetic and theoretical shifts that have been fundamental in framing the virtual in theatre, art and architecture. By providing a detailed context of selected past experiments and movements at the intersection of art, performance, space and technology, the chapter provides historical examples and strategies that can be traced to the works explored later in the book. While the historical precedents in this chapter are not explicitly linked to the contemporary case studies, an argument is made that contemporary digital notions of the virtual, the fragment, the double and the interface between the material and immaterial spaces have roots across antiquity, the Renaissance and more recently in the twentieth century where the arts mirrored society's rapid progression through the mechanical age, information age to the digital age. The chapter concentrates on the 1960s as a decade of pivotal cultural and technical change from Swiss artist Jean Tinguely's superbly analogue self-destroying, twenty-seven-minute mechanical machine-based art performance, *Hommage à New York* at MoMA in 1960 to NASA's creation of the first Digital Twin in 1970 to calculate the recovery of the disabled Apollo 13 spacecraft. The foundational frameworks of new media art and performance established in the turbulent years from 1960 to 1970 in New York are explored, enabled by technology-orientated collaborations between curators, artists, engineers and scientists that facilitated artists' future embrace of digital technologies, extended reality and virtual worlds. The chapter recognizes the origins of architecture's departure from the pragmatics of the post-war modernist programme and the euphoric and utopic visions of future worlds that followed typified by the architecture of the Italian Radicals. The chapters' initial focus is on the events that led to the formation of the Engineering Art and Technology Group (EAT) in New York's 1960s, including the extensive collaborations between Bell Labs, AT&T's research department (today Nokia Bell Lab) and artists such as Robert Rauschenberg and experimental composer John Cage. The critical role Bell Lab engineer Billy Klüver and MoMA curator Pontus Hultén played in orchestrating the evolution of New Media Arts is weaved into this chronology of events, starting with Swiss artist Jean Tinguely's self-destructing machine *Hommage to New York* at The Museum of Modern Art (MoMA) in 1960 through to a detailed look at the seminal New York performance series *9 Evenings: Theatre and Engineering* (1966) and Hultén's curated exhibition *The Machine as Seen at the End of the Mechanical Age* at MoMA in 1968 and on to EAT's work in realizing the Pepsi Pavilion at the Osaka Expo in 1970. Pivoting through the Osaka Expo from a decade of experimentation in the electronic arts to a decade of future architectural visions realized as a utopic vision tempered by the creative turbulence of the 1960s, this chapter co-opts architecture's established expertise in producing utopic worlds, allowing for the appropriation of architectural concepts, including site, territory and imaginaries. It establishes distinctions between architectural imagination, visionary architecture and architectural and socio-technical imaginaries, tracing the origins and development of the term imaginary and relating it to socio-political and spatial aspects of the territory that this project postulates. In the context of a discussion on the virtual model as dispositif, it puts forward critical propositional and visionary aspects of architecture, allowing for an examination of architecture's adoption of performative and media art strategies to disseminate architectural concepts via exhibitions, installations, models and the moving image. Discussing the utopic urban propositions of London-based architecture group Archigram and the Italian Radical Architects, Florence-based architecture collectives Superstudio and Archizoom Associati, an arc is drawn to contemporary UK research agency Forensic Architecture's critical methodology by utilizing architectural and socio-technical imaginaries, architectural methodologies and 3D modelling to scrutinize cases of state violence and genocide while employing exhibition and new media art strategies for display and dissemination.

New York as site for experimental art and technology

The 1960s saw the emergence of a unique relationship between New York's established art scene, the Museum of Modern Art (MoMA) and Bell Labs, the research and scientific development arm of telecommunications giant American Telephone & Telegraph Company (AT&T). These collaborations served as central vectors in the post-industrial-revolution re-convergence of science, engineering, music, performance and the visual arts, typified by the founding of the American collective *Experimental Art and Technology* (EAT) in 1966. Initially informal and initiated by individual artists and engineers, these cross-disciplinary collaborations began to break down the siloization that characterized mid-twentieth-century professional fields in both art and engineering. By charting these early non-hierarchical collaborations between artists and engineers, frameworks emerge for subsequent collaborations focused on art and technology and provide the historical and technical context for artworks and artists working with digital technologies and virtual realms into the twenty-first century. Against the background of late (post) modernism, student protests, radical politics and a vibrant art scene situated between the decline of abstract expressionism and the emergence of pop art, a re-examination or transgression of the limitations of disciplinary silos occurred. Beginning in the 1960s, Bell Labs and numerous other research labs were, in the decades to come, instrumental in formalizing art and technology partnerships by adopting strategies of engagement through residency programmes and integrating artists into the research environment through project-based collaborations that, over time, resulted in cross-disciplinary works that investigated the confluence of art and new technologies. Bell Labs, established in 1925 as Bell Telephone Laboratories Inc., was a leading technology-focused research lab across the twentieth century.

In 1927, Bell researchers first transmitted live television images over extended distances. Ten years later, they developed fundamental theories underpinning digital systems' development, including data quantification, encoding and transmission. Heralding the information age Bell engineers invented transistors in 1947, and in 1954, they created the first functioning solar call, followed by the invention of the laser and optic fibre, enabling contemporary telecommunications. Bell Lab physicist Edward Zajac produced the first computer-generated animation, *Simulation of Two-Gyro Gravity-Gradient Attitude Control System*, an 11-minute, 16mm film computed by an IBM-7090 and drawn using a Stromberg-Carlson 4020 recorder in 1963. Bell Labs computer scientists Ken Thompson and Dennis Ritchie pioneered the UNIX operating system in 1969, the basis for operating systems such

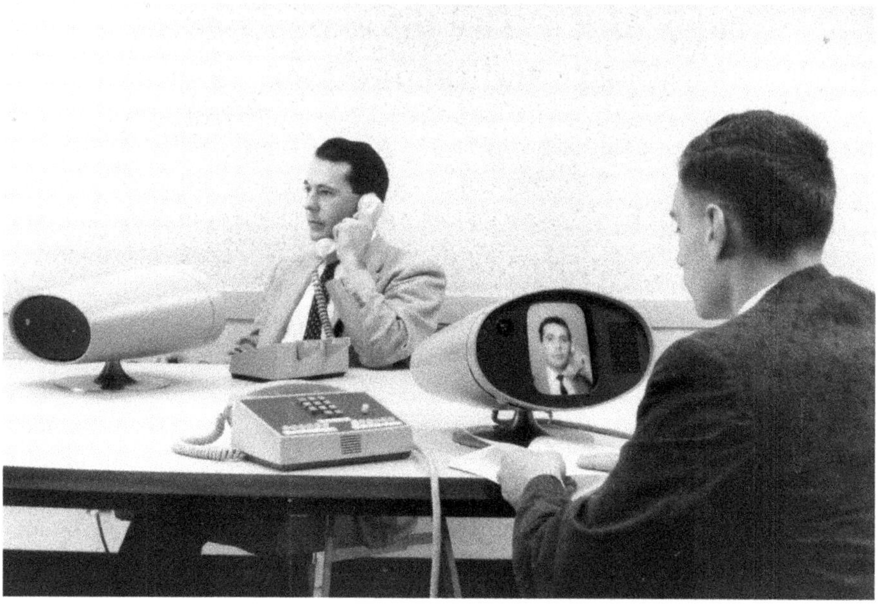

FIGURE 2.1 *The* Picturephone*, which added video to telephone calls, was debuted at the AT&T Bell System pavilion at the 1964 New York World's Fair. Courtesy of RBM Vintage Images / Alamy Stock Photo. Photo: AT&T Photo Service / United States Information Agency / RBM Vintage Images.*

as Android, MacOS and IOS (Georgescu 2022). Overall, the inventions and implementation of technologies developed by Bell Labs remain critical for much of the digital technology and networked systems used today. Pivotal in brokering the working relationships between Bell Labs engineers and the New York art scene was Swedish Bell Lab electrical engineer Billy Klüver (1927–2004), who, from the late 1950s, facilitated and actively supported cross-disciplinary collaborations and projects. Klüver worked with curators, artists, scientists and engineers, transversing the different disciplines to realize numerous performances and exhibitions across the 1960s. Klüver's interactions with Swedish curator Pontus Hultén (1924–2006) from the late 1950s were vital in connecting the art world with the researchers at Bell Lab, allowing the emerging work across art and technology to be made highly visible and impactful in the American and European art worlds.[1]

At the request of Hultén, Klüver collaborated with Swiss artist Jean Tinguely (1925–1991) on what would become a career-defining project for all involved. Their collaboration culminated in Tinguely's 1960 self-destroying, twenty-seven-minute mechanical machine-based art performance, *Hommage à New York*. The performance was staged in the sculpture garden of the MoMA, and even though aspects of Klüver technology failed to operate as planned, this had little impact on the desired overall effect. The performance featured a large, complex machine composed of bicycle wheels, motors, a player piano, a go-cart, a bathtub and other found objects (MoMA 2024a), which self-destructed in front of a live audience. The event showcased Tinguely's fascination with indeterminacy, movement, entropy and ephemerality: 'Industry and automation dominate us and impose a rhythm on us [. . .] My work must move to remain vital, to avoid obsolescence' (Tinguely in MoMA 2024a). *Hommage à New York* brought conceptual art, kinetic art and performance together in a work that is regarded as a seminal contribution to the emergence of new media art, capturing the audience and the critic's imagination and opening a new decade of experimentation between art and technology supported by established institutions such as MoMA.

Facilitated by Hultén, whom Klüver had met a year earlier, *Hommage à New York* was Klüver's first significant project with MoMA, Tinguely and the New York art scene. According to Hultén, the project had given 'him a crash course in contemporary art', after which 'he generously accepted to act as a liaison between the Moderna Museet [in Stockholm] and American artists' (Obrist 2023). Klüver worked with Hultén both in New York and in exhibitions realized at the Moderna Museet Stockholm. Their early collaborations included the 1961 kinetic art exhibition *Bewogen Beweging,* where Tinguely had twenty-six works alongside Rauschenberg, Duchamp, Calder and many others, also shown at the Stedelijk Museum Amsterdam, which explored kinetic art. In 1962, they collaborated on the exhibition *4 Americans*, highlighting emerging American artists and the transatlantic exchange of artistic ideas. In 1964, they mounted the exhibition *Pop Art*, showcasing the emerging movement. In parallel to the exhibitions in Stockholm, Klüver continued working on New York projects, providing technical assistance with the neon lighting for Jasper Johns's *Zone* (1962) and *Field Painting* (1964). In 1963, he developed a small radio transmitter and throat contact microphone for Yvonne Rainer's performance entitled *At My Body's House,* in which Rainer wanted to 'redefine the boundaries of dance' (Mccray 2020: 96) and for 'the audience to hear the sound of her breathing' (Mccray 2020). In July 1965, Klüver collaborated for the first time with composer John Cage and dancer and choreographer Merce Cunningham on *Variations V.* This performance premiered in the Lincoln Center for the Performing Arts as part of the New York Philharmonic's French American Festival. In a performative staging strategy that Klüver used in future projects, engineers joined the performers on stage to operate the light and audio sensors that made up the digitally interactive technology that gave the dancers 'near-instant control of the light, film projection and sound' (Mccray 2020: 97).

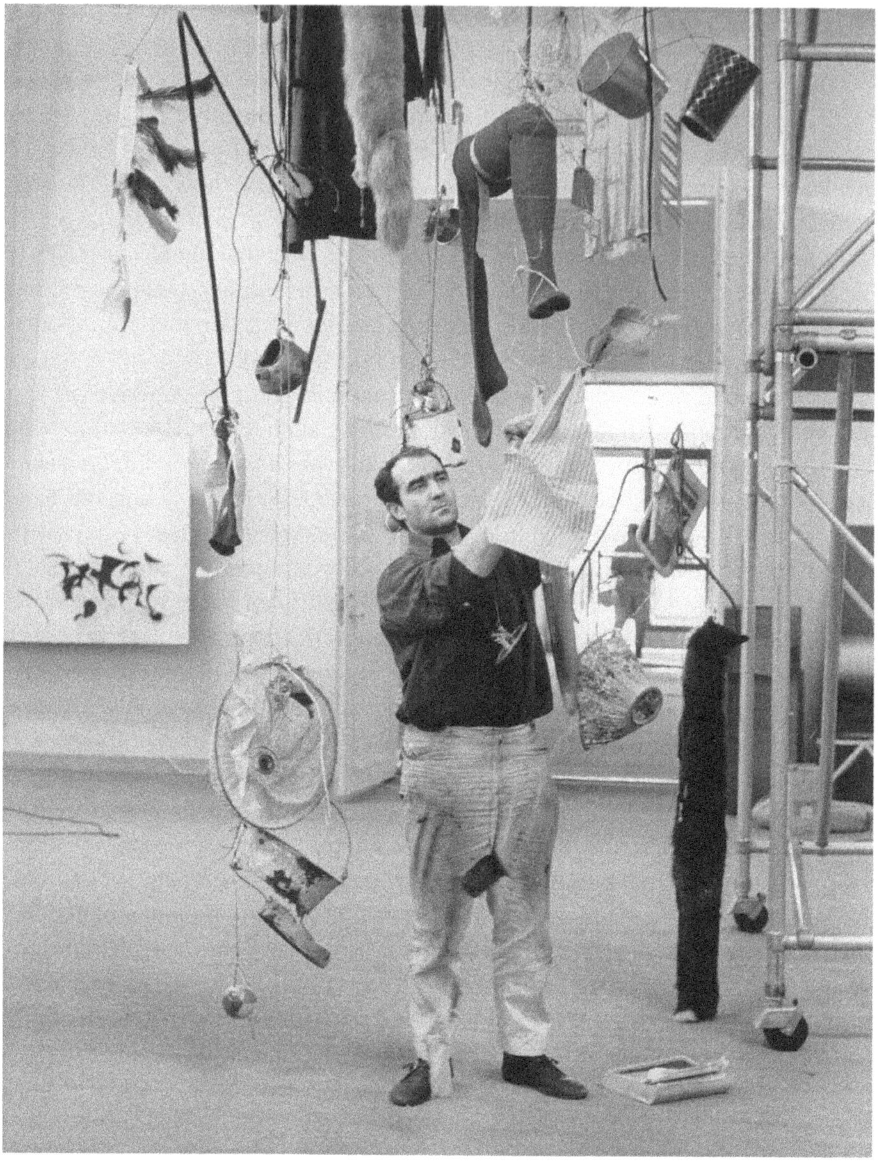

FIGURE 2.2 *Swiss artist Jean Tinguely with his sculpture* Ballet des pauvres *at the Modern Museum (Moderna Museet), Stockholm, Sweden, as part of the exhibition Bewogen Beweging curated by Pontus Hultén, 16 May 1961. Photo: Austrian Archives / Scala. Image courtesy of Austrian Archives / Scala Florence.*

9 Evenings: Theatre and Engineering

In January 1966, instigated by Klüver and visual artist Robert Rauschenberg, thirty engineers from Bell Labs and ten artists began a collaboration that culminated in October of the same year in a series of performances staged over nine evenings and titled, fittingly: *9 Evenings: Theatre and Engineering*. As a central case study in this chapter, *9 Evenings* was notable for its diverse and prescient approaches to performance and technology by some of the most influential artists of the time in revisiting some of the initial artist statements that reveal an overwhelmingly rigorous search for new forms of communication between body, sound and space through the integration of technology that was to be custom-built and tailored to the requirements of each of the performances. The project remains pivotal in the emergence of a genre of experimental digital performance through to the present day. The participating artists, each of them already established at the time in composition, sound, visual arts, dance and theatre, were Steve Paxton, Robert Whitman, Alex Hay, Deborah Hay, David Tudor, Öyvind Fahlström, John Cage, Yvonne Rainer, Lucinda Childs and Robert Rauschenberg. Conceived as an experiment that brought together artists, industry and engineers on an equal footing, *9 Evenings* aimed to expand artistic expression with new technologies and to stimulate industry research towards new products and new use of existing products. An ambitious project with no precursor, its initial phase of introductory meetings, the first one having taken place in Rauschenberg's New York loft, was slow to take off until, as Klüver reports, 'one engineer suggested to another: Let's tell them about something they can use' (1966: 3). A lively exchange between what artists would like to do and what engineers were able to offer, to modify and create, followed and, in the next step, dancer and choreographer Simone Forti, whose meeting and production notes have proved to be essential testimonials of the project, was tasked with finding a performance venue. The choice fell on the drill hall on the first floor of the 69 Regiment Armoury on Lexington Avenue in New York City. Not only had the armoury been the site of the infamous 1913 *International Exhibition of Modern Art*, where Marcel Duchamp first showed his cubist-inspired painting *Nude Descending a Staircase* to a US audience, but it also demonstrated the emergence of a counterculture in the visual arts in the United States as the exhibition had been organized and financed entirely by a group of young artists without any public funding. This history, as well as the armoury's enormous dimensions of approximately 41 x 63 metres across with balconies on all sides and a barrel vault ceiling with a height of 38 metres that would allow for a large public to attend, appealed to artists and engineers alike yet access to the space was only possible five days before the opening on 13 October. Initial concerns regarding the space's poor acoustics with a reverberation time of 6 seconds that meant it would take six seconds for sound energy to decrease by 60 dB comparable to the behaviour of sound in a large church or cathedral with an average reverberation time of up to 10 seconds were dispelled by the engineers who were confident they could cope, also considering that only one of the artists would need for spoken language to be transmitted clearly. The project collaborations that followed were one-on-one relationships between artists and engineers united by the intention to create new hybrid works for live performance. During two months of initial meetings, artists, responding to Klüver's challenge to state what they would like to do, put forward more than seventy items on their technology wish list, of which not all were realized in the end. However, it quickly became evident that an overarching control system was needed to coordinate all technologies involved in the ten performances. The *Klüver/Martin Archive* hosts a website entitled *Experiments in Art and Technology* that assembles extant documents of the origins, the planning and preparation and the actual performances. It describes the research and development of such a control system that, ideally, was to be wireless and networked.

> The engineers then began to design and develop the Theatre Electronic Environmental Modular (TEEM) system for wireless remote control of lights, sound, video, and other effects. It was comprised of nearly three hundred components and was used in some manner in each artist's piece. Lights, sound and other elements of the performances could be pre-programmed and activated remotely. Klüver described TEEM as the first electronic system built for onstage use and a step toward the possibility when the computer could be part of an actual performance.
>
> (EAT 2024)

Engineer Herb Schneider devised structural diagrams for each performance that combined the artistic and technical aspects, translating these into individual diagrams that TEEM would control live. Over two weekends, EAT, artists and engineers put the TEEM system to work and aligned it with individual performances and the overall evening, not in the armoury but in a Brooklyn gym, as it was the only testing space available. In retrospect, the innovative spirit of artists and engineers, their enthusiasm and creativity in overcoming disciplinary distances and the immediate recognition of the importance of finding a common language through concrete experimentation are still remarkable and unique some sixty years later. Several performances are discussed here as to their significance at the time and into the future, their innovative use, expansion and adaptation of existing and emerging technologies and their rethinking of modernist notions of narrative, character and material.

9 Evenings opened with the performance *Physical Things* by dancer Steve Paxton in collaboration with performance engineer Dick Wolff (so the titles of the engineers in the programme). Described by Paxton as 'a dance with a set' (E.A.T. 2024: 9) the piece comprised a large, transparent polyethene inflatable structure that took up half the floor space of the armoury hall (2000 square metres) and rose with a tower-like extension to its roof. In *Physical Things*, Paxton and Wolff wanted to explore visual and auditory immersion that aligned with the visitors' movements through the structure. Manually controlled film and slide sequences of natural environments were projected on the walls of the tunnels, and 500 transistor radios were transmitting a prerecorded soundscape by composer Robert Ashely from hung audio rings to spectators standing underneath. The seemingly arbitrary sound collage, ranging from animal noises to sports commentators, 'followed' the audience as they moved in and between the tunnels, weaving between the partially concealed performers (see Bonin 2006 FDL). Paxton and Wolff merged improvised live-action and prerecorded sounds and images into a participative and interactive performance with many of its cues controlled by the TEEM system. *Physical Thing*'s scenography depended on each element, including the astro turf's tactility that covered the inflatable structure's ground, contributing to the overall sensorial audiovisual and kinetic composition. In the early meetings with the participating engineers, choreographer and dancer Lucinda Childs had wanted to translate the body's movement energy into another kind of visualized energy and through her collaboration with performance engineer Peter Hirsch, a 70kHz Doppler Sonar was built to allow for the data of movements of props, lights and the three performers to be processed as, typically, a Doppler effect changes the frequency of a sound wave when it touches an obstacle, whether static or moving, whether human or nonhuman. Hirsch then used this data to create the sounds and to manipulate the lighting in real time. The second 'instrument' Childs wished to use in her performance, titled *Vehicle*, was a ground effect machine, which, in its most common use in industry, makes it possible for a heavy object to glide above the ground using the air pressure between the ground surface and the object. In her artist statement, Childs describes how performance engineer Per Biorn 'installed two vacuum cleaner motors onto this platform so that I am in effect on a cushion of air when I use it' (Childs in Hultén 1966: 5). With these two 'instruments' as she called them, Childs could realize what, to her, constituted dance: the movement of bodies and static entities for any length of time. Thus, Childs' expanded understanding of dance rendered nonhuman elements equal to performers on her stage in an early articulation of a new materialist choreography and scenography that affords degrees of autonomy to the nonhuman actors. At the time, *Vehicle's* interplay of dance and technology highlighted the potential for new media in performance in ways that have since become mainstream. Equally, dancer and choreographer Yvonne Rainer's statement of intent as related to her performance *Carriage Discreteness* with performance engineer and programmer Per Biorn describes her concept as a 'dance consisting of two separate but parallel (simultaneous) continuities and two separate (but equal) control systems' (E.A.T. 2024: 10). In the large expanse of the armoury, twelve performers, wearing tiny wrist receivers, were moving set pieces of different shapes, volumes and materials such as wood, aluminium, cardboard and plywood throughout the performance according to Rainer's instructions via Walkie-Talkie. Rainer devised the choreography for these directed movements based on a grid structure of the space, numbered into twenty areas, with their respective numbers written on the floor in chalk. This 'board game', however, had two parallel control systems operating at the same time. The first control system saw Rainer choose movements and actions to be realized by her twelve performers and communicate to them via Walkie-Talkie. The other control system saw TEEM organize and display many prerecorded movie excerpts, details of performers, recorded spoken text, slide projections and diverse lighting configurations, including ultra-violet light that rendered the performers mere silhouettes. In *Carriage Discreteness*, the exploration of the play is one between levels of control and freedom (for the performers) and an inevitable loss of control having given over the organization of cues to the machine and, dramaturgically and formally, between one visible system of control and one that remains invisible to the viewer.

In two parts, Rauschenberg's monumental performance piece, *Open Score*, gave over control to a tennis game between professional tennis player Mimi Kanarek and artist Frank Stella with an audience of several hundred seated on bleachers on three sides. The armoury had been used for tennis tournaments before; however, this time, the game's duration was not controlled by the players but by an interactive situation between their modified racquets and the lighting in the hall. Engineer Bill Kaminski had developed a miniaturized FM transmitter and fitted it into the racket's handle. With a contact microphone fastened at the top of the handle and the antenna for the transmitter strung around the racquet head, a loud sound was heard each time the racket hit a ball, amplified by the racket strings and transmitted to the lights. One by one, with each hit of the ball, one of the forty-eight overhead 1000-watt lights went out. The first part of the performance finished when all the lights had gone out. In the second part, several hundred people from a neighbouring community school entered the central space in total darkness. Infrared television cameras picked up their movements, choreographed live by Rauschenberg through Morse code-like torch signals. The seated audience could barely see the group and their movements, yet their transmitted images on three giant

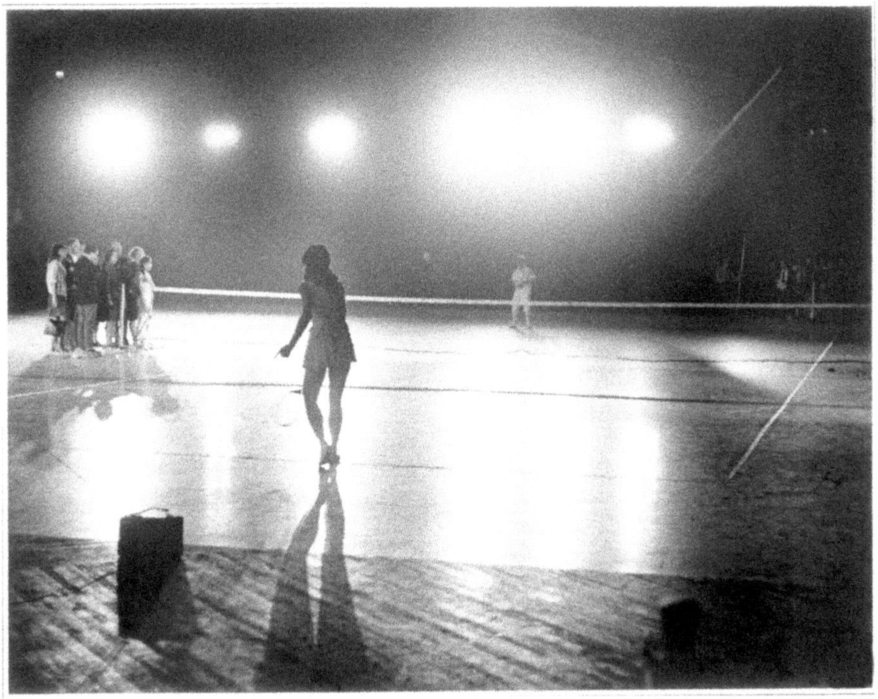

FIGURE 2.3 *Robert Rauschenberg's performance,* Open Score, *1966, starts with a tennis game between professional player Mimi Kanarek and artist Frank Stella in 9* Evenings Theatre and Engineering. *Photo: Peter Moore. © Northwestern University.*

screens made their presence known. According to Rauschenberg, tennis is a 'movement' and a 'formal dance improvisation' (E.A.T. 2024: 11). Interested in what was visible and what was invisible in the two parts of the performance through different systems of control, the artist speaks of a 'double exposure of action. A screen of light and a screen of darkness' (E.A.T. 2024) that was mediated, yet not controlled, in both configurations by the players on the stage. Against dual categories of control and freedom, minimalist, experimental composer John Cage continued his engagement with indeterminacy and chance elements in his electro-acoustic performance in collaboration with performance engineer Cecil Cooker titled *Variations VII*. Cage describes his project as

> indeterminate in form and detail, making use of the sound system which has been devised collectively for this festival, [. . .] using as sound sources only those sounds which are in the air at the moment of performance, picked up via the communication bands, telephone lines, microphones

> together with, instead of musical instruments, a variety of household appliances and frequency generators.
>
> (E.A.T. 2024:4)

With a duration of forty-one minutes and designed for 'any number of musicians using photoelectric cells and electronic equipment', so the text score, *Variations VII*, amplified biological sounds of the body such as heartbeat, breathing and artificial sounds from Geiger counters emitting sounds that were transformed into sounds, radios, televisions and telephone lines. Musicians were free to improvise; however, only sounds produced during the performance were relayed in real-time, with the performer's movements and actions triggering sounds, such as dialling numbers on the phones. Clarisse Bardiot points out that *Variations VII* and the previous works *Variations V* and *VI* can be seen as belonging to Cage's *Theatre Pieces* (Bardiot 2006). Musically, *Variations V* comprised short-wave radios and tapes with prerecorded sounds of household items controlled by photocells that activated switches to turn the audio on and off. Klüver (1966) describes the performance's interactivity as involving dancers whose movements controlled the switches. In addition, ten capacitive antennas picked up the sound of the dancers' bodies moving. In *Variations VII*, with the musicians as the only performers, Cage referred to the principles of shadow theatre. Set up at the back of the stage and obscured by large white canvasses, the musicians operating the equipment were backlit, and their shadows were projected onto them. As Bardiot describes, 'Lights placed under the tables played a twofold role, sending a signal to the photoelectric cells and creating giant shadows that took up almost the entire stage area of the New York Armory' (2006). The audience was free to walk around, approach the tables or be seated on the bleachers. Cage's approach of utilizing aleatory compositional strategies, improvisation and his research into non-instrumental sounds such as sirens, household drains, televisions and radio were seminal in the *Variation* series (*Variations I–VIII*, 1958–67) that persisted on the simultaneity of sound, action and film and video projections resulting in highly theatrical audiovisual performances. Cage's non-hierarchical treatment of the components of the *Variations* series made the composer a leading representative of the 1960s experimental movement in music and performance. Resulting not in engineering patents or entirely new products, the innovation gained from *9 Evenings* for Industry was the surplus that emerges when expanding, appropriating, subverting and misusing technology to adapt to artists' ideas, made even more challenging by the demands of the project's live character. The examples are numerous, and their repercussions are still felt today in the necessary miniaturization of components for live use by performers and audiences, as seen with Paxton's mini transistor radios or Rauschenberg's modified tennis racquet and more subtly with the development of TEEM as the prerequisite controlling system for the organization and coordination of the scenographic elements of remote movement, audio, film, TV and video projection. The parallels to media art of the 1970s and 1980s are evident: artists often used equipment they had no prior knowledge of an opportunity to use. With industry cooperation, as in *9 Evenings* or of funded and specialized institutions, access to high-tech and expensive technologies became possible. With it came the possibility to play, expand their use, deliberately misunderstand their functions and, in short, apply the *what if* that is so fundamental to artistic and scientific creativity. Perceived at the time as 'a critical success by some, a selling out of the avant-garde by many, and a box office flop by most' (Garwood 2007), yet seen by more than 10,000 people over the two weeks with one repeat performance for each of the ten shows, *9 Evenings* remains a critical event in the history of art and technology collaborations. Experimental, non-commercial and fuelled by both industry and artists wanting to test ideas that would eventually find entry into the interactive media art pieces and live performances of the following decades, *9 Evenings* foreshadowed the contemporary desire for the integration of complex technologies into live performances and the redefinition of dramaturgy, narrative, body, scenography and sound. *9 Evenings* was revisited as an exhibition and catalogue at the MIT List Visual Arts Centre in 2006, curated by Catherine Morris and formed the second in the museum's series of exhibitions on technology, engineering and the arts. Much of the material for the exhibition at MIT was drawn from the archive of software *Softimage* director Daniel Langlois's (1957–2023) Foundation for Art, Science and Technology, which was established in 1997 with the aim of 'Exploring and revealing the interdependency between ourselves and our omnipresent technological environment' (FDL 2024). The MIT exhibition reinforced the legacy of *9 Evenings*, strengthening its stature as a pivotal moment in the history of performance, the art and technology movement and the emergence of new media art. *9 Evenings* unprecedented use of custom-built new technologies, sensors and media prefigured later developments in interactive and immersive installation performance. The range of performance projects presented in *9 Evenings* simultaneously reflected on theatre's historic adaption of technology, from Adolphe Appia's work with light to Josef Svoboda's 1958 *Laterna Magika* with its multi-screen immersive projections synchronized to stage action, while providing a lexicon of technology-focused performative strategies and contributed to a technical and visual grammar for new media art and performance moving into the twenty-first century. As Klüver remarks at the end of the programme book, '9 Evenings is an experiment in the true sense of the word: its results are open for the future' (Klüver 1966: 3). In parallel to *9 Evenings* and supported by Hultén, Klüver cofounded Experimental

Art and Technology (EAT) together with electrical engineer Fred Waldhauer (1927–1993) and New York artists Rauschenberg and Whitman, establishing one of the largest, earliest and most influential organizations dedicated to the integration of art and technology in the twentieth century. Officially launched in 1967 at Rauschenberg's studio in New York, the organization rapidly grew to over 5,000 members and twenty-six branches, attracting prominent visual artists such as Andy Warhol and Jasper Johns to its ranks (see Tate 2024).

The machine as seen at the end of the mechanical age

In the following year, Hultén curated an exhibition at MoMA titled *The Machine as Seen at the End of the Mechanical Age* that included contributions from EAT. The 1968 exhibition was vital in framing the historical relationships between artists and scientists from the sixteenth century into the twentieth, documenting the shift, as the title suggests, from the rise of the machine to the advent of the digital era through a curatorial approach that assembled 'a collection of comments on technology by artists of the Western world' (Hultén 1968) and acted as a 'requiem to *L'Homme-machine*, the famous book by the eighteenth-century philosopher La Mettrie about the machine age' (Hultén and Obrist 1997). Arguing that the exhibition title 'reflects a crisis within technology itself' (MoMA 2024), Hultén's exhibition articulated the cultural shift from the material to the immaterial at a time when

> the mechanical machine, which can most easily be defined as an imitation of our muscles is losing its dominating position among the tools of mankind, while electronic and chemical devices which imitate the processes of the brain and the nervous system are becoming increasingly important.
>
> (HULTÉN 1968)

The exhibition offered a chronological exploration of the twentieth century's technological and artistic achievements, including the automobile. Divided into seven components: art, reconstruction 1, invention, car, camera, reconstruction 2, and EAT (Experiments in Art and Technology), the structure provided a historical examination of the interplay between mechanical invention and artistic expression. Notable inclusions were Buckminster Fuller's 1933 *Dymaxion Car*, a reconstruction of Vladimir Tatlin's 1920 *Monument for the Third International*, highlighting early twentieth-century constructivism's political aspirations and an actual STP #70 Lotus 56-3 Indy Race car, a collaboration between the CEO of STP (Scientifically Treated Petroleum) Anthony Granatelli and Lotus cars founder Colin Chapman. Artists, including Eadweard Muybridge (*Kicking a Hat* 1885) and the Lumière brothers

(*Cinematographie* 1895), represented advances in cinematic techniques and technologies. Sculptural works by Alberto Giacometti (*the captured hand* 1932), five mobiles by Alexander Calder (including *the motorized mobile that Duchamp liked* 1932) and eight works from Jean Tinguely including a physical remnant from *Hommage à New York* 1960 displayed a direct relationship between the artworks and modes of production, while works by artists Man Ray (*Object to be Destroyed* 1932 and *Indestructible Object* 1923) and René Magritte (*The Anger of the Gods* 1960), a painting showing a racehorse on a car, represented surreal and alternate views of the machine. László Moholy-Nagy's drawing of a *Kinetic Constructive System* 1922, Lyubov Popova's stage model for the *Magnificent Cuckold* from 1922 and Oskar Schlemmer's *Study for the Triadic Ballet* (1921–23) represented studies of mechanical extensions of the body within a performative context. Also included in the exhibition were some of the winners from a competition organized by EAT at the request of Hultén, who sought out 'the most inventive use of new technology as it evolves through the collaboration of the artist and engineer' (Hultén 1968: 199). This section of the exhibition highlighted the artist and engineers' collaborations realized in New York throughout the 1960s, re-evaluating the importance of interdisciplinary collaborations. Initially, Hultén had been asked to curate an exhibition on kinetic art by MoMA director Alfred Barr but had argued that 'the subject was too vast, and instead proposed a more critical and thematic exhibit on the machine' (Hultén and Obrist 1997). Hultén argued that 'the machine was central to much of the art of the '60s, and at the same time, it was obvious that the mechanical age was coming to an end, and that the world was about to enter a new phase' (Hultén and Obrist 1997).

Architectural imaginaries

EAT's and Klüver's interest in collaboration with industry was realized on a large-scale with the commissioning of EAT to produce the Pepsi Pavilion for the 1970 Osaka Expo, enabling a collective decade of artists working with art and technology to represent the movement in a utopian vision of a future city in Japan. American cultural theorist William Gardner describes the Osaka Expo as 'the most striking and significant science fictional presentation of a utopian "future city" to emerge in postwar Japan' (Gardner 2020: 87). The Expo masterplan was designed by eminent Japanese architect Kenzo Tange (1913–2005), who had previously designed the Hiroshima Peace Centre and the Tokyo Olympic Park. With the optimistic central theme of *Progress and Harmony for Mankind*, the official starting point was ambitious in the light of the sixty-four million visitors who visited the site over the 183 days that the Expo was open.

As a global summation of the technologically driven dreams and euphoria of the 1960s achieved through 'its integration of advanced technology, immersive multimedia environments, and eye-popping architecture, the Osaka Expo projected Japan as a simulation site for a future society' (Gardner 2020). Across the Kita Osaka Express railway line that divided the site, EAT's *Pepsi Pavilion* represented a large-scale collective artistic vision commissioned by PepsiCo, one of two non-Japanese corporations represented on the site. The pavilion featured a dome structure with origami-like folds enveloped in a cloud sculpture by renowned Japanese fog artist Fujiko Nakaya (1933–). The forecourt featured seven pill-shaped moving objects called *Floats* by kinetic artist Robert Breer which emitted sound and changed direction if you touched them. A large sculpture entitled *Suntrak* emitted a three-metre-wide *sunbeam* to a fixed point on the pavilion, visibly cutting through the Nakaya cloud sculpture that intermittently surrounded the pavilion; this was supplemented by a moving elliptical mirror and a stationary triangular mirror that reflected sunlight. Breer, who had been previously involved in *9 Evenings*, was responsible for the initial contact between David Thomas, Vice President for Marketing and Distribution at Pepsi-Cola and Klüver from EAT, which led

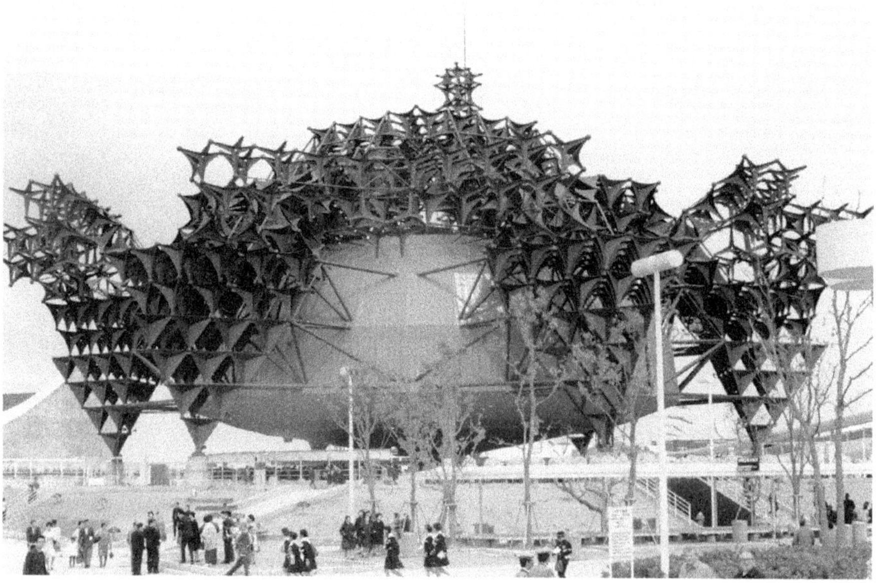

FIGURE 2.4 *The Toshiba* IHI Pavilion *at the Osaka Expo'70. April 1970. Photo: Takao Marui. This image is licensed under the Creative Commons Attribution-Share Alike 2.0 Generic license.*

to the commissioning of EAT to realize the Pepsi Pavilion. Klüver had asked Forrest Myers, Robert Whitman and David Tudor to design different parts of the building infrastructure. The building shell was designed by Japanese architect Tadashi Doi of Takenaka Komuten Company. At the same time, sixty-three engineers and scientists collaborated on designing and implementing a range of technological devices on the outside and inside of the pavilion (FDL 2002). The thirty-six-metre white dome-shaped pavilion was made of white polyvinyl chloride panels on a steel frame. People entered the pavilion through a round tunnel, where they were received by silver-clad hostesses who provided visitors with a small headset that picked up sound from audio loops embedded in the floor. The tunnel ended in a darkened preshow space called *the clam* that transitioned visitors into the central space. Dominated by a 27-metre 210-degree reflective dome made of aluminized mylar foil, the space, designed and installed by Robert Whitman, created a unique visual phenomenon where 'the virtual image and the real image (. . .) seem to come out of mid-air and the walls of the dome itself' (Whitman in Saarinen 2011). On the floor of the central area, various zones were established by the use of contrasting flooring materials and an associate audio loop played through the individual headphones, including asphalt floor with city sounds, grass floor with bird sounds, and other areas covered in rubber, wood, lead and stone. The construction of an elevated platform allowed

> the visitor to merge with the images, isolating himself from the rest of the real and image worlds. Looking out through the spherical mirror, the visitor sees enlarged right-side-up images of people and objects standing in the outer regions of the floor. These images are not 'real' in that they appear on the other side of the mirror.
>
> (GARMIRE 2016)

Similarly, the dome's acoustic properties and technical set-up allowed sound to float in space, alternating between point, line and immersive soundscapes programmed by 'changing teams of four people, composed of artists, scientists, and people from other professions' (Garmire 2016). According to Hultén, the overarching concept for the pavilion was inspired by John Cage's idea 'that a work of art could be like a musical instrument' (Hultén in an interview with Obrist 1997). Hultén goes on to speak about the deterioration of the relationship between Pepsi and EAT after the opening of the pavilion. The disagreement centred around Klüver's strategy of inviting rotating groups of artists, engineers and scientists to programme the audio and visual systems, thus generating an ever-changing spectacle based on evolving collaborations, while Pepsi's insisted on a pre-programmed show. The dispute ultimately put *The Pepsi Generation,* as represented by EAT, in conflict with *Pepsi The*

Corporation and pointed at the differing ambitions and intent from this and many other future partnerships between corporations and artists.

The general format of the Expo included seventy-six national pavilions, curated and conceptualized to represent the nation-states through cultural or scientific achievements and several mostly Japanese-sponsored corporate pavilions, such as EAT's *Pepsi Pavilion*, the science fiction-themed *Mitsubishi Future Pavilion, the Hitachi's Pavilion* journey into the unknown or persuasive technological visions of the future such as the *Electric Power Pavilion*'s promotion of nuclear power sponsored by the Federation of Electric Power Companies. The host organization designed and curated central areas, thematized zones, transportation and general infrastructure. In subtle resistance to the official optimistic tone of the Expo, Japanese theorist and artist Okamoto Tarō (1911–1996) co-curated the central *Symbol Zone* with its muted hints of a dystopian future through works that reflected on Japan's experiences of nuclear and environmental devastation through his dominating, and still standing, animistic 70 metres high *Tower of the Sun* that he designed as a central element and that became an unofficial symbol of the Expo. Similarly impactful was the West German pavilion's blue spherical concert hall, based on a concept by Karlheinz Stockhausen (1928–2007) that put forward a state-sponsored, singular artistic vision from one of Germany's foremost and controversial composers, who had

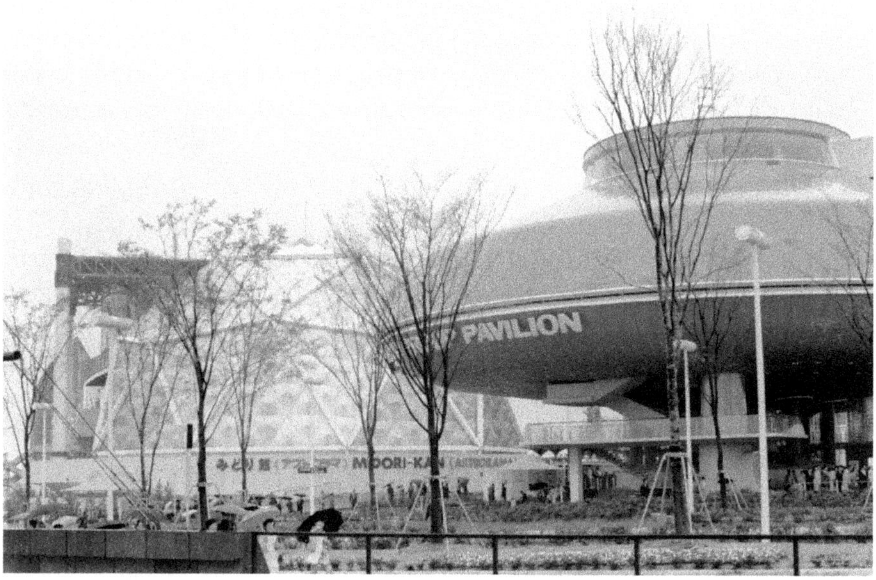

FIGURE 2.5 *The Hitachi Pavilion* Invitation to the Unknown *at the Osaka Expo'70, April 1970. Photo: Takao Marui. This image is licensed under the Creative Commons Attribution-Share Alike 2.0 Generic license.*

convinced German architect and scenographer Fritz Bornemann (1912–2007) to move away from a conventional auditorium design and place the audience in the centre of the sphere surrounded by the lateral loudspeaker groups. Seven concentric and sequential layers of loudspeakers were attached to the interior walls of the sphere and controlled from a console that could project the voices and instruments in moving circles or lines, allowing the technicians to guide the movement and spatialization of sound. Stockhausen presented a daily five-and-a-half-hour programme of his work, including a work composed specifically for the sphere entitled *Expo* for three performers and short-wave radios. The thirty-metre-high Italian pavilion was designed by Rome-based architects (Gilberto and Masino Valle and Sergio Brusa Pasqué from Studio Valle), who acknowledge in their design statements (Valle 2016) that the experimental, utopic and proposals of UK architect group Archigram, Italian collective Superstudio and the Japanese Metabolists directly informed the theoretical and tectonic aspects of the design of the pavilion. Argued as a microcosm 'able to recreate the complexity of the urban image through the expansion of spaces, perceptual stimuli and speed of travel' (Valle 2016), the pavilion embodied concepts of a technologically determined urban future. It condensed into built form the utopic visions of the Italian Radicals, Japanese Metabolism and British High Tech. Evoking the utopic urban proposals of Archigram and Superstudio, Studio Valle's pavilion articulated a physical system that asserts the possibility of infinite duplication, characteristic of Superstudio's urban vision. As a fragment of a megastructure, the pavilion physically embodied the unbuilt concepts of young architects in Belgrade, Italy and London and paradoxically made material the vision of infinite urban continuance. Studio Valle's megastructure represented concepts around the city as a machine while embracing a utopic technologically determined future where the 'interstitial spaces of the project (of the city) become 'the space" of the exhibition' (Valle 2016).

Overall, the 1970 Osaka Expo architecture comprised a collection of propositional and temporary structures that were more about the *idea* of architecture than architecture itself. Driven by space-age aesthetics, domes and tensile structures and influenced by the aesthetic of the Japanese metabolic movement with their megastructures and repetitive biomorphic forms, the Expo became a 'physical as well as an intellectual node or connecting point for a diverse network of architects, authors, artists, and academics exploring issues of futurity [. . .] and articulating a vision of the coming information society' (Gardner 2020: 88). Supporting radically new forms that leapt out from the designer's imagination, influenced by science fiction, pop art and utopic vision of the future, the pavilions broke from the uniformity and rationalism of late international modernism into a collection of dazzling original forms that were at the 'convergence point in the articulation of ideas of the future' (Gardner 2020: 96). The Osaka Expo represented and reflected on the global social, artistic and architectural upheavals of the 1960s, a decade positioned between the decline of international modernism[2] and the rise of postmodernism and starchitecture.[3]

As evidenced by the Osaka Expo 1970, on the fractured border between the imagined, physical and virtual territories, architecture has, in its expanded practices, taken on aspects of theatre and art's conceptual performative and ephemeral qualities. Collectively and retrospectively termed *architectural imaginaries* in this project, the case studies discussed are firstly in the broader context of the established terms social and socio-technical imaginaries and then on the utopic and dystopic propositions by the Italian Radical Architects such as Superstudio and their earlier London counterparts Archigram in the 1960s and early 1970s, with iconic works of playful, ironic and critical visionary urban and architectural collages, installations and exhibitions. The term architectural imaginaries, put forward here, conceptualizes a new category of such architectural schemata that branch from but still rely on individual fictional, visionary or imagined architectures, cities or landscapes and operates in opposition to the imaginary of smart urbanism that 'lacks the higher concepts discussed and invoked by [German Philosopher] Horkheimer: ideals such as justice, happiness, and democracy' (Cugurullo 2019: 120). Following Jasanoff's definition of socio-technical imaginaries as

> collectively held, institutionally stabilized, and publicly performed visions of desirable futures, animated by shared understandings of forms of social life and social order attainable through and supportive of advances in science and technology.
>
> (JASANOFF 2015A: 11)

These imaginaries are potent instruments in projecting and demarcating the porous border between the virtual, the imagined and the real, which can formalize the imagined within an advanced technological and cultural frame. The 1970 Osaka Expo, seen by almost half of the Japanese population and institutionally stabilized by the varying controlling bodies, proposed a radical model of a utopic future city, which remains an example of an architectural or urban imaginary remarkable in its scale and proposition. On the other hand, *imagined* architecture as a subjective vision of the future has a long-standing tradition in literature, scenography and the visual arts. The imagined city appears in the utopic writings of Francis Bacon's *New Atlantis* (1626) through to Italo Calvino's *Invisible Cities* (1972), and Giotto's (c. 1267–1337) frescoes in the Upper Church of the Basilica di San Francesco in Assisi where the painter both imagined and represented the city and its architecture. Baroque scenographer Ferdinando Galli-Bibiena's 'stage designs emphasize views that exaggerated the monumentality of structures they loom dramatically in ways that never could be visible when projected from the ordinary horizon line' (Stewart 2021: 165) and serve as an early example of imagined architectures realized on the stage. In the engravings of Italian architect, archaeologist and artist Giovanni Battista Piranesi (1720–1728), the attention moves away from fictional architecture as background to imagined architecture as subject, where 'paper architecture becomes a paper archaeology – an often imaginary, and for the most part speculative, account of the long destiny of a Roman space' (Stewart 2021: 186). In 'visionary architecture' (a term coined by curator Arthur Drexler in his 1960 exhibition at MoMA of the same name), French neoclassical architect Etienne-Louis Boullée (1728–1799) and Italian Futurist architect Antonio Sant'Elia (1888–1916) both proposed improbable structures that lay outside of the technical or societal possibilities of their time, yet they resonate into the architectural imagination of the twenty-first century. The term architectural imaginary, argued here, is a variation of a socio-technical imaginary focused on technology, society, architecture and the urban, inseparably linked to the architectural imagination as an instrument to pierce the virtual. Its primary function is to collectively place its authors into future yet undefined worlds, allowing for inclusive strategies to shape and transform our response to challenges ranging from climate to the emergence of posthuman viewpoints and future affinities with emerging technologies, including, of specific relevance here, artificial intelligence and virtual worlds. Further characterizing the architectural imaginary is its use of established architectural visualization strategies, including models, drawings, collages and 3-D modelling to generate persuasive visual media to communicate and project both utopic and dystopic urban futures.

Utopic vision of a future city

Beyond the duration of its temporary existence, the experiments between architecture and technology at the Osaka Expo 1970 influentially contributed to a utopic vision of a future city where Archigram had been highly invested during the 1960s. Archigram were 'reading space comics, and we were influenced by Buckminster Fuller' (Cook in Hobson 2020). Architecture and automobiles designed by American poet, philosopher, inventor and system theorist Buckminster Fuller (1895–1983), such as the Dymaxion car (1933), the 100 sqm hexagonal Dymaxion House (1920), or the proposed three kilometre geodesic dome covering Manhattan (1959), provided Archigram with concepts and inspiration for lightweight modular structures and megastructures that emerged as fictional structures in their work. As a group of loosely aligned architects, Archigram's dissemination of their architectural ideas initially relied on publishing, exhibitions and drawings.

Hypothetical projects like the *Walking City* (lead author Ron Herron 1964), *Living Pod* (lead author David Greene1965) and *Instant City* (lead author Peter Cook) informed Archigram's best-known propositional project, the *Plug-In City* (lead author Peter Cook 1964 onwards). Archigram's members collaborated and influenced each other's ideas within specific aesthetic and ideological frameworks; however, they retained individual authorship, and many had notable careers in realizing built architecture (notably Sir Peter Cook). While operating outside a defined movement, Archigram has been aligned with the British High Tech (see Fierro 2024) exemplified by Norman Foster and Richard Rodgers, where the influence of their propositional work can be seen in built form culminating perhaps in Peter Cook's involvement in *The Line*, a 170 km long 200 metres wide and 500 metres high linear smart city megastructure across the desert of Arabia announced in 2021. In 1963, Archigram mounted its first exhibition at the Institute of Contemporary Arts (ICA) in London entitled *Living City*. According to Peter Cook in a recent interview, it was only after that exhibition that people began to refer to them collectively as Archigram (Hobson 2020). Archigram was optimistic about embracing and achieving a technology-determined future with projects such as *Plug-In City*, which gathered previous

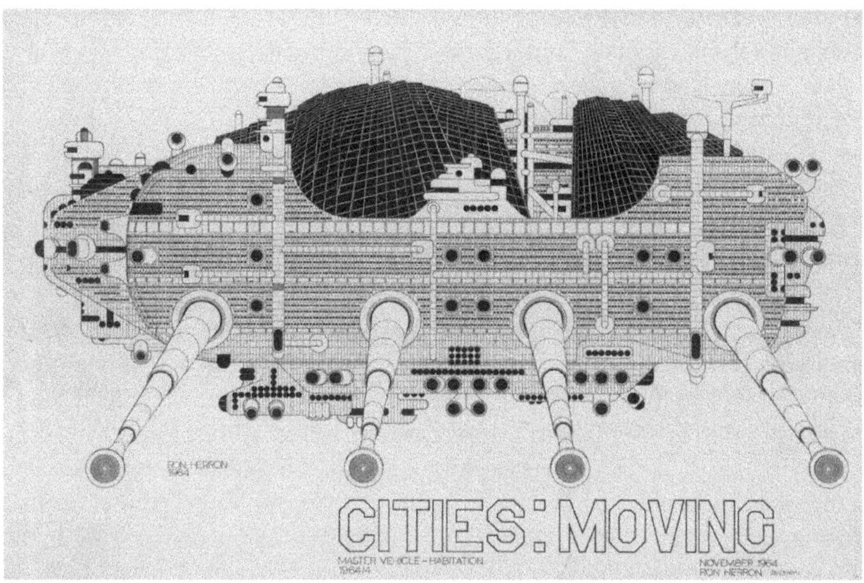

FIGURE 2.6 Cities: Moving, Master Vehicle-Habitation, project. *Aerial Perspective, 1964. Notes, ink and graphite on tracing paper 21 3/4 × 32 3/4' (55.2 × 83.2 cm). Image courtesy of the Museum of Modern Art, New York / Scala, Florence.*

projects from the group into a proposed modular grid into which functional modules could be plugged in and swapped out of a central infrastructural mega-machine as required. Their proposed megastructures employed fictional technologies and modular building processes to propose a flexible, adaptable urban environment. Conceived to evolve and transform dynamically, *Plug-In City* proposed an architecture that underwent continual re-configuration in reaction to technical developments and societal needs. Arguing against the notion that architecture is permanent and fixed, Archigram reimagined the city as an organically evolving structure where ultimately the 'megastructures dissolved into ubiquitous bots, virtual effects or, at its extreme, simply ambiance' (Fierro 2024: 5). While Archigram earnestly proposed technologically advanced cities, and with Peter Cook's involvement in *The Line*, may achieve it, Florence-based architecture collective Superstudio, established in 1966, proposed wild concepts from planet-size megastructures to post-architectural nomadic social structures that were 'at the level of infrastructure; it's a premonition of the Internet today. At the level of social structure, it may be a fair prediction of augmented reality tomorrow' (Keats 2018).

Superstudio became aware of Archigram through a self-published architecture magazine of the same name; the magazine was a London-based platform for youthful architectural discourse and concepts driven by

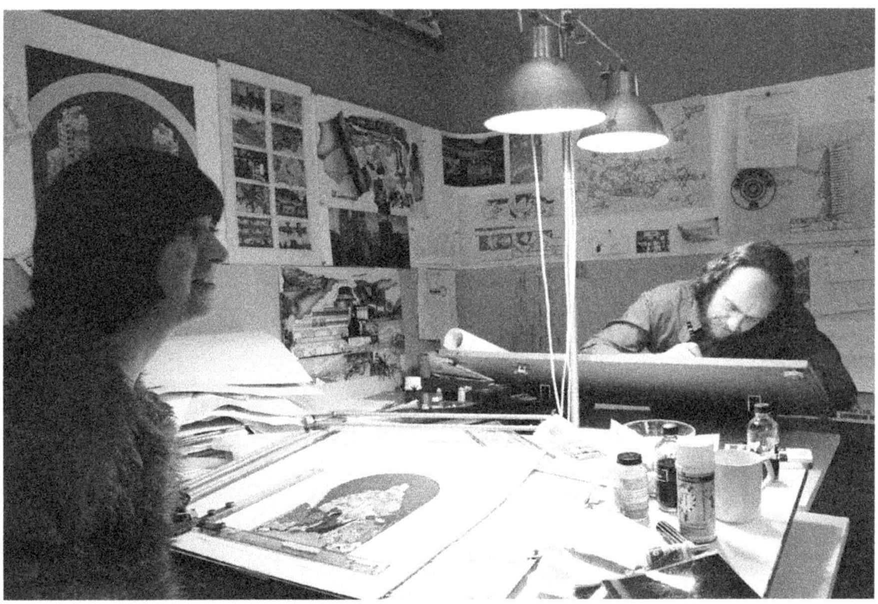

FIGURE 2.7 *Archigram Architects member Ron Herron at his drawing board in the Archigram Endell St office, 1972, London, UK. Photo: Kathy deWitt. Courtesy of Kathy deWitt / Alamy Stock Photo.*

popular culture and technology in the form of spaceships, submarines and oil rigs. Superstudio was a founding collective of a movement of architects and designers in Italy in the mid to late 1960s, whose work was described as *architettura radicale* (radical architecture) by the architecture critic Germano Celant in an attempt to gather diverse utopic experimental studios mainly in Florence under a single name. Organized in collectives aligned with the anti-capitalist political, cultural and social counter-cultural movement of the time, the Italian Radicals opposed the modernist myth of the single architectural visionary, breaking with a tradition predicated on providing a literal relationship between the schema and its construction or adhering to traditional concepts of historical context or modernist ideals of unbridled progress. In contrast to preceding architectural movements, the Radicals framed architecture entirely as a socio-technical phenomenon, remaining propositional and imagined, disseminated through exhibitions, installations, architectural competitions, text, collages, design objects and drawings.

While infinite grids are synonymous with the visual collages of Superstudio's concepts of post-architecture existence they also became the framework for the all-encompassing megastructures that, by their very scale, negated themselves as architecture per se, but rather become an ironic commentary on international modernism taken to its absurd conclusion, their improbability reinforcing Superstudio's utopic vision of a nomadic existence on a plug and play energy grid. Far from operating in a cultural vacuum, Superstudio were astutely aware of and influenced by the emergence of pop art and technology-driven art projects in New York, the work of Viennese Architect Hans Hollein with his 1968 proclamation that *Alles ist Architektur* (everything is architecture) where Hollein argued that architecture was not necessarily a building and could be simulated without it via media and technology. Liberated from the tectonics of building 'real' architecture, the Radicals were free to engage with critical and socially progressive urban agendas in a pivotal decade marked by youth-driven counterculture and profound social, political and artistic shifts providing both a vision of the future and a hyperreal hallucinatory reflection of an imagined alternate space of the present. Aligned with science fiction imagery, future technologies and early computer graphics, which were employed to propose radical new ways of living and societal structures, the Italian Radical Architects utilized visual graphics, collages and films. Their collages of infinite gridded worlds populated by nomads who inhabited fragments of a photo-collaged reality, or the continuous repetitive universal megastructures, recall the porous and interstitial border between the real, the virtual and the fictional that this project advances. Unlike most twentieth-century professional architects that preceded them, the Radical's intent was not to propose built form but to propose utopic worlds and uncompromisingly critique existing socio-political frameworks, freed from the pragmatics of construction and the rationale of capitalism. Initiated by the two prominent Italian Radical collectives Superstudio and Archizoom Associati, the 1966 exhibition *Superarchitettura*, realized at the Jolly 2 gallery in Pistoia near Florence, is generally regarded as the defining moment in the birth of the Italian Radical movement overall. The exhibition reflected the rise of pop art and counterculture aesthetics in Italy, with its curvilinear sofas and collection of modular and colourful organically shaped furniture and fittings complemented by conceptual and aesthetic explorations presented in the form of installations. Accompanying the exhibition was the *Superarchitecture Manifesto,* which established the strategy of playful, ironic rhetoric for the movement, proclaiming that

> Superarchitecture is the architecture of superproduction, of superconsumption, of superpersuasion to consume, of the supermarket, the superman, of superoctane gasoline. Superarchitecture accepts the logic of production and consumption, and works for its *demystification.*
>
> (SOZZANI 2007)

In parallel to Superstudio and Archizoom Associati, other Radical collectives formed, including Florence-based Design Studio *UFO,* whose members were influenced by the semiotic teachings of University of Florence semiotician Umberto Eco and the Florentine group *Gruppo 9999* that focused on issues around ecology and sustainability and were 'especially interested in research on the theater as applied to architecture' (Ambasz 1972: 276). *Gruppo 9999* manifested their position through design happenings, including light projections on Florence's Ponte Vecchio, media installations in the *Space Electronic* night club and *The Separate School for Expanded Conceptual Architecture (S-Space),* cofounded with Superstudio in 1971, which presented *the Vita, morte e miracoli dell'architettura = life, death and miracles of architecture* Festival in November 1971. In Turin, *Gruppo Strum* (Group for Instrumental Architecture) prioritized 'the use of architecture as an active instrument for political propaganda' (Ambasz 1972). Superstudio's projects *Continuous Monument* (1969) and Archizoom Associati's project *No-Stop City* (1969–72) converge in their exploration of radical, utopic and speculative concepts of urban futures, questioning the established role of the architect and launching utopic concepts around future human inhabitation while reacting against modernist architecture in favour for a 'more imaginative, science-fiction-like approach' (Mcquaid et al. 2002: 178). Provocatively, Archizoom Associati's, borderless *No-Stop City* (1969–72) asserted that people's actions should be able to reconfigure their personal space, simultaneously freeing the individual from architecture's controlling aspects while imposing a centreless, non-hierarchical, homogeneous urban landscape, realized as an endless grid of prefabricated units where all and any urban operations could be housed in an entirely interchangeable city. *No-Stop City*'s unending urban fabric ironically alluded to future technologies and industrial production to assemble an infinitely extendable city that expanded 'the model of the factory to society itself' (Stauffer 2020: 104). In the collages of Archizoom Associati, ironic utopia, rhetorical strategy and acuteness of critique produced 'a gloomy reality brightened by the poetry of the irrational' (Stauffer 2020:106). Conceptually, the blankness and repetitive nature of the proposed urban landscapes were intended to allow the individual to operate autonomously from any central political power, living a nomadic existence and indulging in anything from radical consumerism to digital nomadism. The characteristics of *No-Stop City*, *Continuous Monument* and other radical projects included a deliberately open-ended approach. The projects evolved without fixed completion dates, with exhibited installations appearing to be a work in progress towards a collective future vision represented by a body of work rather than by single works. This approach allowed for collective contributions and a dynamic convergence with other Radical Studios, ultimately leading the movement to evolve a distinct ideological framework and a recognizable artistic visual language across design and architecture. Typical of the open framework that permeated the radicals' approach, Archizoom Associatis developed a strictly geometric, non-gendered clothing concept entitled *Dressing Design: Nearest Habitat System*, intended to be worn in the *No-Stop City*. A prototype was exhibited as an animated film and shown at the 1973 Milan Triennale at the International Exhibition of Industrial Design. Curated by designer Ettore Sottsass (1917–2007) and Archizoom Associati's co-founder Andrea Branzi (1938–2023), the exhibition prioritized the immaterial over the material, exhibiting design objects through film and other audiovisual experiences. The design objects' placement within the wider architectural or urban spaces and the interchangeability of disciplines were to become a defining quality of the Radicals. Consequently, Superstudio's negative utopic model of total urbanization, the *Continuous Monument*, symbolized a form of transnational conformity by connecting diverse cultures, languages and geographic locations through a unified architectural megastructure. Evolving from an early concept titled *Supersurface*, where architecture was removed entirely, and the planet was wrapped in an energy grid populated by nomads that could access it simply by plugging in, *Continuous Monument* visualized a continuous, repetitive three-dimensional grid structure encircling the earth. Its intentional, ironic use of the international style[2] and monumental black-and-white blocks critiqued modernist architecture's agenda and the harrowing homogenizing consequence of globalization, capitalism and technology on society if left untethered. The endless Cartesian grid became a recurring motif in their work, reducing architecture to an infinitely scalable, dimensionless abstract field and, through its impossible scale, not a proposition on architecture but a proposition against it.

The Italian Radicals' work arguably gained, to use Jasanoff's term, *institutional stability* and international exposure through the 1972 MoMA New York exhibition entitled *Italy: The New Domestic Landscape*. Curated

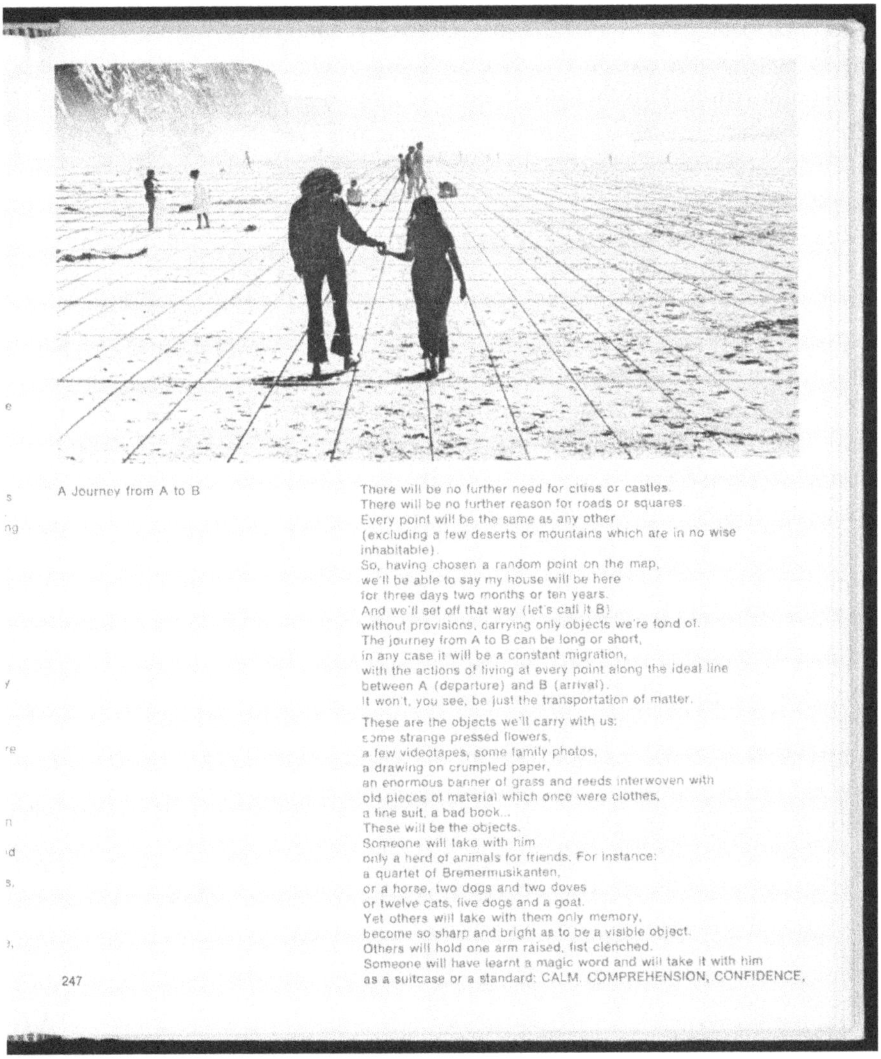
A Journey from A to B

There will be no further need for cities or castles.
There will be no further reason for roads or squares.
Every point will be the same as any other
(excluding a few deserts or mountains which are in no wise inhabitable).
So, having chosen a random point on the map,
we'll be able to say my house will be here
for three days two months or ten years.
And we'll set off that way (let's call it B)
without provisions, carrying only objects we're fond of.
The journey from A to B can be long or short,
in any case it will be a constant migration,
with the actions of living at every point along the ideal line
between A (departure) and B (arrival).
It won't, you see, be just the transportation of matter.

These are the objects we'll carry with us:
some strange pressed flowers,
a few videotapes, some family photos,
a drawing on crumpled paper,
an enormous banner of grass and reeds interwoven with
old pieces of material which once were clothes,
a fine suit, a bad book...
These will be the objects.
Someone will take with him
only a herd of animals for friends. For instance:
a quartet of Bremermusikanten,
or a horse, two dogs and two doves
or twelve cats, five dogs and a goat.
Yet others will take with them only memory,
become so sharp and bright as to be a visible object.
Others will hold one arm raised, fist clenched.
Someone will have learnt a magic word and will take it with him
as a suitcase or a standard: CALM. COMPREHENSION, CONFIDENCE,

247

FIGURE 2.8 Superstudio, A Journey from A to B, *1969, pencil on photomontage. Illustration from* 'The New Domestic Landscape' *catalogue of MoMA exhibition, 1972. Photo: Aldo Ballo. The Museum of Modern Art Library, ref. no. :300062429_0251. Image courtesy of The Museum of Modern Art, New York / Scala Florence.*

by US-Argentinian architect and industrial designer Emilio Ambasz, it brought together twelve leading Italian designers, half of whom were part of the Radical Movement, in a single show. Being presented as a coherent and institutionally endorsed vision at MoMA, the Italian Radicals had, in the space of six years, consolidated their ironic techno-spatial imagined urban landscapes into 'cohesive and publicly performed visions of desirable futures' (Jasanoff 2015a: 11), even if those futures relied on entirely fictional advances in society, science and technology, taken forward by successive generations of architects and designers and probably only realizable within the virtual realm. In a late iteration of *Continuous Monument* for the 1972 MoMA exhibition *Italy: The New Domestic,* Superstudio joined fellow Radicals, Archizoom Associati, Gruppo 9999, Gruppo Sturm *and* Ugo la Pietra, in a curatorial section called *Counterdesign as Postulation*. The five selected Radical collectives were invited to realize a 16-foot x 16-foot environment, a film and a catalogue essay, and in the two other significant sections of the exhibition, entitled *Design as Postulation*, six leading Italian designers, including Ettore Sottsass and Gae Aulenti, developed projects to the same brief in a curatorial strategy that played with the internal dynamics of the Italian design scene. A third section, *Design as Commentary*, comprised a fictional future narrative by Italian architect Gaetano Pesce describing the findings of a future excavation of a small city from the late-twentieth century in an epoch Pesce describes as the *Period of the Great Contaminations,* a satirical account of societies disregard for a sustainable future. Through a 'model of a mental attitude' (Ambasz 1972: 242), Superstudio presented in the exhibition that they termed a Microevent/Microenvironment defined as a 'critical reappraisal of the possibilities of life without objects'(Ambasz 1972). Their model within the 16-foot cube occupied around a third of the floor area. The exhibition intended to 'present an alternative model for life on earth' (Ambasz 1972). The model included Superstudio's signature Cartesian grid, to be 'understood not only in the physical sense but as a visual-verbal metaphor for an ordered and rational distribution of resources' where 'Nomadism becomes the permanent condition' (Ambasz 1972: 242), and resources distributed evenly regardless of location. Like many of the Radicals projects, Superstudio's schemes are not supposed to be scaled into reality but present a 'visual rendition of a critical attitude toward (or a hope for) the activity of designing, understood as philosophical speculation' (Ambasz 1972: 242).

In this, Superstudio's visualization of the spatial interface between humans presented a strangely prescient vision of a seemingly virtual space of inhabitation where notions of time and the logistics of existence become immaterial. These qualities have an unnerving similarity to the virtual territory imagined in this project and, thus, provide an analogue visual and conceptual precedent to grasp the contradictions of an interstitial border between the virtual, the physical and the imagined. Several recent exhibitions and publications, including *Radical Design* at the Vitra Design Museum, *Superstudio 50* at the MAXXI in Rome, *Yesterday's Future* at the Deutsches Architekturmuseum, *Utopie Radicali: Florence 1966–1976* at the Canadian Centre for Architecture (CCA), *Archizoom Superstudio – Superarchitettura* at the Fondazione Sozzani in Milan, *Radical: Italian Design 1965–1985* at the Yale Architecture Gallery and *Radical Disco: Architecture and Nightlife in Italy, 1965–1975* at the Institute for Contemporary Art in London's as well as the 2021 *Expo Superstudio Migrazioni* at CIVA in Brussels have secured the Italian radical movement's notoriety and legacy, reinforcing that the conceptual thinking is as relevant today as it was then. These exhibitions have re-examined the Radicals in the light of current discourses around extended reality, climate change adaption, human rights and social equality and highlighted their prescient understanding of networked digital technologies. For architecture, the exhibition format, through the appropriation of performative and media art strategies together with models and drawings, continues to be the primary site where concepts of inhabitation and new forms or architectural imaginaries emerge and are communicated. The exhibition format allows ideas to be partially built, fragmented and scaled models of impossible urban landscapes and buildings presented as ideas, speculations and experiments. In this format, socio-technical futures are also prototyped and made visible. Architecture exhibitions have been a feature of the architectural discourse across the twentieth century, both in Europe and the United States, with the Deutscher Werkbund and the Bauhaus developing architectural exhibitions to express the material reality and the ideas and concepts behind the work. Ranging from museum-scale exhibitions of models, drawings and interiors to exhibitions of completed buildings, such as Marcel Breuer's butterfly roof house on the roof of MoMA in 1949, to entire housing estates exemplified by the Deutscher Werkbund's exhibition *The Dwelling* at the Weissenhofsiedlung, Stuttgart, Germany, in 1927 that included designs from seventeen European modernist architects including Le Corbusier, Mies van Rohe and Bauhaus founder Walter Gropius. The overwhelming intent of architectural exhibitions until the 1960s was the exploration of modern forms and materials as they related to actual physical buildings and building costs. This self-proclaimed mandate began to shift in the 1960s with a series of exhibitions at MoMA, including the 1960 *Visionary Architecture* exhibition curated by Arthur Drexler, followed by *Architecture Without Architects* in 1964 and *The New City: Architecture and Urban Renewal* in 1967. Italian Architect Aldo Rossi directed the architectural section *Architettura Razionale* of the 1973 Milan Triennale, which laid the groundwork for architecture's inclusion in the Venice Biennale in 1980. The first Venice Architecture Biennale curated by Italian Architect and theorist Paolo Portoghesi (1931–2023) was an exhibition entitled *The Presence of the Past,* which is still today regarded as a critical point in the international exposure of post-modern thought and a foundational model for architecture exhibitions and biennales worldwide. Since 1980, Biennales and Triennale of architecture have been established in places as diverse as Teheran, Chicago, Moscow, Seoul and Lisbon and have provided a natural site for architectural imaginaries, propositions and speculations. Often utilizing display strategies from the media arts, theatre and design, this global exhibition network has provided the discipline of architecture with a multifaceted platform on which to imagine and disseminate architectural ideas. The installations and interventions have articulated a vast array of architectural thought located between theoretical texts and tectonics. In recent editions of biennales worldwide, issues of sustainability, climate adaption and social justice within a posthuman theoretical frame have come to the fore, echoing earlier work and corresponding governmental frameworks where politics, technology and sustainability have become inseparably intertwined.

Forensic architecture's virtual models

Antithetical to the visionary propositions of imagined architecture, virtual spaces for gaming or contemporary speculative architecture of virtual worldbuilding is the work of UK research group Forensic Architecture's (FA) unerring focus on the political imaginary through the investigation, visualization and presentation of physical sites of conflict and violence. Founded by architect Eyal Weizman in 2010, FA is committed to investigating human rights abuses with digital technologies. They describe themselves as an 'interdisciplinary agency operating across human rights, journalism, architecture, art and aesthetics, academia and the law' (FA 2024) that develops, employs and disseminates new techniques, methods and concepts for investigating state and corporate violence (FA 2024). Working at the intersection of architecture, technology and human rights advocacy, FA uses the digital tools of architecture to virtually construct sites where human rights incidents and other violations have occurred and build evidence around them. FA's investigations are either self-commissioned or commissioned by news outlets such as Al Jazeera in the case of Hind Rajab's death in Gaza in 2024, lawyers representing bereaved families in the case of the 2017 Grenfell Tower Fire or NGOs, grassroots organizations or governmental agencies such as Amnesty International or the European Centre for Constitutional and Human Rights (ECCHR). The resulting, often highly visual analysis forms the basis for dissemination through exhibitions, web platforms and legal processes, parliamentary inquiries and UN human rights reports. FA's stunningly designed website is a highly transparent, current and exhaustive project archive, presenting the most accurate primary material available. It includes team members commissioning parties, exhibition and event sites, methodology and detailed description of all projects laid out systematically.

The research agency works with architectural techniques and tools of site analysis and visualization to advocate, challenge and call out actors of human rights and other abuses. Utilizing digital XR technologies, additive modelling, fieldwork, shadow analysis, data mining, audio analysis, open source intelligence (OSINT), Geolocation and photogrammetry, FA coalesces fieldwork with extant photographic, film and audio sources into a virtual site model to build a geospatial configuration that, together with the analysis of satellite images, audio files, media and social media, personal testimonies and

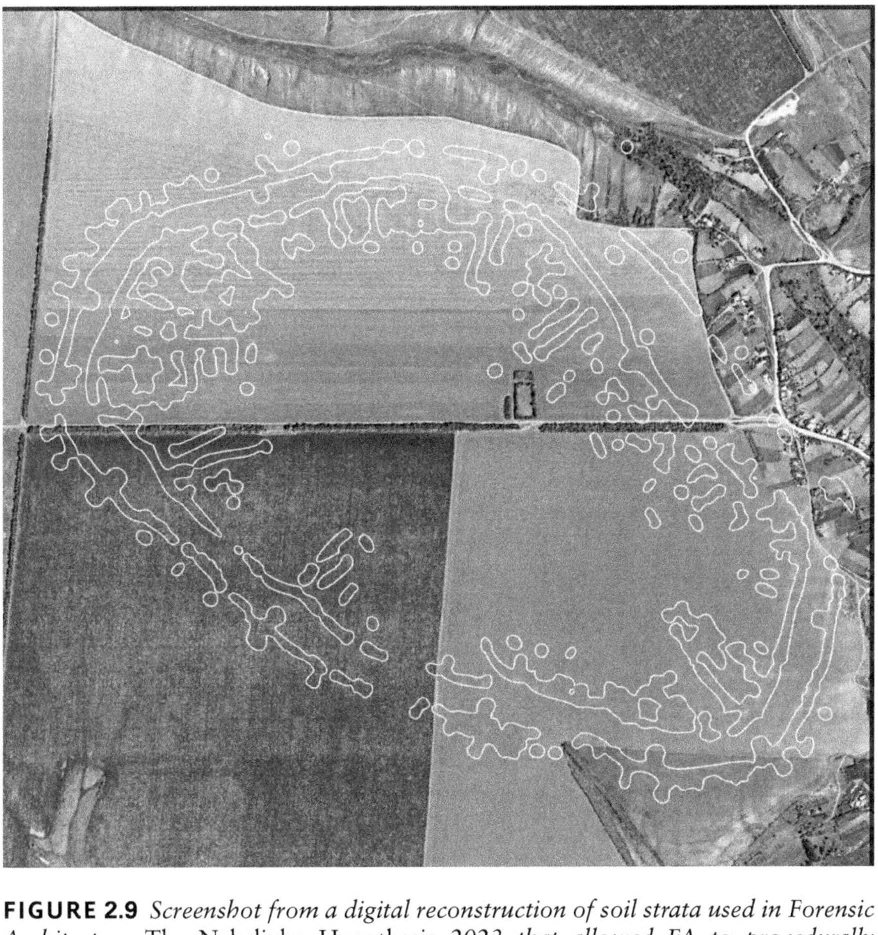

FIGURE 2.9 *Screenshot from a digital reconstruction of soil strata used in Forensic Architects –* The Nebelivka Hypothesis *2023 that allowed FA to procedurally recreate in 3D the structure of the soil covering the settlement. Image © Forensic Architecture.*

newspaper reports, harnessed as technical evidence of the incident, its site and complexity in time. To this effect, FA has developed specific and relatively complex methodologies that ensure accurate reconstructions of events and record and follow interconnected events over time. These methodologies aid in reconstructing, enhancing and understanding current and historical incidents of violence, displacement, destruction and environmental degradation. Taking a specific FA case *1.88 Resituating Evidence: Genocide and Reparations in German Namibia dated 1904–1908,* investigated in 2022, FA outline their process as follows

> Working with Ovaherero community members and oral historians, we (FA) employed a technique we refer to as 'situated testimony'. This involves the re-configuration of a navigable game engine such that it serves as a digital platform in which traditional and collective forms of memory can be enacted. The result, in this instance, is a series of immersive models of historically important locations within the wider landscape, collaboratively reconstructed to appear as they were before the early 20th century period of German colonisation, and during the genocide of 1904–8.
>
> (FA 2024)

Further methodologies such as Additive Modelling, Fieldwork, Situated Testimony, Geolocation, GroundTruth (matching the results of Photogrammetry and remote sensing to an actual physical site), Remote Sensing (data from satellite and aerial imagery) and Photogrammetry were employed to reconstruct acts of genocide committed by the then imperial power Germany between 1904 and 1908 against the Hereru, Mbanderu and Nama peoples in present-day Namibia. This project was undertaken in collaboration with 'genocide activists from descendant communities to merge archival photographs and oral testimony within advanced 3D models of sites of atrocities' (FA 2024). The findings of this project are intended to be used as supporting evidence for future land claims and reparations. Projects such as the ongoing investigation of migrant drift-back in the Aegean and violent pushbacks of asylum seekers from Greece into Turkey are projects funded by the Safe Passage Foundation, Allianz Foundation and Open Society Foundation (OSF) in collaboration with AF's Berlin office Forensis, or, as in the case of a young woman from Iran experiencing illegal pushback, has been commissioned by the European Centre for Constitutional and Human Rights (ECCHR 2020). FA disseminates its findings through its website, media and the courts and in staging exhibitions that document specific projects or more significant themes. Since its foundation in 2010, FA has participated in or featured solo in forty-four exhibitions worldwide in architecture biennales (Venice 2023, Rotterdam 2024 and many others), museums, visual art venues and cultural centres, among them the ZKM (Centre for Art and Media Karlsruhe) 2023 Mumbai part of Peter Weibel's and Bruno Latour's *Critical Zones* exhibition project (see Chapter 5 for a detailed discussion of Weibel and Latour's genre of the 'thought exhibition') as well as public institutions. Forensic Architecture has become present in the closed selection processes for Biennales and international exhibitions, a development that could not remain without comment and some critical reflection. Art historian and critic Claire Bishop's reflection on FA's exhibition practice in the context of her 2023 Artforum article 'Information Overload', art critic Claire Bishop groups the collective into the 'vanguard of research-based art' (Bishop 2023) and strongly critiques what she calls the 'monodirectionality' (Bishop 2023) of their work that, while, as Bishop contends, presenting valid counterhegemonic research that often unsettles dominant narratives, the viewer's reception of the work is predetermined by the way FA navigates them through the large amounts of data visualized in highly persuasive formats. Indeed, not neutral, with strong opinions and openly advocating for the marginalized, occupied and colonized, and with research that uses digital tools and virtual models to find the other side of 'truth', FA's work, however, exists independently of their exhibitions and whether the assignation of 'art' to their collective, as Bishop does, is applicable or appropriate is another question. FA's mandate is evident in its mission statement:

> We investigate states and corporate entities – including militaries, police forces, government agencies, and companies – for their violent acts, including repressive policing, civilian deaths in conflict, structurally racist policymaking, violence against migrants and refugees, and historical and contemporary colonial violence, including the destruction of traditional environments and life worlds.
>
> (FA 2024)

Investigation and its documentation, while traditionally not a distinct artistic or aesthetic category, has come to the fore in artistic practice with the rapid rise of digital. Far from being overloaded with information and unable to navigate their path and form their own opinion, contemporary audiences are data and digital literates. Bishop's critique of research-based art falls short in that she underestimates the audience's widened attention span in the digital age and their desire not for 'the truth,' not for 'post-truths' but for standpoints independent from state actors and their associated media and that, arguably, all art is research-based. FA argues,

> In the pursuit of accountability, we seek to work across forums, from courts and parliamentary inquiries, citizen's tribunals, international media

> and exhibitions. [. . .] In courts, we struggle for the admissibility of citizen-produced digital evidence; in cultural institutions, we employ art as an investigative and political medium.
>
> (FA 2024)

In an installation, created in association with archaeologist David Wengrow and University of London Goldsmith's Centre for Spatial Technologies (CST) and disseminated in the form of an exhibition, a book and an extensive media gallery on their website, presents as a research exhibition embedded in a site-specific scenographic installation thus heightening the scientific materials' presence and persuasive power. Exhibited at the Venice Architecture Biennale in 2023, *The Nebelivka Hypothesis (NH)* takes as its departure point the findings of archaeological excavations in Nebelivka, Ukraine. The archaeological remains of the 6000-year-old city showed a settlement without an architecture of power – without a centre. Seemingly proving a light ecological footprint, the excavations pointed to a concentrically organized settlement with domestic buildings around an empty, open space in its centre. The implications for architecture, urbanism and sociology are obvious: Was this a society of equals? FA's *Nebelivka Hypothesis* posits that 'egalitarian societies have existed on an urban scale and that cities could also enhance the vitality of the land they inhabit' (FA & Wengrow 2023: 34). Their methodology for this project comprised additive modelling, Ground Truth, Photogrammetry, Remote Sensing and Simulation (digital models that imitate operations or processes). Far from providing archaeological information in a detached modus, the installation was sited in a large, dimly lit space of the Arsenale building dominated by an excavated rectangular structure filled with soil. Downward projection onto the bordered structure showed the archaeological findings and detailed documentation of each step of FA's digitally based research. The text projected at the opposite wall explained succinctly the meaning of this project beyond an aesthetic and informative experience, namely: 'If Nebelivka is a city, then our genealogy of the city – rooted in extraction, predation and hierarchy – must change.' Digital technologies and, in particular, what this project calls the virtual in that certain modes of production and dissemination carry within them 'possibility' and, in the case of *the NH*, can visualize and communicate this 'possibility' to a non-specialized audience – both the central findings and above all a proof of concept with wide-ranging implications about what a city was, is and could be. FA's exhibition and web-based work highlight the critical capacity of the virtual model as dispositif able to reveal power structures and politicized narratives. In staging their research through exhibitions, FA makes both visible and tangible existing socio-technical and architectural imaginaries to the public and opens these up to scrutiny.

Performance, media and architecture

This chapter investigated the dual and connected histories of technology and new media in New York in the 1960s, where individual engineers, visual artists, composers and choreographers began to collaborate with the aim of expanding both disciplines through the integration of new technologies into live performance. Remarkable in its scale, ambition and rigorous playfulness, the performance series *9 Evenings: Theatre and Engineering*, conceived by Bell Lab engineer Billy Klüver and visual artist Robert Rauschenberg, is discussed as foreshadowing developments in media arts, technology and performance concerning interactivity, improvisation and the representation of body and machine that have since become mainstream. The continued collaboration of artists and scientists in specialized institutions had its origins in the open-ended experimentations of the performance series *9 Evenings* and the founding of EAT. Revisiting two decades of experimentation from the founding of EAT to the propositional architectures and new technologies exemplified by the 1970 Osaka Expo allows for the historical arc that continued into early media arts on one side and the notion of a radical, unbuilt architecture on the other hand, to become visible. The introduction and positioning of imagined and imaginary architecture at the border between the real and virtual, together with theatre and art, allowed for a discussion on the territories they inhabit, the inferred fragmentation and the material and immaterial spatial doubling inherent in the continuous mirroring between worlds and the architecture exhibition emerged as the primary vector in the communication and dissemination of the imaginary of architecture and its utopias. Fiction, as the third realm between the virtual and the real, continues to be the carrier of the narratives of hierarchical architectural and socio-technical imaginary and manifests in the futurist plug-in cities and nomadic gridded future worlds of the Italian Radicals. Today, the socio-technical imaginary is exhibited in the political advocacy projects of the research group Forensic Architects (FA). The virtual model operates in their digital worlds of architectural tools and methods as the dispositif that asks the viewer to recognize and critique the fragmentary, distorted and hijacked narratives of political power. With Braidotti, this chapter affirms the significance of *other* stories told by those *becoming-minor*. This conversation is continued in Chapters 3 and 4 with close readings of artists' and artists' collectives' contemporary works where the human-machine interface provides the foundation of a criticality toward anthropocentric and binary imaginaries. Writings and case studies collide through theoretical proximity and diverse geographic and gender identities on this territory's porous border between the material and immaterial worlds clustered momentarily within this monograph as a conduit to other worlds both created and yet to come.

3

Performing the virtual model in the material world

Deconstructing nation, gender, race

Focusing on contemporary artists and artist groups from Asia and the Middle East who perform across virtual spaces and physical environments, creating innately blended landscapes of human and nonhuman activity and invention while utilizing motion capture and other interactive technologies in live performance configurations, the chapter explores the performative dimension of the virtual model and its potential to construct and deconstruct site, nation, gender, race, culture and history. Concepts, technologies and aesthetics are discussed in relationship to space, time, narrative and body. Often positioned in blurred genres between performance, installation and exhibition, these artists are engaged in pressing social and environmental issues and hold a critical position in reframing the use of technology in artistic contexts. Working with extended reality technologies (XR) and digital postproduction technologies extracted for display in a performance or exhibition setting,[1] the artists reflect on and articulate critical positions on technology. The Japanese artist collective Dumb Type, whose international installation and performance practice between 1992 and 2024 is discussed, represents an international trend of artists' adoption of technology to create spaces and articulate new narratives in mediated environments using advanced technologies to produce digital scenographic elements while retaining the physical body of the performer on the stage. In contrast, in Chinese artist LuYang's artworks, the physical body is dematerialized into code via motion capture systems and exists conceptually in the virtual realm. The physical body is captured, mapped and digitized, creating avatars and landscapes inspired by Buddhist cosmologies, which become both the site for the body's existence and the location of the installation, performance and video. US-based Iranian-Kurdish artist Morehshin Allahyari's practice oscillates between physical manifestations of the immaterial and virtual representations of the material within a conceptual base that both reclaims material cultural remnants and immaterial Middle Eastern mythology in a practice that spans performance, objects, video and virtual reality and activism. As a self-declared *preenactor*, Berlin-based Jewish artist Yael Bartana uses the virtual model in mixed media installations to create artefacts within dystopic and utopic worlds as reimagined kabbalistic mythologies. Humankind's departure from a destroyed Earth or remigration to historical geographies of genocide are shown as conceptual possibilities to rethink and transgress contemporary ideologies of nation, race and environment. In coalescence, the artists and case studies discussed here explore shifting notions of body, heritage, identity, gender and location through an array of technologies.

Theoretically, no common bonding through a shared experience of techno-anxiety or environmental collapse is assumed, but rather one that discards binary oppositions of human and nonhuman, male and female, flora and fauna, while embracing ideas of a multiplicity of species and transversal connections. Rosi Braidotti posits that the 'most important' of 'all the set criteria for Posthuman Critical Theory [is] the tactical method of defamiliarization, that is to say, disconnection of the subject from familiar and habitual patterns of identity' (Braidotti in Alemani 2022: 220). This position, aligned with queer-feminist philosophical frameworks, demands radical action that entails the cutting of links with established hierarchies of human and nature, human and history, human and culture, human and machine and opens a field of political and materialist philosophical inquiry. The artists and artist groups discussed here are united in their *becoming minor* in the Deleuzian sense of 'minority as a universal figure or becoming – everybody/everything (*devenir tout le monde*)' (Deleuze and Guattari 1987: 470). They are contemporaries in deterritorializing the political imaginary[3] as an artistic strategy from their own conceptual perspective and distinct aesthetics. In the works discussed in this chapter, humans and machines enter diverse and different, often symbiotic relationships, marred by interferences and uncertainties propelling the audience on journeys that are urgent and relentless, frequently overwhelming in their visual or acoustic elements, and overall, affording critical agency through the human-machine interface. The power of conceptual thought and creative practice to articulate, contextualize and reimagine historical and contemporary inequalities based on sexuality, race, ethnicity or gender through the deliberate use of the digital is outlined and affirmed. Performance, while not the only mode of representation in the works introduced, nevertheless operates as a central part of Yael Bartana, Morehshin Allahyari, LuYang and Dumb Type's body of work and is a discursive element within a thematic series in the form of lecture-performances or working with the dramatic and spatial tension between the real and the virtual in physical space.

Liminal spaces – dumb type

As early adopters of the implementation of new media on stage, Japanese art and performance collective Dumb Type experiments with prerecorded video and live projections as scenographic and narrative elements since the mid-1980s; their latest productions include AI-enabled installations and mise-en-scènes that embrace advanced technologies and cinematic and audio elements generated through postproduction tools, including digital data-driven modelling software and virtual environments made visible to the audience via large screens or projections on stage or in exhibition spaces. Highly articulate in their positions on nature, inclusion, identity and the alienating aspects of technology, Dumb Type excels at 'perpetually shifting and evading fixed categorization', preferring instead to enact a sort of scanning across a 'spectrum of possibilities' (Lentini and Takatani 2022: 16). Such deliberately performed instability extends to the shifting membership of the group, the way projects evolve into each other and their refusal to be classified by medium or artistic form and rather embracing performance, new media and installation in a body of work that operates in a 'liminal zone between two states or spaces' (2022) and speaks of the zones between inclusion and exclusion, material and immaterial, life and death not as binary opposites but through a rigorous exploration of the fragility of human existence immersed in artificially constructed worlds. This perpetual shifting between the differing forms of artistic expression – installation, theatre and performance – and the reuse of conceptual, literary and visual motifs across three decades of practice give Dumb Type's body of work remarkable coherence. Collaborators come and go, installation merges into performance and decade-old motifs are rediscovered and reinterpreted; literary sources cross from performance to installation, where one work blurs into the next, resulting in a body of work that, rather than being a discreet set of works, arguably reads as a singular artistic statement. Dumb Type Theatre (renamed Dumb Type in 1987) first emerged in Kyoto in 1984 as a non-hierarchical, multidisciplinary, inclusive collective that retains relevance until today through its prescient understanding of future societal, technological and aesthetic trends in Japan and internationally. Influenced by filmmakers such as Stanley Kubrick, Derek Jarman and Andrei Tarkovsky for their visually rich depiction of ultimately tragic human desires, Japanese Noh theatre for its treatment of voice, gesture and time and contemporaries such as Laurie Anderson, Robert

Wilson and Pina Bausch for their staged experiments into time and narrative, Dumb Type became known for its 'performative approach to the information age' (Miya 2017: 123) where technology became a 'dreamscape into which people enter' (Rugoff in Rovner 2022). Their central themes, including gender politics and a positive engagement with the AIDS crisis within its conceptual framing of the relationship between the human body and the vagaries of technologies, inform a collection of highly politicized work that differentiated (and, at times, alienated) itself from its 1980s and 1990s technology-oriented contemporaries. The performance and installation series *S/N* (1992–96) explicitly dealt with the HIV-positive status of Teiji Furuhashi, one of Dumb Type's founding members, at a time when a pervasive silence, or, as one of the projections in *S/N* reads, a *conspiracy of silence* surrounded the topic in Japan. The first iteration of *S/N* was an installation in the exhibition *The Binary Era* at the Museum of Ixelles in Brussels. Further iterations followed in Japan, Vienna and San Francisco in 1992. The initial *Seminar Show for S/N* was first staged in March 1993 at the Artspace Mumonkan in Kyoto and at the Shonandai Culture Center Civic Theater in Fujisawa, near Tokyo, as an 'open production process' (Lunsing 2017: 103) by interspersing a talk show format, a panel conversation on sexuality, AIDS and gender with fragments of the yet-to-be-staged *S/N* performance (that premiered the following year). The seminar began with a group of performers labelled as Black, Japanese, HIV+, Homosexual, Deaf, American or Male with yellow stickers in capital blue letters stuck on their immaculate suits. At a certain point, Peter Golightly, the *Black American Homosexual*, turned to the audience and said (in English), 'I am sorry to tell you that we are not actors, but we are this' (Lunsing 2017: 97) and proceeded to point at and read the content of each of the yellow stickers of his fellow performers. As most of the Dumb Type collective identified as heterosexual, this work was not a departure into gay activism but rather a response to Teiji's letter to his collaborators that made his HIV status known and his request that, with the time left for him, that 'dumb type members help him create *S/N* under his direction' (Lunsing 2017). Teiji's biography and personal history aside, both production and *S/N* themes sat directly within Dumb Type's established focus on critiquing exclusion and stereotyping.

The opening section of the performance ended with Alex (Ishibashi Kenjiro) screaming into the microphone SEX, DEATH, LOVE, MONEY, LIFE – five words that would recur in Dumb Type's work through to the 2022 immersive AI-driven installation *TRACE/REACT II* at the *Haus der Kunst* (Museum for Contemporary Art) in Munich. The splicing of a talk show, a panel discussion on the AIDS crisis and other related topics with fragments of an unfinished, highly mediatized performance triggered a debate in Japan on the appropriateness of the medium of performance to address issues on AIDS, gender and identification. The performance *S/N* premiered at the Adelaide

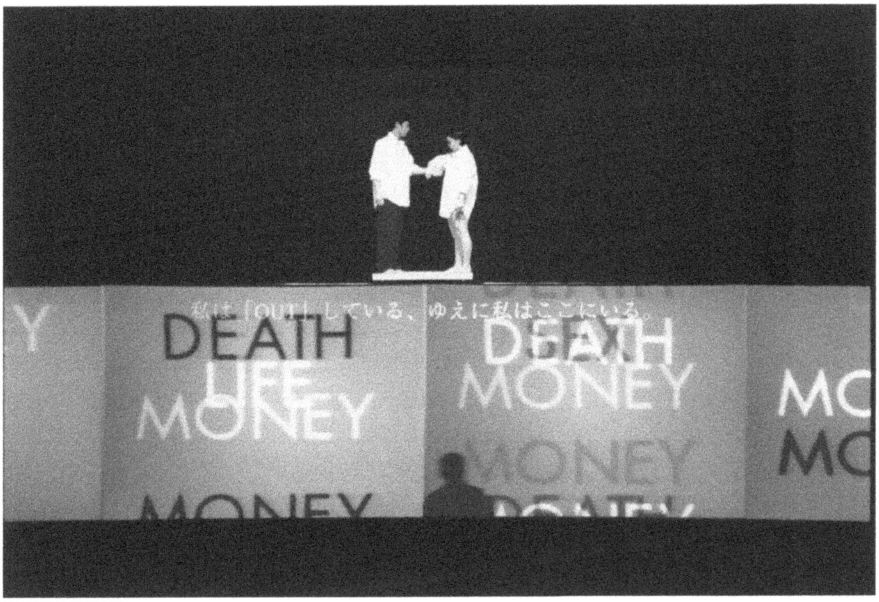

FIGURE 3.1 *Dumb Type Performance of* S/N, *1994. Photo: Kazuo Fukunaga. Image and permissions courtesy of dumb type.*

Festival in Australia in 1994 and travelled internationally to over twenty venues from 1993 to 1996. The set-up was a horizontally split stage, providing two levels for performers: a stage level directly in front of the four back-projected images with performers being silhouetted or highlighted depending on the lighting and a platform receding away from the top of the projection surface to the back of the theatre that allowed the performer as if to *float* above the video images. The deceptively simple set-up allowed intense play between the performer and the moving image. Dumb Type has toured performances and exhibited work internationally since 1988, including collaborations with Danish production house Hotel Pro Forma and New York interdisciplinary design studio Diller + Scofidio. However, this period of intense creation of new performance work and international touring slowed in 2002, and an eighteen-year gap ensued during which no new works were created; however, the performance *work Voyage* was restaged, and the installations *OR* (1997), *Memorandum* (1999) and *Voyage* (2002) were re-exhibited primarily in Europe, as was a collation of works entitled *Memorandum OR Voyage* displayed on an elongated ultra-high-definition screen that had premiered in that form at the Museum of Contemporary Art Tokyo in 2014. Dumb Type's 2002 programme note alludes to the reasons for their silence, arguing that an 'unprecedented atmosphere of opaque uncertainty surrounds us. If you try to dismiss it or paralyze your mind, it stays with you like a second skin of anxiety and fear' and ends with the question, 'is performance a true substitute for such mutual resonance? Once again, we find ourselves questioning the very essence of performance' (Dumb Type in Cesta Cursach 2002). In many respects, this is also a question that *the Seminar Show for S/N* unintentionally provoked in Japan in 1994. The commissioning of a solo exhibition, *DumbType, | Actions + Reflexions,* at the Centre Pompidou-Metz (2018) and the performance entitled *2020* created for the ROHM Theatre Kyoto for the International Arts × Science Festival reassembled the collective and propelled them out of hiatus. Following this, Dumb Type represented Japan in the Japanese Pavilion at the 59th International Venice Biennale with a work entitled *2022, where* famed Japanese composer Ryuichi Sakamoto was welcomed as a member. Concurrently, a significant exhibition comprising three room-size installations entitled *Memorandum OR Voyage*, *Playback* and *TRACE/REACT II* at the Haus der Kunst in Munich (2022), curated by Damian Lentini, represented one of the largest exhibitions of their work in Europe. Due to the pandemic, *2020* was staged without an audience, resulting instead in an outstanding documentation video of the entire performance available through the Japan Foundation's programme *Stage without Borders*. *2020*, in contrast to *Voyage*, is calmer in character and explicitly acknowledges two critical influences on the group, Pina Bausch and Robert Wilson, as well as giving Dumb Type's collaborator, electronic composer and visual artist Ryoji Ikeda a platform to embed his visual data aesthetic through large-scale projections in dialogue with the performers. Comprising a highly contemplative and self-referential work that distils the group's decade-old themes in new ways, *2020* reflects on their body of work and is a precursor of future directions. The stage has a central void, a conceptual and physical device seen in *TRACE/REACT II* at the Haus der Kunst and the Venice Biennale project. Elaborating in the Venice Biennale catalogue text, Dumb Type explains, 'In contrast to the discourses that surround it, the centre of the room is a space – a place that exists nowhere, but at the same time a place that could be anywhere. We live in a time of post-truth and liminal spaces. The centre is void' (Dumb Type in Alemani 2022: 82).

The stage of *2020* comprised a white projection surface at the back of the stage, supplemented by three smaller square screens that could fly in and out of the centre stage; in one scene, thousands of surveillance feeds combined to reveal the faces of figures such as Donald Trump and Vladimir Putin, and in another, a live feed of a record player on the stage was projected, a reference perhaps to *playback*. The performance began with a large single lantern swinging over the void, a solitary figure and a disembodied voice asking seemingly simple questions that came from the same 1856 geography textbook, *First Lessons in Geography*, by James Monteith, that was to be the source of the laser projected text fragments in Venice. Questions from the book, such as 'What is the shape of the earth, what is an ocean, what

FIGURE 3.2 *Dumb Type Performance entitled* 2020. *World Premiere at the KYOTO STEAM – International Arts × Science Festival. Photo: Yoshikazu Inoue. Image and permissions courtesy of dumb type.*

is an empire, what is a mountain, who governs an Empire?' (Dumb Type in Alemani 2022), alluding to a shifting understanding of geospatial mapping, colonization and national identity reinforced by its visual exploration in the second part of the first act with a downward projection with a circular black void, a compositional device first seen in Ikeda's installation *point of no return* (2018). The circular scanning movement of the projection made way for a larger projection of a visualization of a Lidar laser virtual point cloud data set, identical to the one Ikeda also used in the *Data-Verse* trilogy first shown at the 58th Venice Biennale in 2019. In the final scene (around twelve minutes long), a solitary figure returned to the stage and the audience was presented again with a body caught between themselves and the 'scanning' of a map, in this case, the subantarctic. This in-between between humans and technology was further made immediate by placing the audience member in a black room with mirrored floors surrounded by a word cloud of text fragments generated by an AI bot instructed to scour the internet to create associative text strings starting from Dumb Types rallying cry from *S/N*, Love, Sex, Death, Money and Life. The overall experience was one of disassociation as one is immersed in a set of open signifiers where the loss of agency in decoding what surrounds one was overwhelming. The autonomous AI bot was set free to explore the net and report back through this immersion into a text world that

> operates across representational, iterative, and autonomous model typologies in that it is an abstract representation of the human self, undergoing rapid iteration while not proposing a future structure other than further iterations of itself.
>
> (BREJZEK AND WALLEN 2022)

The installation made tactile the abstract nature of a fragmented virtual text space, reinventing its future in real time and constantly proposing future iterations of itself. Dumb Type's installation was not an endorsement of virtual worlds but rather a critical reflection that asked when and where the simulation terminates. In such a post-representational approach, reality and representation, i.e. the map and the territory, do not proceed with each other but are relational; in other words, they are co-produced. In terms of extended reality, the co-production of physical and virtual spaces is implicit in the future development of large-scale ubiquitous virtual environments. Dumb Type's use of technology and its simultaneous critique, where the human body remains central while employing a highly considered approach to the relationship and form of physical elements to the immaterial media elements (including AI and other programmed components), gave the work currency in the contemporary discourse on the digital society. In this, the topics of inclusion and diversity have gained crucial importance. They are relatable to the aspirations of a generation of emerging artists whose work straddles extended realities, technology overload, environmental concerns, societal issues and activism in a context where such concerns are no longer optional but urgent and foregrounded.

Body and code – LuYang

Tokyo-based Chinese artist LuYang's frantically paced, intense techno worlds take the viewer on perilous journeys that transcend space, time, body and gender in a desperate search for the self between the relentless workings of the cognitive mind and the inescapable cycle of reincarnation. LuYang (born 1984 in Shanghai) creates immersive installations, 3D animated films, video game installations, holograms, virtual reality projects and live motion capture performances, and his multidisciplinary practice integrates and collages Buddhist cosmology and anime, goth style, manga aesthetics, science fiction, dance and electronic music into the central elements of a virtual realm influenced by the artist's research into neuroscience and the workings of the human brain. Born female but referring to themselves as he/him as a direct response to their experiences of gender bias in the media, born a Chinese national but not identifying as belonging to a specific nation, an internationally successful practising artist but not wishing to be defined by a singular aesthetic language or brand, LuYang belongs to a new generation of media artists that no longer identifies with existing gender norms, nation-states and media or aesthetic categorizations. With its infinite possibilities of the seamless transcendence of the limitations of body, time and space, the virtual realm presents an ideal hub for post-identity multimedia artists such as LuYang. Beyond Western binary or essentialist traditions and definitions of the self or subject as stable, singular and coherent, LuYang's XR practice performs the notion of the self as fluid multiplicities and as a 'nomadic subject' that Braidotti, with recourse to Deleuze, defines as 'a materially embedded and embodied, affective and relational collective assemblage, a relay-point for a web of complex relations that displace the centrality of ego-indexed notions of identity' (Braidotti 2017: 140).

In LuYang's digital practice, nomadism or 'becoming nomad' occurs as doing away with subjectivity understood as individual property but instead embracing

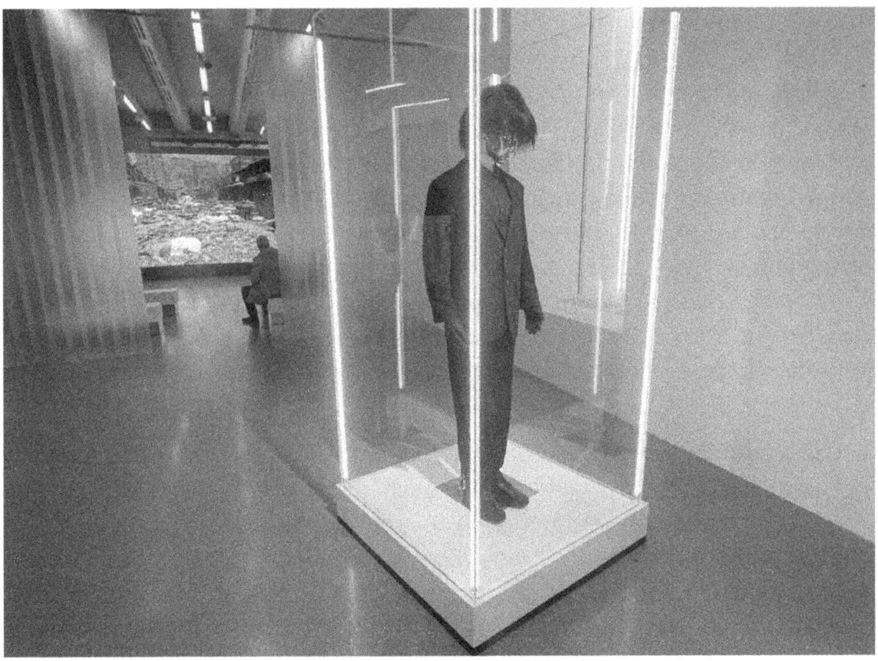

FIGURE 3.3 *LuYang exhibition view from* LuYang: DOKU Experience Center *at PalaisPopulaire, Berlin 2022. Photo: Lawrence Wallen. Courtesy of LuYang Studio.*

difference and collectivity before the background of a hypercapitalist panorama of social, political, gender and visual heteronormative appearances. In an interview with the *New York Times*, LuYang articulates his sense of belonging and identity as one of abandonment, 'By living on the Internet, you can abandon your identity, nationality, gender, even your existence as a human being. I rather like this feeling' (LuYang in Qin 2015). Deeply steeped in the Buddhist tradition of samsara, the cycle of reincarnations and karma, the result of one's actions that determines the level of rebirth, and visually reimagined in richly detailed techno-infused utopias and dystopias, the six versions of LuYang's most recent video series *DOKU* are centred around an ungendered avatar named Dokusho Dokushi, chosen after the Buddhist saying, 'We are born alone, we die alone'. The figure of DOKU is presented as a cyborg, an amalgamation of a biological organism and a machine in a virtual world whose overall aim and meaning is the exploration of the Buddhist concept of the material world as responsible for the eventual destruction of the universe. Its abbreviation, *DOKU,* denotes LuYang's digital avatar or reincarnation, modelled via motion capture technologies of traditional Balinese dancers who performed DOKU's dance movements. While DOKU's face is modelled after LuYang's features, their facial expressions and eye movements are those of the dancers. A solitary figure, *DOKU* travels at a frantic pace through the six Buddhist realms of existence, from the earthly human *DOKU* Human to the utopic DOKU Heaven, to the demigod realm of the *DOKU* Asura who fights with the gods, followed by the *DOKU* Animal of suffering and primitive consciousness, the invisible yet constantly craving Hungry Ghost, and *DOKU* Hell, the realm of extreme suffering in intense heat or cold. All realms in Buddhist belief are temporary and cyclic states; only the state of nirvana can liberate the individual from the system of karma and samsara. LuYang's techno-futurist reimagination of Buddhist belief and iconography is more than a dramaturgical and aesthetic mode of practice but is rather grounded in his culture and upbringing. In an interview with Emily Mc Dermott from 2024, the artist describes his visualization of the Buddhist concepts of heaven and hell as intrinsically linked to human suffering

> This method [of the narrative of DOKU] involves imagining oneself experiencing the true suffering of each realm not only the pain of hell but also the suffering in heaven, eventually developing a renunciation of all these attachments. Many religions aim for heaven as the ultimate goal, whereas Buddhism's ultimate goal is to escape all cyclic existence – including not even desiring heaven – because any attachment to pleasure still causes suffering.
>
> (LUYANG IN MCDERMOTT 2024)

The six *DOKU* versions are deliberately impersonal, and while inviting identification with the artist through *DOKU*'s facial features, their journeys are as if programmed towards predetermined destinies and outcomes, set in the clearly defined spatial typologies of their respective realm with their recognizable attributes. In contrast, LuYang's 2020 narrative video *DOKU: The Self* is a first in that the artist incorporates episodes and events from his personal life, such as a near-death experience during a lightning storm on a plane trip. Premiered at the 2022 Venice Biennale in curator Cecilia Alemani's exhibition, *The Milk of Our Dreams*, the High-Definition Video Installation *DOKU: The Self* was presented in a three-channel version in the final section of the Arsenale exhibition space that was dedicated to the figure of the cyborg, the creature that is both human and machine. This fifth and last section showed works by women artists who, beginning with Dada and Bauhaus until today, imagined and articulated a future where emerging, existing and futurist technologies merge with the human body in performative configurations, photography, film, sculpture, painting, video, XR and gaming. Donna Haraway inscribes to the cyborg a critical faculty in that it is not the product of a Western tradition of binaries, between nature and culture or man and woman. The cyborg, to Haraway, has no origin or history, and in particular, no history of the Western concept of unity and thus has no desire to return to one (see Haraway 2003: 9). Thus, as an ahistorical and genderless creature of science and fiction, the cyborg can construct new forms of difference and heterogeneity. Matthew Biro identifies the cyborg throughout the twentieth century as a (cultural) 'producer' (Biro in Alemani 2022: 500–5) in opposition to its conventional image as a necessarily sterile hybrid. Biro, like Haraway, emphasizes the cyborg's political agency through its inherent ability to subvert and transgress traditional definitions of body, mind and ownership towards critical posthuman positions in articulating the threat of surveillance, domination and control.

LuYang's digital alter ego and avatar, DOKU, presents as a cyborg in a genderless world of destruction and renewal, life and death, heaven and hell. Yet, in the virtual worlds that the artist creates, these binary oppositions exist only as temporary states of human pain and suffering in the timelessness of the universe. Trapped in the Buddhist wheel of reincarnation, fighting the gods and searching for self, the cyborg *DOKU also* appears as the manga-inspired *MaterialWorldKnight*, a romantic figure searching for release from the material world. In the XR performance version of *DOKU*, titled *DOKU: Binary*, which premiered in Sydney and Hong Kong simultaneously in 2022, two dancers onstage in full-motion capture suits in Sydney and Hong Kong, respectively, controlled the cyborg's movements while their surrounding 3D environment and soundtrack were mixed live. Set up on three central screens

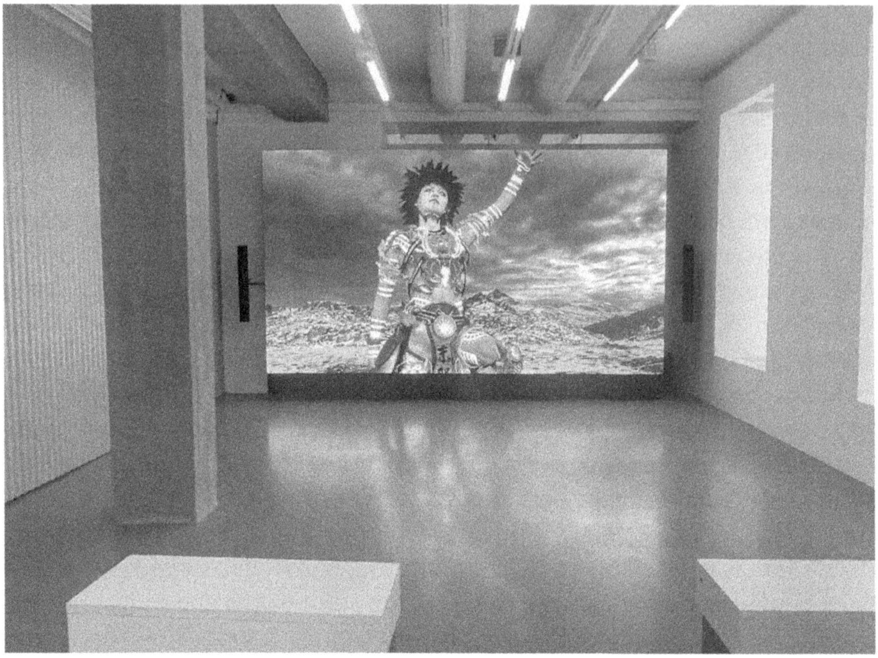

FIGURE 3.4 *LuYang exhibition view from* LuYang: DOKU Experience Center *at PalaisPopulaire, Berlin 2022. Photo: Lawrence Wallen. Courtesy of LuYang Studio.*

with a small forestage and the technical production desk on the right-hand side, the seated audiences in Sydney and Hong Kong followed *DOKU* through the six realms of existence, and the two dancers took turns portraying first Heaven, followed by Human, Asura, Animal, Hungry Ghost and Hell. After the sequence of inescapable reincarnations was concluded with the red-hot, violent *DOKU* of Hell, a new sequence began, a kind of epilogue or synthesis that showed both dancers on the central screen, now moving in dialogue with each other. What started as a slow, peaceful dance between Heaven and Hell in a bright, icy landscape quickly sped into a close struggle for dominance, now on a rapidly rotating disc, the mandala wheel of life. The audience was fascinated and challenged in their close observation of the live dancer in the black full-motion capture suit with only the body sensors glowing in the dark. In its energetic embrace of popular culture and mass media that afforded identification and its differentiated articulation of the existential loneliness of the post-modern subject, the performance's conceptual, technical and aesthetic complexity kept shifting the audience's focus. Initially, the body of the live dancer captured the audience's full attention, their attire, position on the stage and their seemingly both improvised and choreographed movement concerning their costume and environment on the central screen. Next came transitional moments, when the live dancer very slowly removed themselves from the central position on the forestage and moved into an invisible position on the left of the stage while the other live dancer took up position on the central screen. Once the audience was familiar with the dramaturgical set-up of switching scenes and dancers simultaneously, attention focused on the technicality of the live motion capture and the process of translation from the body to screen observed in its precision as well as noticing the slight time delay to the screen. At the beginning of the last section of the performance, the 'binary' duet between Heaven and Hell, all attention was on the interaction of the two dancers, one present on stage in Sydney and the other in Hong Kong. Whereas in the previous six scenes, each dancer moved their avatar, it now appeared as if two avatars were fighting each other, and the human element steering them was no longer of interest to the audience. The audience saw two cyborgs roaming in their utopic-dystopic universe, outside and beyond karma's sequence and inevitability, thus demonstrating Heaven and Hell's coexistence in LuYang's posthuman, genderless world. The fight that Heaven and Hell fought was a symbolic representation of the post-modern subject yearning for release from the material world. The second episode in the DOKU series, the 50-minute video titled *DOKU: The Flow,* premiered as both video and spatial installation at Fondation Louis Vuitton's (FLV) *Open Space* in Paris in 2024. LuYang stated in an interview with FLV that for his installation that he was inspired by the layout of the *Open Space*, which comprises a single exhibition room with a high ceiling and an atrium-like cutout in the ceiling. LuYang placed a large-scale, mounted LED screen at the far end of the space and surrounded it with a floor of large pebbles and a small waterway in their midst. On the floor, close to the perimeters of the screen, the artist positioned several Tibetan *mani* stone mounds, spiritual objects from rocks, stones or pebbles that traditionally are placed by pilgrims in the rocky high mountain areas of Tibet and that are carved with Buddhist mantras and prayers. From the ceiling, natural plant vines intruded into the space, completing what LuYang calls his 'decoration' and inspired, as he said, by DOKU's fall from a cliff (LuYang 2024). In *DOKU: The Flow*, the artist's avatar again presents as a solitary figure on a spiritual search. Trapped in the material world, DOKU is seen shouting and crying from the tops of mountains, speeding across post-apocalyptic cityscapes and rocky cliffs down to a deserted posthuman world around him, but, for the first time in the DOKU series, he shows the character in this episode entirely still in a long single-shot sequence, naked, in a seated Lotus-like Buddhist meditation position and gazing directly at the viewer. In this sequence, DOKU inhabits a cave-like interior, their body visibly ungendered, their forearms resting on their knees and their face half-obscured by shoulder-length hair on an otherwise hairless body. DOKU's facial expression reads as exhausted, defeated or resigned as if to counteract their serene meditative pose. The end of the fifty-minute video comprises a spoken prayer for world peace words underlined with chanting by LuYang's Tibetan guru.

> May I become a refuge and guide for all sentient beings
> Food for the hungry, and sweet water for the thirsty
> Clothing for those suffering from cold, and cool breeze for those affected by heat
> A friend to the lonely, a helper to the helpless
> A healer and medicine for the sick
> A support and a ferry for those without a shelter (LUYANG 2024)

LuYang created the DOKU series as his alter ego, a cyborg yearning for release from human suffering. He placed the protagonists in a shocking, intriguing world of screaming video arcades and Buddhist iconography. However, in his second, most recent episode, this world comes to a stillstand in the meditation scene, followed by the prayer for world peace. For the first time, in a world of hypercapitalist consumerism and environmental destruction, DOKU's *spiritual* search is foregrounded in both image and sound, marking the artist's urgency in being heard. With new earnestness, still rather than frenzied, his 2024 Paris installation may mark the artist's desire for inner peace and an overall concern for the world. The virtual model enables the subject in his works, which is and is not him, to become a nomad, to become an animal, to transform from one to another and to leave the physical world behind and, with it, the binary hegemonies of identity and gender.

Digital colonialism – Morehshin Allahyari

Transformation, gender fluidity and the reimagination of prescriptive gender assignations, cultural hegemonies and hierarchies from a queer-feminist perspective define the artistic and activist practice of Iranian-Kurdish media artist and activist Morehshin Allahyari. Born in 1985 in Teheran and based today in Oakland and New York, the artist utilizes spatial digital technologies, including 3D scanning, photogrammetry, additive printing and data sharing, VR and modelling technologies in her aim to reclaim and reimagine myths, mythological creatures and artefacts of the Middle East and reveal censorship and suppression in both her native Iran and in the United States, where the artist lives and works today.[2]

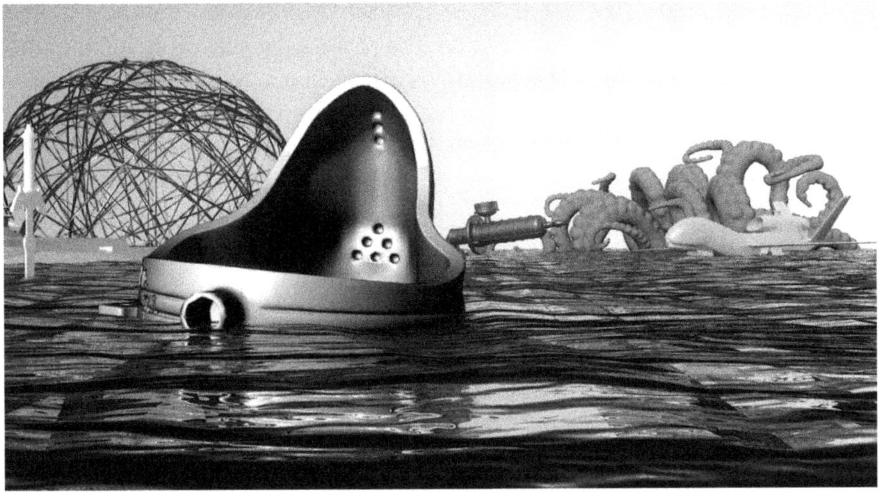

FIGURE 3.5 *Morehshin Allahyari and Daniel Rourke,* The 3D Additivist Manifesto. *Video still 2015. Sound design from Andrea Young. Image courtesy of the artists.*

As part of her activist and feminist engagement, Allahyari is in the process of creating a digital archive and library where she collects and organizes 'underrepresented and misrepresented female mythological figures' (Allahyari in Paquette et al. 2022, 254). In a related second strand of work, the artist focuses on Middle Eastern cultural artefacts and archaeological remains, specifically from the conflict zones in Iran, Iraq and Syria and adds geospatial technologies such as Lidar (geospatial) laser scanning, GPS and geographic information systems to her vocabulary of digital technologies. Allahyari employs what she terms 'Digital Colonialism' as a critical framework to document the use and misuse of spatial and geospatial technologies that, she argues, continue to perpetuate colonial power relations and 'their use/misuse in the construction of endangered or lost artefacts and cultural heritage of the Middle East' (Allahyari 2022). Allahyari extends pioneering VR artist Char Davies's 1990 critique of the aesthetics of Virtual Reality; as Davies succinctly points out, virtual reality was not developed as an artistic medium, but rather, 'its origins lie deep within the military and the western-scientific-industrial-patriarchal complex' (Davies 2004: 72). Davies argues that conventional thinking dictates virtual reality technology, leading to a complex she classifies as the 'hard-edged-objects-in-empty-space syndrome' (Davies 2004: 79). Visually, this aesthetics embraces and utilizes the Italian Renaissance perspective outlined by Alberti, Cartesian space described by Descartes and Euclidean geometric models defined by Euclid around 300 BCE that reinforced a particular way of 'being in the world' (Davies 2004) defined by a long-standing

Western worldview formalized to a dogma of viewing, measuring and constructing the world and its artefacts. The resultant visual experience of the vast majority of VR aesthetics is argued as a 'one-to-one mapping of the visible surfaces of the world onto the picture plane, and from there to the eye' (Coyne 1994: 68), creating a 'literal re-enactment of Cartesian ontology' (Coyne 1994). In articulating the cultural bias of spatial and geospatial tools, Davies opens up the potential question of how an impartial non-Western or even a nonhuman eye might construct the virtual. Allahyari's concept of Digital Colonialism (Allahyari 2020) is further supported by Haraway's position on the significance of author, intent and criticality, where she states that 'It matters which stories tell stories, which concepts think concepts. Mathematically, visually and narratively, it matters which figures figure figures, which systems systematize systems' (Haraway 2015: 160). Allahyari's critique of Western technology companies and institutions for creating replicas (both virtual and physical) of artefacts lost to the conflicts in the Middle East while simultaneously creating her own is without contradiction because, as Haraway points out, it 'matters' who controls the narrative, in this case, – the colonizer or the colonized. In an ongoing project entitled *Material Speculation: ISIS* (2016–present), Allahyari refabricates objects that had been destroyed or lost in the Middle East's conflict zones through 3D models in resin using extant prints of artefacts. The artist embeds a flash drive that contains all the documentation needed to reconstruct the artefact, its history and its cultural and mythological meaning into the scaled, three-dimensional artefact. A series of violent actions by ISIS in Syria and Iraq caused Allahyari's project, *Material Speculation,* to address and counteract the erasure of parts of the cultural history of the Middle East through ideology and warfare. The intentional destruction of artefacts in the Museum of Mosul in northern Iraq and sites at Nimrud and Hatra had been carefully planned by ISIS, documented and distributed via social media, with these violent performative actions provoking the desired international outrage and displaying the negative power of Islamic extremism. In the period preceding the destructions, predominatelyWestern Institutions and technology companies had devoted significant resources to recreate what was lost, including the reconstruction of a 5.5-metre-tall scale model (2:3) of the 1800-year-old Arch of Palmyra unveiled in London's Trafalgar Square before travelling to New York and Dubai. The marble model was constructed in Italy using additive printing technologies and was controversial due to some commentators seeing it as a Disneyfication of lost ruins. Its inauthentic material construction and the project's inability to contextualize the event (including the significant loss of life surrounding this conflict) is dismissed by Allahyari as a 'techno-utopian simplistic binary reading of political events' (Allahyari 2017). To undo such Western reading through her practice, Allahyari has worked with the digital art and culture platform *Rhizome* and the *New*

Museum in New York, both as a venue for her lecture-performances and as a platform to release a digital model of a destroyed sculpture of King Uthal, which had been demolished by three men with sledgehammers in the Mosul Museum in 2015. This work highlights her concern about the lack of public access to the digital and other assets that make up the material needed to recreate the Middle Eastern past. Allahyari argues that the rise of 'tech heroes, holding their 3D scanners in their hands and defending this shared heritage' (2017) is a Western fictional narrative and obscures the fact that it marks a 'new era of colonialism in ways we have not experienced before' (Allahyari 2017). In her research projects, exhibitions and lecture-performances spanning more than a decade, Allahyari employs a feminist methodology to precisely articulate the violent patriarchal gestures of ownership and destruction in the political and cultural actions of both Middle Eastern andWestern configurations. In making visible through art and technology what has been destroyed or forgotten, cultural artefacts as much as the dark mythologies of powerful female monsters and goddesses of Middle Eastern traditions, Allahyari performs what Braidotti calls the 'composition of an assemblage between women and LGBTQ+ as the others of "Man" and the other "others" in the form of non-whites (postcolonial, black, Jewish, Indigenous, plants, trees, viruses and bacteria), and so forth into – a colossal hybridization of species' (Braidotti 2017: 14). The hybridization Allahyari engages in is one between human and nonhuman, between Western digital technology and century-old oral histories and iconographies from the Middle East. In composing an analogue-digital, live and archived terrain, the artist creates new artefacts, hybridized, reclaimed and reimagined, aiming to articulate activist counter positions to the traditional narratives of cultural heritage and digital reconstruction. By doing so, Allahyari affirms the 'thing-power' or *conatus* that Jane Bennett speaks of (Bennett 2010: 2) and imbues her creations with vibrancy, vitality and critical presentness through performance and audience immersion into XR environments. Throughout the research project *She Who Sees the Unknown* (2016–present), Allahyari imagines Middle Eastern dark goddesses, female figures and monstrosities. She refigures their aesthetics and stories in a decolonizing, queer-feminist and activist act. She continues to build a virtual 3D model archive of these figures that are both female and genderless. Based on the artist's visual and historical research into the figure of the *Jinn* in Arabic manuscripts, predominantly from the late fourteenth century, and descriptions from contemporary writings,[3] Allahyari creates bold, strong figures that exude mythical power and strength. Utilizing 3D fabrication methods and VR as well as storytelling in the format of lecture-performance, she weaves tradition, myth and contemporary political, patriarchal, colonial and environmental critique (see Allahyari 2022) into a unique genre of *new materialism* performed in that she creates things and stories in real-time for a live audience. Citing from Donna Haraway's *Kinship of Feminist Figurations* (2004), Allahyari reinforces the significance of storytelling and the calling up of figures as links to real and imaginary worlds rather than rigid ideologies.

> Figures collect up hopes and fears and show possibilities and dangers. Both imaginary and immaterial, figures root people in stories and link them to histories. Figures collect up hopes and fears and show possibilities and dangers. Both imaginary and material figures root peoples in stories and link them to histories. Stories are always more generous, more capacious, than ideologies; in that fact is one of my strongest hopes.
>
> (HARAWAY 2003: 1)

Currently, there are five reimagined Middle Eastern mythological figures in Allahyari's digital archive, realized as 3D models, figures, videos and (VR) installations where figure and video projection are aligned in diverse constellations and, at times, complemented by constellations of small hanging objects displaying symbols between figure and screen. These figures operate between present, past and future and use their powers so the artist can confront and balance contemporary fears, horrors and catastrophes. By embracing their monstrosity, the artist refigures their *Otherness* as a productive force to restore balance, confront violence and subvert patriarchal and colonial power structures (Allahyari 2022). Refiguring the past is thus seen as an act of imagining a different present and future.

The figures Allahyari reimagines are the jinn, spirits and shapeshifters composed of air and fire originating in pre-Islamic Arabia, unseen and hidden, regarded as good or evil, both feared and revered. Though without a perceptible material body, jinn have senses and can possess humans, mirror the social life of humans or act as their alter egos. As supernatural, mythical creatures, tales of jinn are frequent in people's lives across the Middle East, in children's bedtime stories and, with the Quran dedicating a sura to the jinn (Surah Al-Jinn 1–28) also part of the Islamic belief system. According to folk tales and myths, the jinn often live in dark places, in shadows, caves and desolate places and appears in the form of snakes, lizards, scorpions or even humans. Jinn is said to inhabit the Hammams, Middle Eastern bathhouses segregated for men and women, themselves hidden places where storytelling and intimate conversations take place. In *She Who Sees the Unknown: Kabous, The Right Witness and the Left Witness* from 2019, Allahyari reimages the figure of the jinn Kabous, who, according to myth, causes nightmares and sleep paralysis. Designed as a physical installation with a VR film, two 3D sculptures of fictional characters surrounding the mythical fable and a physical daybed reminiscent of Allahyari's childhood room in Iran, Allahyari catapults the viewer into the VR

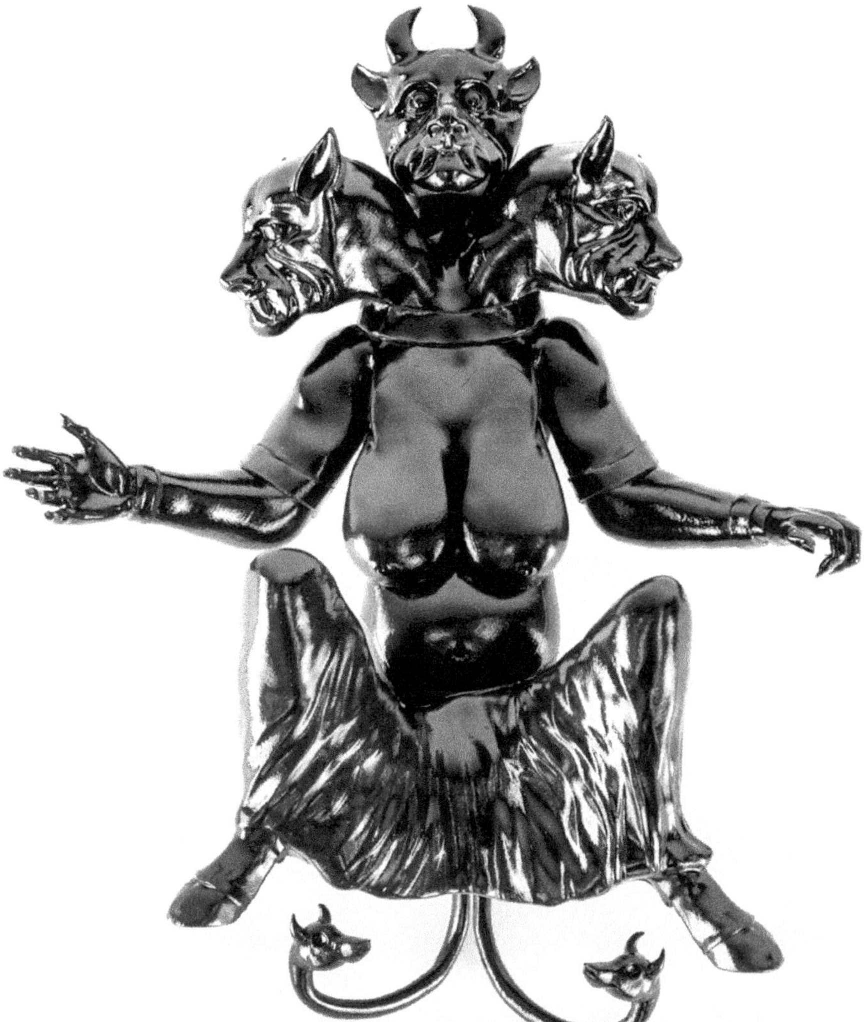

FIGURE 3.6 *Morehshin Allahyari,* She Who Sees the Unknown: Huma, *image of a 3D printed Sculpture 2016. Image courtesy of the artist.*

space of a women's Hammam and, from there on, into various architectural spaces while in a sleep-like position on the daybed. As if possessed by Kabous, the participant is taken into the narratives of three past generations of Iranian women and one imaginary future. In these, myth, fiction and trauma experienced during the Iraq-Iran war (1980–88/1990–91) are both evoked and driven by the morally ambiguous character of the jinn. The fourth and final narrative set in an imaginary future evokes an 'imagined monstrous daughter who is birthed to heal our ancestors and our future generations of daughters to come' (Allahyari 2022). As the only work in Allahyari's jinn series that utilizes a VR film in coalescence with a physically inhabitable object and accompanying 3D figures, *Kabous* presents a compelling work through the immersive quality of the VR and the engaging personal-political narratives. Performative in character and constructed with a chronological dramaturgical structure (from past to future), the virtual model of Kabous is actualized in the visitors' live experience and enters a dual temporality, creating a world between a past myth and an embodied presence. In Allahyari's recent installation project *Moon-faced* from 2022 onwards, past and present merge over time into an unsettling, ever-moving portrait created using a multimodal AI model inputting text and images that the artist trained on nineteenth-century Persian Qajar dynasty portraiture. Culturally, Allahyari states, referring to an article by Iranian historian and gender theorist Afsaneh Najmabadi, that notions of gender and gendered beauty were markedly different during this period and while reflecting Western technological influence through the availability and use of photography in composition, the portraits appear to deny a binary, clearly gendered identity to its subjects (Najmabadi 2005). To generate portraits and feed specific portraits into the system to 'undo' them (Allahyari 2022), Allahyari trained the AI model on words and phrases. Such undoing reveals both the Qajar tradition (of genderless portraiture) and the Western cultural bias of the AI model and Allahyari explains, 'If I would put in a phrase like, "two lesbians holding hands" for example, immediately it would add a rainbow' (Allahyari 2022). Queering Western technology, the artist demonstrates the AI model's struggle as faces, bodies and clothing change and merge relentlessly with no original or final representation to affirm a single subject, gender or narrative. While the portraits, constructed in the format of the nineteenth-century large-scale frames of Western portraitures, present the result of specific research, Allahyari also shares videos of her AI process with a live audience that explicitly demonstrate the impossibility of the binary in contemporary culture in that her image production is infinite (Allahyari 2022). Her engagement with a cultural counter-tradition that reveals gender norms as reflected in Western art history and the algorithms of AI as artwork and political research projects posit a single, significant critical statement about Western culture and technology. In a practice that reaches far beyond the visual richness of her work and that, with Haraway, acknowledges storytelling as a political act, Allahyari resituates dominant power relations and cultural hierarchies exploiting the virtual model as dispositif. Its performance enables her to visualize and reimagine displaced, destroyed and misinterpreted non-Western mythological figures and artefacts beyond gender.

Imagining the future – Yael Bartana

The reimagination of political histories through storytelling and imagining possible futures through recourse to culturally specific mythology is a critical feature of Berlin-based Israeli artist Yael Bartana's work. Bartana (born 1970 in Afalu, Israel) describes herself as an 'observer of the contemporary and a pre-enactor' (Bartana 2024) in terms that define both the method and intent of her mixed media practice. Concerned with the present, her work foregrounds possible futures in predominantly performative settings. In her films, installations, performances and videos, she aims to provoke and question national identities, trauma and dislocation through the staging and playing out of present and future, utopic and dystopic scenarios. Art, to Bartana, acts as a forensic instrument to name and represent historical, social, cultural and political phenomena of power relations and to heal through redemptive powers. Through performance, whether live or mediated, Bartana both reenacts and deliberately mis-acts history in the form of fictional multi-format constructions, games, public rituals and collective assemblies. Bartana engages with Jewish history and identity throughout her work and calls out racism and political violence, anti-Semitism and Zionism through the confronting appropriation of totalitarian aesthetics and dramaturgies. The artist came to prominence as Poland's representative to the Venice Biennale in 2011 with a provocative trio of films that envisioned the repatriation of three million Jews to Poland, created between 2007 and 2011. In her contribution to the Berlin Biennale in 2012, Bartana created a fictional Jewish Renaissance Movement in Poland (JRMiP) that met in the form of an initial congress in the Hebbel Theatre in Berlin. Faced with the question of how Europe views the 'Other', the staged in-person congress continued Bartana's strategy of self-reflexivity in an artwork – a mise en abyme that, as art historian Juli Carson writes in an article on the JRMiP project, comprises the 'productive space of doubt' (Carson 2012). What Carson refers to by inscribing a space of doubt into Bartana's scenarios may be interpreted as what the viewer or participant perceives in her work: the space of doubt lies in the radical opening up, the visualization and above all, a dramatization of contested histories, of Jewish existence within a global context as a possibility, as a 'What if. . .'. There lies the productivity of such a space of doubt, of the 'What if. . .' that is the seed of utopia suggested in an otherwise dystopian world. The JRMiP's call for three million Jews to return to Poland, their former homeland yet a place of historical and present racism and anti-semitism, carries the seed of redemption and presents a transgression of national borders, histories and othering. Twelve years later, Bartana conceptualizes another *call*, the call articulated in the Hebrew Bible or Old Testament's Book of Isaiah, 42: 6.

> I am the Lord, I have called you in righteousness, I have taken you by the hand and kept you; I have given you as a covenant to the people, a light to the nations.
>
> (ISAIAH 42:6)

Bartana's mixed media work, *Light to the Nations, Generation Ship* (2023), takes its name from the above passage from the sixth chapter of the Book of Isaiah, the book of prophecies attributed to Isaiah. It records the calling of Isaiah to be the messenger of God to the people of Israel and is regarded as a book of hope and warning. The verse cited calls for Isaiah to be a mediator of an accord between God and its people. Embedded into an overall scenario of humans departing from the planet Earth due to its destruction, either artificial or in the aftermath of a natural catastrophe, Bartana's work features a spaceship whose design and interior navigation and programme are based on the kabbalistic tree of life with its ten nodes known as the Sephirot. Jewish biochemist Isaac Asimov, author of science fiction novels,

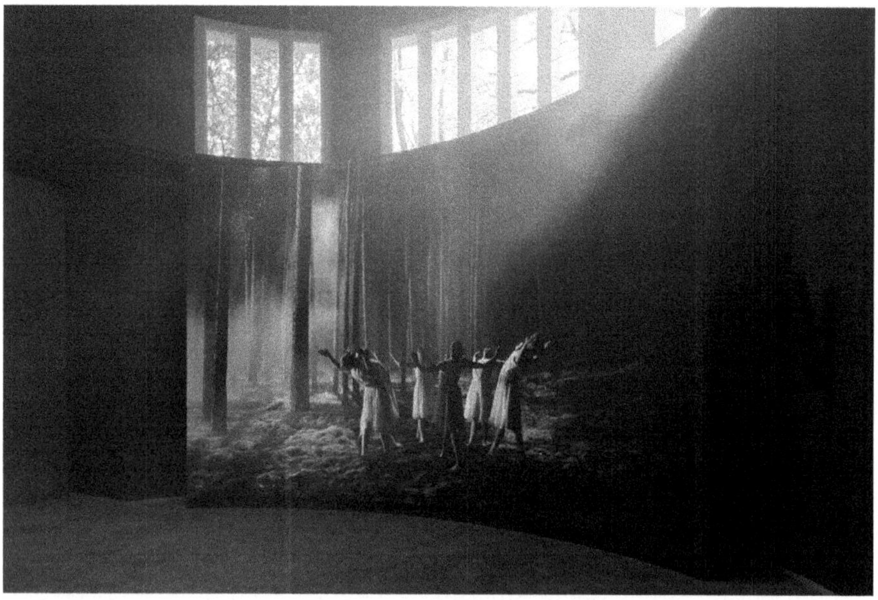

FIGURE 3.7 *Yael Bartana, Installation view of* Farewell, *2024 as part of* Light To The Nations *2022–2024. Single channel video, 15.20 minutes. German Pavilion, 60th International Art Exhibition – La Biennale di Venezia. Photo: Andrea Rossetti 2024. Courtesy of the artist and LAS Art Foundation.*

including *The Foundation Trilogy*, has pointed to the relationship between Jewish sacred texts and Science Fiction, concluding that 'the Holy Writings lead the way to science fiction' (Asimov as cited in Cohen 2019: 1213). What this 'way' entails is the search of the Jewish people for a (new) homeland and for the Messiah to lead the way. Bartana's 2024 version of *Light to the Nations, Generation Ship* was first shown at the Center for Digital Art, Holon, Israel, in 2023 and expanded for the German Pavilion at Venice Biennale in 2024; it articulates both hope and redemption with the inclusion of the 2023 single channel video *Farewell* that, so Bartana, 'portrays a ceremony preceding the departure of the generation ship Light to the Nations, destined for distant galaxies' (*Thresholds* 2024: 10). The generation ship, carrier of survivors from Earth to an unknown destiny, presents both as a physical model (in the first room) and a virtual model in the final room, its design also sketched in chalk depicting the structure of the Sephiroth as its ground plan and the new functions of the spaceship superimposed on the Sephiroth's ten spheres. Çağla Ilk, the curator of the 2024 German Pavilion, asks, 'Is abandoning the earth the ultimate consequence of the failure of humanity as a collective?' (*Thresholds* 2024: 24). In Bartana's artistic vision, space travel appears as a provocative response to Ilk's question, and, at the same time, a possibility linked with the rich connotations of Jewish kabbalistic mysticism, the Sephiroth, that promises at its crown *Ein Sof*, the Infinite. The contradiction of human failure and messianic promise unites a work in which the virtual model is both carrier and vessel, introduced in two of the four sections of the installation where departure, travel and life in the spaceship are presented. Entering through a side entrance to forego the centre entrance of the contested building of the German Pavilion due to its expanded monumentality during the Nazi era, the visitor moves through the anteroom towards the centre apsis that Bartana shares with a scenographic construction by stage director Ersan Mondtag that speaks of a different kind of migration through the personalized account of a Turkish immigrant, his grandfather, to Germany. While the visitor is irritated at first by Mondtag's three-storey tower filled with dusty extant materials and populated with several actors that crowd the main space, Ilk's concept of the sharing of space in *Thresholds* becomes clear: to present migration in a performative and discursive format at the threshold between past, present and future in physical objects and people (Mondtag) and in virtual representation (Bartana). The interrogation of migration as an experience of a threshold is also inscribed with the possibility of crossing the threshold, the doorway, the border and the deliberate making of 'space into other space' (Chude Sokei in *Thresholds* 2024: 26). To Ilk, the fragmentary tale of the current state of an 'earth [is] in motion, utopian, utopian, uncontrollable, vulnerable' (*Thresholds* 2024: 24). In motion is also a physical model of Bartana's spaceship, encountered when turning left from the anteroom. Hung at 2.5 metres off the ground and lit in colours of golden, blue and purple with a length of 7 metres, it depicts a so-called generation ship, a vehicle of salvation and utopia. Modelled at a scale of 1:5000, the physical spaceship would be 32 kilometres long at full scale. Slowly spinning, with its front pointing directly towards the visitor, the physical model takes up an entire blacked-out room. The encounter with this mysterious and immensely beautiful and detailed spaceship model begins the artist's seduction, and the visitor's desire for a departure is awakened.

Moving into the central space, Bartana's video work *Farewell* shows a ritualistic, slow-moving departure ceremony for the impending journey. Set in a lush green forest at night, a group of dancers dressed in white, flowing garments move in synchronous circles, arms outstretched towards heaven or pointing down to the soft forest floor. Electronic rhythmic sounds increase in volume and intensity as the dancers seem to sense and evoke a nearing presence through their continued body formations reminiscent of Laban's movement studies in the 1920s and 1930s and German *Ausdruckstanz* (expressive dance).[4] Rapidly moving shadows and directed light beams indicate the 'arrival', and the dancers disappear as if sucked into the yet invisible spaceship. When the ensemble reappears now on a clearing beyond

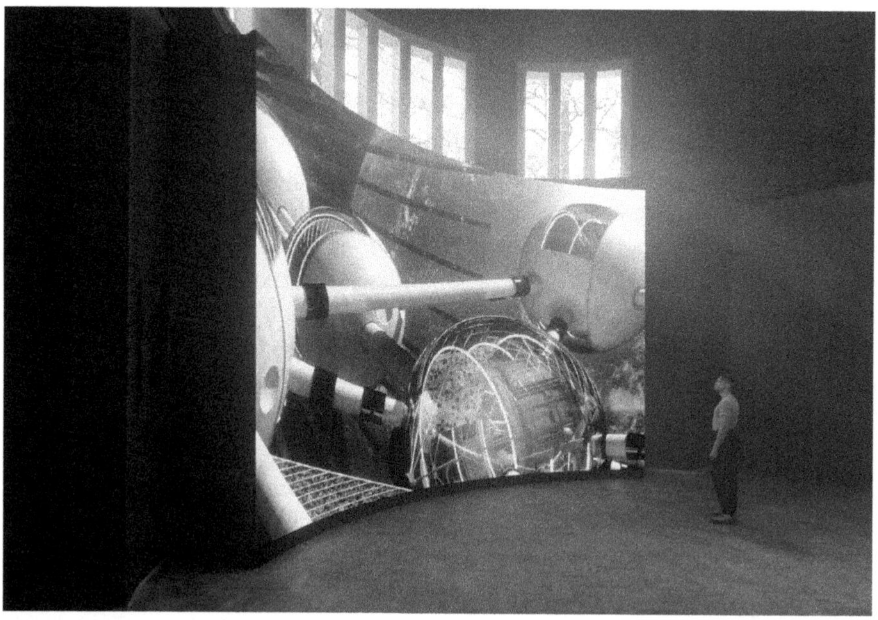

FIGURE 3.8 *Yael Bartana, Installation view of* Farewell, *2024 as part of* Light To The Nations *2022–2024. Single channel video, 15.20 minutes. German Pavilion, 60th International Art Exhibition – La Biennale di Venezia. Photo: Andrea Rossetti 2024. Courtesy of the artist and LAS Art Foundation.*

the forest, under a full moon and boasting animal heads, continuing their solitary ritual, the scene changes to the arrival of a heroic-looking bare-breasted, clean-shaven torch bearer, a direct citation from Leni Riefenstahl's 1938 Nazi propaganda film *Olympia* whose first part is called *Fest der Völker* (Festival of Nations). Bartana's torchbearer, in contrast to Riefenstahl's assumed herald of a new regime, is the messenger of the arrival of the spaceship that now glides ever so slowly across the screen. Superimposed onto the dancers, their slight frames draped in white flowing garments, they disappear into its capsule that consequently docks onto the mother ship. Aesthetically and formally, Bartana's fifteen-minute video cites the heroic sports and movement films and photographs of the 1920s and 1930s and the preceding *Lebensreformbewegung* (life reform movement) that began in Germany and Switzerland and strove for a return to nature and liberation of the (civilized) body towards its natural state as well as the National Socialists and socialists ultimately cynical portrayal of beauty and youth in propaganda films and photography. The melodrama of *Farewell*, in its exaggerated rituals of waiting, invocations, deliberate slowness and synchronized movements, and its climax, the arrival of the spaceship, demonstrates the human desire for the dissolution of all that is earthly into the virtual. *Farewell*'s narrative continues into the Pavilion's next room, bracketed by a video interview with Berlin-based Israeli art historian Doreet LeVitte-Harten, adviser during the production of the installation. In her contribution, LeVitte-Harten contextualizes Bartana's work regarding the history of Sci-Fi, especially a history of Jewish Sci-Fi via its link to colonial practices of conquest and submission of those encountered and the uptake and significance of Sci-Fi scenarios in the liberation movement of Afrofuturism, defined by curator Ingrid LeFleur as 'a way of imagining possible futures through a black cultural lens' (2012). African American scholar Louis Chude-Sokei, whose work has been instrumental in the afrofuturist movement, posits that 'slaves were essentially *prosthetics* for a white, allegedly more rational intelligence and deemed incapable of reason, their status hovered in a zone between human, animal, and also machine' (Chude-Sokei 2017). From this position, Chude-Sokei refers to early science fiction literature such as Samuel Butler's *Erewhon: or, Over the Range* (1872) and his essay 'Darwin among the Machines' (1863) and refutes an assumed binary polarity between race and technology but rather reveals its intersections. His presence in Ilk's overall curatorial project is significant as a 'chronicler' (*Thresholds* 2024: 36–7) of the threshold as metaphor and symbol, as 'physical markers of transition' (*Thresholds* 2024). Stepping into the generation ship means crossing the border from the known into the unknown, from the present into the uncertainty of the future. The virtual model of Bartana's generation ship, the vessel, is meant to lay the ground for the act of *Tikkun Olam*, the kabbalistic myth whose contemporary meaning is the repair of the world. Chalk drawings by Bartana on the wall opposite the monitor showing the interview with LeVitte-Harten overlay the ship's internal functioning with the kabbalistic Sephiroth in diagrammatic representation: the ten spheres of the Sephiroth are renamed as the ten spheres of the spaceship and inhabit different contemporary functions that secure the survival of the passengers such as headquarter, space research, technology, medical centre, teaching centre, agriculture, cultural heritage, public space, residential space and recycling. The interior organization of the spaceship is shown in the last part of the installation when the visitors' journey ends in a final and fourth room with a lounge-type layout and furnishings. Low, cushioned seating is arranged in a semicircle underneath a large 3D dome projection of the rendered interior of the *Light to the Nation*'s spaceship. The grainy projection shows plants, furnished interiors and passengers interacting with each other. The slow tempo and low resolution render the journey as if being watched from far away, or conceptually speaking, as a deliberate citation from a low-budget Sci-Fi movie. On the opposite wall, a round monitor underneath a dome-shaped plastic cover appears to hold video portraits of the crew in Star Trek-like uniforms adorned with what may be the ship's logo that had first been seen in the arrival sequence of the spaceship in *Farewell*. Looking quizzically at themselves, or at the audience, or out of a window of the spaceship towards the expanse of outer space, the audience wonders whether their facial expressions may be disappointment at their mission or a warning to the people left behind on Earth. A disembodied female voice emitted from the dome offers a media release that speaks of the journey of the Jewish people in the search for a new homeland. However, the destination remains unknown, and the journey itself remains the promise. Bartana, appropriating Jewish mysticism into a typical Sci-Fi narrative, wishes to do more than introduce a sheer escape fantasy. At a time where the possibility of both human-made and natural destruction poses more than a distant reality, the virtual model as dispositif acts as the vehicle for the imagination of a future in the reinterpretation and visualization of the Sephiroth-as-spaceship leading humankind to infinity – and salvation.

Other spaces

Linked to the capabilities and the emergence of extended reality in this chapter's research and performance contexts, the virtual model as dispositif operates between the material and the immaterial body. Dumb Type performs the physical body in a mediatized environment – partially immersed and in a constant dialogue with the fragments of figurative and non-figurative projected environments as the material body blurs with the immaterial data body. LuYang dematerializes the material body entirely in the figuration of the cyborg DOKU, who travels through six levels of Buddhist reincarnation. While their movements are based on those of physical dancers in VR and steered by live dancers in a VR performance, DOKU remains the solitary genderless hero in a dystopian world. Allahyari's practice evokes the thing-power of objects lost and forgotten and, through additive fabrication methods, performance and storytelling, reconfigures colonized histories and technologies. Monsters, goddesses and cyborgs populate the physical and virtual stages of the artists discussed here, who conjure in their advocacy for inclusion, difference and equality, thus creating a new relation between body and matter, between the thing and the mind, between physicality and virtuality, gender, race and culture. Critical narratives are constructed and communicated through the virtual model in coalescence with performance and installation configurations that immerse and confront a single viewer and participant or live audience with the politics and aesthetics of Eastern and Western mythologies, gender traditions, national identities and race and their complete dissolution. In Yael Bartana's reenactments or better: preenactments, past and present ideologies are provocatively questioned and transgressed with the visualization and dramatization of possible futures. In her most recent work, these futures are imagined through the virtual model of the spaceship, and the departure of humans from a destroyed planet Earth plays out in a scenographically realized narrative. Whether the work is grounded in Non-Western belief systems and iconographies such as LuYang's highly technified Buddhist cosmology or Morehshin Allahyari's reimaginations of Islamic and Yael Bartana's Sci-Fi reimaginations of Jewish mythology, or how Dumb Type's data bodies and electronic sounds give an overwhelming presence to the void of a post-truth contemporary existence, the artists introduced continuously work, rework and expand an artistic vocabulary that embraces the virtual body in the material world. Fuelled by the richness and diversity of belief systems and mythologies and developing critical processes to feed these aesthetic and conceptual elements into the present popular culture, artists discussed in this chapter imagine the future through the virtual model as dispositif. On the web title page of her project, *She Who Sees the Unknown*, Allahyari cites the queer-feminist *Out of the Woods Collective* (2017) with the words, 'We need to engage with dystopian fiction that extrapolates from the white, able-bodied, colonial, hetero-patriarchy that structures our world'. The Collective defines itself as 'a transnational political research and theory collective, a loose grouping of decolonial, small-c communist, antiracist queer-feminist thinkers working together to think through the problem of ecological crisis' (2017), and this citation highlights the subversive capacity of dystopian fiction, and, in extension, aligns with the theoretical (political) and artistic point of departure for the artists discussed in this chapter. Dumb Type, LuYang, Morehshin

Allahyari and Yael Bartana create other spaces and other worlds through digital technologies from the threshold position of being 'other' and act as observers of the contemporary, as collectors of histories and stories and as translators. The other spaces and other stories thus created owe their vibrancy to their makers' methodology of 'becoming minor' as an act of subverting, reimagining, revealing and recomposing existing power relationships and narratives.

4

Immersion, animism and technology

Between the virtual and the real

The intersections between physicality, virtuality, experience and memory are introduced in this chapter that focuses on artists and artist groups experimenting with new narratives between humans and non-humans, AI bots and human avatars in fully virtual environments, and between robots and humans in live art environments. Several key works are examined for their unique and performative relationships between the virtual and the real, space and memory, immersion and experience presented as film, scenic installation, projection performance, theatre performance, installation, music video, concert and app. With the focus on perception and experience, participation and interactivity, the use of technology in the works introduced does not define the artists' overall oeuvre but rather points to specific concepts and specific reasonings that lead to mechanistic, digital and virtual, performative configurations.

In the confronting and iconoclastic theatre performances of Romeo Castellucci, technology acts as a metaphor and symbol for a wide range of uses. In the highlighted work, mechanistic technology is a deconstructive, scenographic actor and digital technology an immersive and animistic agent imbued with sentience. While immersion as an active aesthetic and technological strategy and practice transcends a Cartesian body-mind and object-subject divide, contemporary animism or techno-animism affords a permeability of human and nonhuman worlds and opens towards a distinct critique of binary concepts of nature and culture, human and animal and physicality and virtuality. Both strategies, immersion and techno-animism, permeate the works of Icelandic artist and singer Björk through her symbiotic relationship with digital and VR technologies in creating a fluid persona, and the works of Thai filmmaker Apichatpong Weerasethakul whose scenic installations and projection performances oscillate between dreams and wakefulness utilizing and queering the vocabulary of virtual reality. While the performer Björk uses her body, face and voice as material for continuous virtual transformations between human and nonhuman, Weerasethakul's film material emerges from his cultural history and personal memories and an innate affinity to the liminal worlds of Thai ghost stories and Buddhist fables. In his installations, virtuality is linked to a path to one's inner world, inner states and dreams, transformations between human and animal, animate and inanimate. Whereas Weerasethakul's biography, cultural beliefs and eclectic cinematic influences shape his approach to *nature-culture* as a single mysterious entity, Björk's animism reflects her reception of Timothy Morton's postphenomenological philosophy that posits that the apocalypse has already happened (so there is hope now) and is reflected in her masked and monstrous stage characters that evolve from and with nature. Morton's object-oriented ontology (OOO) speaks from the perspective of 'after the collapse of the Earth'. It presents as an invitation 'to participate with other beings in a realm that has something more playful than we expected. Eventually, ecological awareness means being able to "smile"' (Morton in Eliasson 2015b: 5). It is *with a smile* that Danish Icelandic visual artist Olafur Eliasson embraces virtual reality in a continuation of his aim to create specific atmospheres and enable individual experiences and journeys within a given virtual world that is not prescribed but allows for discovery and wonder. However, whereas Eliasson offers an open invitation into his skilfully researched and realized 'friendly' virtual creations, Björk takes the viewer and participant on a journey into the depths of her search for identity, her pains and sufferings and merges these with her transforming into dangerous, threatened or loving creatures all at the same time, made possible through her close collaborations with VR artists and labs. Castellucci's darkness is a different one: fuelled by intellectual rigour and a messianic energy that reaches back to Societas Raffaele Sanzio's early, angry days in the 1980s, technology to him offers the desubjectification that communicates the void of representation – animism as a theoretical concept, not a spiritual belief. To Weerasethakul, in contrast, the seamless transformations that the (virtual) model offers are of a similar fluid quality as one's drifting thoughts in meditative practice or in that transitional state between wakefulness and sleep that psychology calls hypnagogia, in which intense sensory perceptions can be experienced. The chapter thus addresses virtuality as a methodological, dramaturgical and aesthetic strategy capable of depicting, expressing and communicating transformative processes, individual journeys and communal experiences from a posthumanist and postphenomenological standpoint, where technology, nature and culture interrelate and inspire rather than 'other' one another.

Deconstruction and myth – Romeo Castellucci

Technology presents as a co-producer of a theatre that is performed by machines, projections, lights and sounds with the actor-body and actor-voice manipulated to perform as material and media rather than as psychologically formed characters in Romeo Castellucci's radical theatre and his collaborations with the collective Societas Raffaele Sanzio (SRS). Castellucci continues to stage his struggle with and against representation in performances that shatter aesthetic expectations and explode the conventionalized theatrical vocabulary of meaning-making since the 1980s. Founded in 1981 in Cesena, a small town in Emilia Romagna, Italy, through the artistic collaboration of siblings Romeo and Claudia Castellucci, and Chiara and Paolo Guidi, SRS has conceived more than fifty productions and toured worldwide with a repertoire that includes theatre, opera and installations. Leveraging their educational backgrounds in painting, scenography and art history, SRS's projects are centred on the visual aspects of performance and, starting with the image, relentlessly configure, reconfigure and, often violently, dissolve space, body and narrative. Language appears dematerialized, fragmented and automated as the Western medium of history, myths, ideologies and hierarchies. Citing the performative qualities of the medieval oratory and epistemic techniques of *ars memoria* and *ars combinatoria* (see also Chapter 1), SRS performed and deconstructed a new language first developed by Claudia Castellucci for the production of *Kaputt Necropolis* (Biennale Teatro 1984). Termed *Generalissima*, 'the alphabet of all possible thoughts' (Castellucci and Guidi 2001: 9). C. Castellucci constructed this artificial language from 800 words from Creole dialects and excerpts from texts by Raimondo Llull, Giordano Bruno and Leibniz to do with questions of truth and, above all, the ontology of Being and the existence of God. Llull, a Catalan theologian, philosopher and missionary, had devised a mechanical machine, the so-called *Ars Magna* from 1305, built to connect fundamental concepts to derive knowledge and truth, first designed in diagrammatic form, then realized as an actual machine comprising rotating concentric rings. The combinations of concepts would act in a single device as a *clavis universalis*, a universal key to all (abstract) knowledge. Lull's construction thus comprised the potentiality of all knowledge, and in turning its wheels and performing its combinations, it promised access to the universal world of knowledge. Computer scientist Ton Sales contends that

> Perhaps the most striking of Llull's anticipations was the idea of having a finite set of rules as well as a finite set of truths – "basic concepts", axioms or whatever you call it –, so that you can then generate from them a (presumably infinite) set of derived truths. Nowadays we would describe the idea more simply and say that Llull had just come across the idea of a generative system.
>
> (SAL 2019: 29)

Castellucci, by rupturing this distinct, generative system of Western philosophy and truth-finding and intersecting (and thus subverting) it with words from Creole, a language that originated as a product of colonialism and migration, opened the systematic and non-systematic aspects of language and lay bare the system of language itself, as pure material. SRS spatialized Lull's machine and rendered it the central scenographic object on the stage.

First in *Kaputt Necropolis* and thirty years later, *Uso umano di esseri umani. Un esercizio in lingua* generalissima ('Human use of human beings. An exercise in the most general language', 2014–2015, various locations), the machine deconstructed the language devised as universal in four scenes with the performers communicating with the words and combinations offered by the machine, initially in complete sentences; however, in time, their

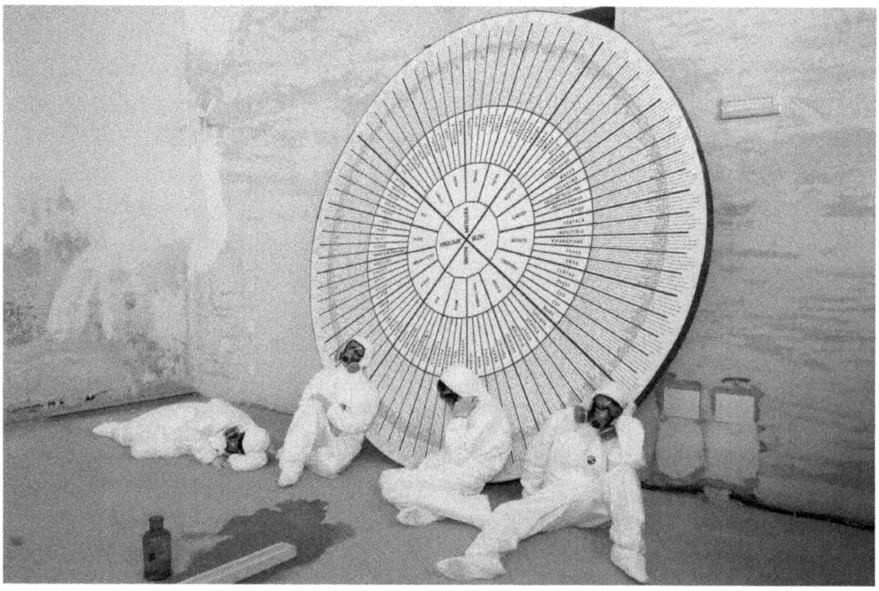

FIGURE 4.1 Uso umano di esseri umani. Un esercizio in Lingua Generalissima, *by Romeo Castellucci – Societas. Special project* e la volpe disse al corvo, *presented by Xing at Ex Ospedale dei Bastardini, Bologna, on 14 February 2014. Photo: Luca del Pia. Image Courtesy of Xing Bologna and SRS.*

communication became utterly dependent on the words the four rings of the machine dictated to them, and syntax and meaning eroded systematically. Language was reduced and abstracted from the first outer ring and moving to the fourth, most inner ring until the machine only showed four letter combinations: *apothem, meteora, agone* and block. While the machine relentlessly reduced meaning to sheer combinations of letters, it intensified the actors' vocal intonation and sound. R. Castellucci explained,

> I find there is true scenic potential in this: in front of the actor who changes his speech through the terms of the purest levels, where fewer and fewer words are available, the spectator is forced to expand their concept of linguistic subject and to perceive in the mantra-like repetition of the finale an unheard and always present phrase that language seems to say: you are mine. Thus, language reveals itself for what it is, an appearance of our belonging to the species.
>
> (CASTELLUCCI IN ARTRIBUNE 2014)

The mechanic deconstruction of language and its performance thus reversed the subjects' assumed hegemony over language. Instead, in this instance, it was language itself that controlled human communication. Castellucci's 2014 performative reimagination of Lull's machine, a technology initially devised to produce truth in the historical belief that there is a universal truth, reduced language to utterances. The machine that made language 'stutter' subverted the assumption of language as a system that is simply representative and, expressed by Deleuze as the notion of 'creation as resistance', provoked the audience to experience 'one's language stutter, face to face or back to back and at the same time to push language as a whole to its limit, to its outside, to its silence – this would be like the boom and the crash' (Deleuze and Guattari 1987: 113).

In Castellucci's 2014–15 version, *Uso umano di esseri umani. Un esercizio in lingua generalissima*, the machine rigorously fulfilled its deconstructivist function throughout four repetitions of the action (one for each 'ring' of words). It acted as the central visual and dramaturgical instrument; the other dramaturgical instrument and plot being the narrative of the awakening of St Lazarus by Jesus. Two performers, Lazarus and Jesus, dressed in contemporary business suits, performed a discourse about the biblical story in which Lazarus is resurrected from death by Jesus. Flanked by a silent group of supporting actors and presented as a station performance in three rooms of a former factory building, Llull's machine reappeared not in its original theological context of proving the existence of God through his *ars combinatoria* but as a kind of test instrument that determined the roles and their reversal in an increasingly charged dialogue about life and death. In the performance and in direct contradiction to the biblical narrative, the performer of Lazarus initially refused to be resurrected, and in the following dialogue, set in front of two large panels that together formed a reproduction of Giotto's painting *The Raising of Lazarus* from 1306 (one year after Llull's *ars magna*), the dialogue between Lazarus and Jesus, the offer of the miracle and its refusal was followed by a reversal of their roles and the resurrection was performed after all. Each of the four scenes was structured according to the dramaturgy and the workings of the language machine; in this version, a large disc on which, in the end, Jesus was carried outside. Repeated four times in increasing levels of abstraction of language, the dialogue between the resurrector and the initial disobedient resurrectant, with the biblical story dramatized by actors taking on the poses of figures in Giotto's painting, took its precision from the ever-present machine. After all, Castellucci presented an exercise demonstrating the systematic breaking apart of language as a system of communication and meaning towards isolated utterances that are repeated but not comprehended anymore. In the context of this project, it is Castellucci's method of the 'minorizing' (see Deleuze and Guattari 1987) of a system through a technology that foreshadowed Leibniz's calculus as much as the contemporary combinatorial algorithms of artificial intelligence. This method was prepared to take the departure from representation to its most rigorous conclusion: the performer's absence through the machine's performance.

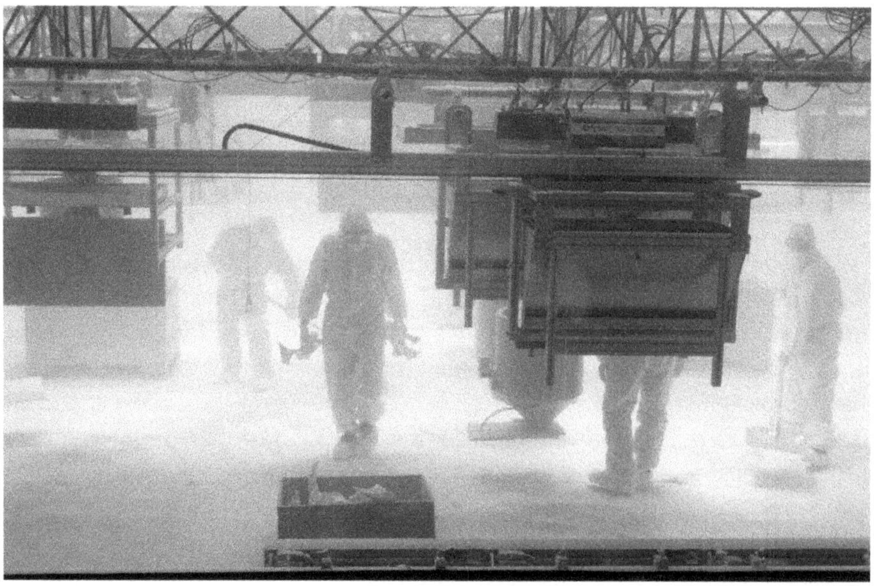

FIGURE 4.2 *Dress rehearsal of Stravinsky's* Le Sacre du Printemps *(The Rite of Spring) 2014, conceived and directed by Romeo Castellucci for Ruhrtriennale, Germany. Photo: Bettina Strenske. Courtesy of Bettina Strenske / Alamy Stock Photo.*

Castellucci's scenic interpretation of Stravinsky's The *Rite of Spring*, performed in Paris and at the Ruhrtriennale in 2014, comprised a project on the disappearance of representation through digital technologies. 'Everything must disappear, language, the artist, the body and even the image in the end' (Castellucci in Solis 2012), posited by the artist two years prior. With *The Rite of Spring*, SRS' self-described 'iconoclastic theatre' (Castellucci and Guidi 2001: 9) took on another historic iconoclast, the Russian composer Igor Stravinsky, whose composition had shocked and terrified the opening night audience in 1913. Largely grounded in Russian folk music and with a score that shows experiments in tonality, expression, dynamics and rhythm, the musical-choreographic work (originally for Diaghilev's Ballet Russes) is structured into two parts, firstly *The Adoration of the Earth* and secondly *The Sacrifice*. The work ends with a young girl, the *Chosen One*, being forced to dance a sacrificial dance until she collapses and dies. The music writer and critic Paul Rosenfeld wrote about the *Rite* in 1920 that it is 'pound[ing] with the rhythm of engines, whirls and spirals like screws and flywheels, grinds and shrieks like laboring metal' (Rosenfeld 1920: 202), a description fitting for Castellucci's interpretation. Set in La Grande Halle de la Villette, a former slaughterhouse, Stravinsky's score was heard from a recording while the audience was seated throughout the performance. Stage and auditorium were separated by a thick plastic curtain filling the stage's width and height. With Stravinsky's music turned up to an overwhelming volume from exceptionally large speakers that pointed the audiences' focus to their technical capacities rather than the music itself, the stage was bare. *Plastikart*, the scenography and special effects company from Cesena that Castellucci has worked with since 1998, realized his design that was centred on the grid (the technical support structure of the rigging for lighting and to 'fly' set elements in and out) to the degree that the grid itself appeared as a giant, threatening machine, as a single mechanical body. The performance started with red LED lights blinking in the grid as a prelude to the computerized operation of forty machines hung in rows and circles on the lighting grid. These machines were constructed to be able to tilt, pivot and slide along the grid and made to look like something between automatic feeding machines for cattle and small cement mixing machines. Like the feeding machines they resembled, this ensemble of forty machines held material and could deposit it in controlled amounts. In the complete absence of dancers, the dancing machines opened their levers. They released differing amounts of a powdery grey substance onto the stage throughout the performance, leaving traces, tracks and mounds of powder on the stage floor. With the machines release of the powder culminating in large sprays, Castellucci projected a text onto the curtain during the death dance of the *Chosen One* that explained in technical detail the procedure of killing cattle and producing bone ash as an organic fertilizer and animal feed in a slaughterhouse in a chilling, last sequence. Only then could the audience correlate Stravinsky's rhythms of the pagan dance with death and sacrifice beyond a protagonist on the stage. Castellucci's deliberate dehumanization of one of the iconic experimental, modernist works of the twentieth-century classical music repertoire shifted the focus from a ballet music, however provocative, to necropolitics, the predetermined socio-political system of managing life and death. Invariably, the audience attempted to humanize the machines in a frustrating desire for identification and mimesis. With a computerized dramaturgy and choreography, Castellucci's *Rite of Spring* remained true to Stravinsky's ritualized brutal narrative yet by technological means. Dehumanized, the production spoke of the cycle of life and death: the fertilizer produced from the dead animal's bones promises renewal and new life for the soil it is scattered upon and nutrition for the animals that feed upon it. In a symbolic sense, thus, the animal, being the source of the animal product can be considered sacrificial. Technology was presented as the carrier of the sacrificial that, in its mechanical dance, evoked the 'animation' of the nonhuman element. 'Technology', so Castellucci, 'is present on the stage as metaphor and spirit. Technology and machines are bearers of phantoms who inhabit the set, the stage – the concept is animistic' (Castellucci 2004: 21). As an anthropological concept that relates to immanence, transcendence and overall, to a way to inscribe sentience to the natural environment and nonhuman actors in it, the concept of animism in this production was expanded towards that of technology that can be 'animated' and that humans can develop social relations with. Contemporary animism, corresponding with Castellucci's scenic proposition, is directed against a modernist, Cartesian body-mind and subject-object dualism. Instead, it considers the question of humans' relationship to and communication with technology. Karen Richardson (2016) coined the term 'technological animism' in her work on humanoid robots in Japan and used it to 'describe the conceptual model of personhood that emerges in the interaction between fiction, robotics and culturally specific models of personhood, which may already include nonhuman persons' (Richardson 2016: 111). In this sense, Castellucci afforded agency to the nonhuman actors in *The Rite of Spring* and acknowledged their capacity to be imbued with sentience and possess the ability to communicate through symbolic and metaphorical means. The effect of the world created through the virtual models that Castellucci's machines are based upon was equally alienating and affecting; they emanated the lives and deaths of animals and were, at the same time, as is Stravinsky's score, life-affirming through a spiritual yet relentlessly performed connection between human, animal and non-humanoid machine. Staging another kind of techno-animism in the Bruxelles episode of his multi-city research project on the ontology of tragedy today, *Tragedia*

Endogonidia (2002–2004), Castellucci placed a small child, unable to speak or walk independently, on the floor of a marble-clad stage space. A humanoid machine was positioned opposite the child on the floor, modelled after the basic features of a human face with two flaps that could open in the position of eyes and one flap in the position of a human's mouth. All-white and comprising the equivalent of a human head and shoulder torso, the machine (or robot) spoke single letters of the alphabet as if to teach language to the child. Ethical questions aside as to the *use* of small children unable to give consent or even depart a threatening or unpleasant situation on their own, this scene in Castellucci's ontogenesis in its totality aimed to dissect human evolution in eleven episodes and staged a beginning of mediality in the form of language and communication. This beginning is shown as one of innocence or unknowing and existential solitude. The friendly-looking robot did not act upon the child's facially expressed fear, discomfort, crying or happy gurgling sounds and the child was unable to communicate with the robot.[4] The scene, however short, became unending and highly emotionally charged in the spectators' perception. Did Castellucci tell the audience that human survival is unsolvable in crisis through technology? The effect achieved through the desubjectification of the human figure and their positioning into environments that act upon them or force them into isolation through technological constructions or configurations was one of the voids of representation. Indeed, the eleven performance stations of the *Tragedia Endogonidia*, named after a self-propagating cellular process, suggested the collapse of humanity trapped in the real. And the real is silent.

Metamorphoses and masks – Björk

Contrasting Castellucci's iconoclastic performances that tear the metaphorical masks off a passive society, Icelandic singer, musician and artist Björk (born 1965) works with physical and virtual masks to hide, transform and make visible relentless transformations between living and non-living, animal and plant. In the merging and transformations of form, colour, being, object and non-being through masks, the virtual model affords the singer the technical and aesthetic capacity where the material itself becomes the actor and identity becomes fluid. In 2019, Björk released an immersive album-length VR music video[1] to accompany her studio album titled *Vulnicura*. Filmed entirely on locations in Iceland's mythical nature of fjords, waterfalls and volcanoes, viewers navigate 360-degree positions above and around the singer, whose body and costuming are constantly transforming. In a personal statement published with the release, Björk wrote,

> I am very excited for you to see the VR videos to Vulnicura, it felt natural to footsoldier into the private circus that virtual reality is, with material like this [. . .] VR is not only a natural continuity to the music video but has an even more theatrical potential, ideal for this emotional journey.
>
> (BJÖRK 2019)

While *Vulnicura VR* was her first album-length VR experiment, Björk had embraced new technologies and new ways to experience her music holistically much earlier. In 2011, she launched the app *Biophilia* for iPad (Björk 2011), an exploration of ten musical and three-dimensional interactive experiences into sound and nature, where users were able to navigate their journeys from atomic to cosmic configurations, not dissimilar to the analogue nine-minute-long cinematic journey from quasars to quarks, *The Powers of Ten* (1977) by Charles and Ray Eames for IBM. The app was included in a retrospective of Björk's work at MoMA (Museum of Modern Art) in 2015 and was the first app in the museum's permanent collection. Curated by Klaus Biesenbach, the show included an eleven-minute sound and video installation, *Black Lake*, filmed in Iceland, featuring the song of the same title. The set-up for *Black Lake* comprised one of the spatial configurations of the exhibition, while the second one was a cinematic setting that screened many of Björk's music videos going back to 2003. The third space was an interactive, location-based audio experience through the artist's songs with an overarching subjective narrative written by the Icelandic writer Sjón. Parallel to the MoMA retrospective, a collection of materials was published under the title *Björk Archives* (2015) with several contributions, among them an essay by philosopher Timothy Morton, whose environmentally focused concept of so-called *hyperobjects*, objects so massive in scale and time that they transcend conventional space-time configurations such as global warming has been influential not only to Björk but also to another artist of Icelandic origin discussed in this chapter, namely Olafur Eliasson. According to Morton, the environmental collapse, or the end of the world, has already happened. Belonging to a school of realist philosophers in the arts and humanities that critiques the project of postmodernism as unfinished but shares the departure from an anthropocentric viewpoint and a push for the agency of objects with certain concepts of phenomenology and Latour's Actor-network-theory (ANT), Morton identifies with Graham Harman's object-oriented ontology or OOO. Morton is mentioned here as Björk (as has Eliasson, see Morton's 2015 essay accompanying Eliasson's Stockholm exhibition *Reality Machines*) initiated an email exchange with the philosopher published in full in *Björk Archives* that (in addition to revealing a respective fandom) demonstrates the singer's powerful desire to name who she is or what her art stands for in philosophical terms, or, more specifically, in an '-ism' (Kane 2015). Taking recourse to his articulation of the hyperobject concept, Morton replies that this could be one of Björk terms, seeing there are so many 'nonhumans' in her work that are alive and also 'not so' alive, a view he describes as 'animistic' (Kane 2015). In his monograph *Realist Magic: Objects, Ontology, Causality* (2013), Morton inscribes art with spirituality and care, and, reiterating, states in an interview from 2015, 'What if art was some kind of magic? Art is charisma, pouring out of anything whatsoever, whether we humans consider it to be alive or sentient or not' (Morton 2015). Art and nature in OOO's view is infused with an energy independent of interaction with humans, which cannot be fully comprehended. Equally, human and nonhuman, living, not living and not quite living, are independent entities that have no agency over each other or 'with' each other. In their sprawling email exchange, the singer and the philosopher found common ground through the notion of animism, a life force in all things, 'in each object there is a soul. and therefore, asks for different reaction to ecology ? each laptop, each bird, each building' (Björk 2015, email 8/24). In an interview from 2024, Björk returns to Morton's (and her) understanding of animism, 'So, not post-apocalyptic but post-optimistic animism. And definitely no elves or puffins' (Björk in Molinari 2024), and she continues by applying the concept towards the meeting point of nature and technology in her work,

> I really like where technology and nature meet. It's a huge part of me, actually. And I really enjoy the places where two areas of plants meet, like when there's moss, and then it becomes a forest. Also, when I do arrangements, I like to have something hyper acoustic and then something really techno. It's the bridge-building between them, not just in one place but in a hundred places. When we were doing all the silicone plants, yes, it's biomorphic, but it also looks fucked up. It looks techno. Also, nature for me is dangerous.
>
> (BJÖRK IN MOLINARI 2024)

In Björk's digital and virtual reality projects, the notion that elements of danger are inherent in nature comes to the fore through her continuous biomorphic metamorphoses between humans, technological creatures, animals and plants, often manifest as indistinguishable. Ovid offers early examples of transformations when he opens his epic poem, *Metamorphoses*, with the lines, 'It is my design to speak of forms changed into new bodies' (lat *'In nova fert animus mutatas dicere formas / corpora*' (Ovid, *Metamorphoses* 2014)) in an all-encompassing but unsystematic history of the creation of the universe and stories from Greek mythology. These have in common constant transformations of form, of time, of human and nonhuman, of stones to humans (Deucalion and Pyrrha), human to stone yet weeping (Niobe) or human into tree (Daphne). Ovid describes the transformation of Daphne into a laurel tree with her father Peneios' help to escape from Apollo's advances in great detail and such that for a while, human and tree are one, intertwined and above all. While the transformation from a human into a tree is seemingly concluded, the tree still has Daphne's heartbeat; it lives, feels and withdraws from Apollo.

> Her prayer hardly finished, a heavy sluggishness takes hold of her limbs; her soft breasts are girded with slender bark; her hair grows into foliage, her arms, into branches; her foot, moments ago so swift, clings fast with unmoving roots; a tree's crown takes her face; a gleam alone remains in her. Phoebus loves this tree too, and with his right hand placed on the trunk he feels her heart still trembling beneath the new bark; and embracing with his arms her branches, like limbs, he gives the wood kisses; but the wood shrinks from the kisses.
>
> (OVID, MET., BK I:525–552)

Björk and Morton do not mention this scene from Ovid in their discussions on nature and ecology of care. However, viewing Björk's digital and VR works, one is struck by the similarity in the seamless process of transfiguration. The digital imagery in the four-minute music video, *Loss* (2019), by example, circles from two human-plant like creatures into increasingly human faces into a face growing fur into a molecular structure and slowly back into the creatures who intertwine with long grass-like facial extensions, yet what had started as a fluid dance becomes confrontational towards the end of song and video. Inscribed into the relentlessness of Björk's digital transformations is the treatment of time as timeless. The virtual model, capable of infinite iterations while simultaneously remembering each of them, never reaches a final state, as the body in flux remains in a process of eternal transformation. And not unlike Daphne, whose heart still beats inside the tree trunk, Björk's digital body carries any possible gestalt of human, nonhuman or not human or all of these and none. In Björk's *Cornucopia* tour from 2019 to 2023, the nonhuman and the human body were inseparable throughout the nineteen-song set. With a creative team that included British scenographer Chiara Stephenson, Argentine film director Lucrecia Martel and Björk's long-time collaborators James Merry and video artist Tobias Gremmler, responsible for co-creative direction and video art respectively, *Cornucopia* was received as a digital theatre that aimed at redefining the popular concert genre. Gremmler produced the video to be shown on ten-meter-high screens before set and costumes were completed. Fashion designers such as Iris van Herpen known for their experimental and eclectic approach to styles, materials and cuts designed the costumes. Stephenson designed the set, which comprised four platforms at different heights with connecting stairs that allowed musicians to move throughout the concert. Inspired by the intricate gills of mushrooms and their umbrella-type form, Stephenson's approach was to scale their microstructure to the large-scale platform stages that could be lit from below. The stage was separated by a translucent curtain constructed from thin silver strings that would soften the image of the actual stage situation but could also be opened for the entire stage to be seen without obstruction. Gremmler's digital video images were projected onto the semitransparent curtain and across the entire back wall. In this way, combined with an intricate lighting design, infinite worlds were created where the performer (and musicians and choir on stage) could either be the focus or merge into the digitally created scenography and be another creature in this narrative. Björk's nineteen songs had an associated video sequence realized by Gremmler, creating a fully digital set focusing on biomorphic forms evoking a distinct visual and sonic world.

> I am using design principles that are very close to nature. It's like planting virtual seeds in the soil of a surface. When the seeds sprout, they deform the surface, crack it, grow along it or develop new shapes.
>
> (GREMMLER IN POWNALL 2019)

In this interview, Gremmler described his design process as an unending and dynamic morphogenetic process where a new form is created out of an existing one yet with new energy. The abundance of visuals in coalescence with Björk's captivating voice, lighting and staging created poetic, hypnotic and eccentric world between natural and artificial life and between analogue and digital creatures. In an interview from 2019, the singer stated

> I personally would like to say that I am trying to carve ways to express the spiritual in the digital. Is that too much of a cliché? I think there is an enormous need to find a place for the soul in our global landscape [. . .] I feel acoustic-ness will go even more intimate, for we crave it and we will find a million different touching points between the two. The more digital we have, the more naked skin and rawness we will want.
>
> (VAZIRI 2021)

Indeed, between Gremmler's digital creations and Björk's physical body on stage, a field of vulnerability is opened up through the deliberate vocal rawness on the one hand and perfect artifice on the other. The transformations of Björk's face, often adorned, hidden and decorated by embroidered masks created with additive fabrication methods, have become a central part of her stage persona. Initially working with embroidery artist James Merry on masks made from various materials that would emphasize and decorate certain facial features or obstruct others, these often resulted in fantastical creations that protruded well beyond Björk's face resembling insect or butterfly details. In 2016, Björk approached Neri Oxman, head of Massachusetts Institute of Technology (MIT) Media Lab's Mediated Matter research group, with the idea of designing a mask for her face. Over the next two years, in collaboration with Björk, Oxman and her team developed a series of masks entitled *Rottlace*, with the overarching theme of 'self-healing or the face without a skin'.

> As in the human body, where continuous, collagenous elements alter their chemical and mechanical properties as a function of the tension they exert or endure, each mask is designed as a synthetic 'whole without parts'.
>
> (MIT MEDIA LAB)

The masks incorporated tunable physical properties, recapitulating, augmenting or controlling the facial form and movement behind them. Inspired by their biological counterpart and conceived as 'muscle textiles' (Björk in Russell 2019), the masks were bundled, multi-material structures, providing formal and structural integrity and movement to the face and neck.

Björk selected one of the masks to wear at a stage performance at Miraikan, Tokyo's Science Museum, which was printed using additive fabrication methods by Stratasys (see Figure 4.3), especially multi-material printing.

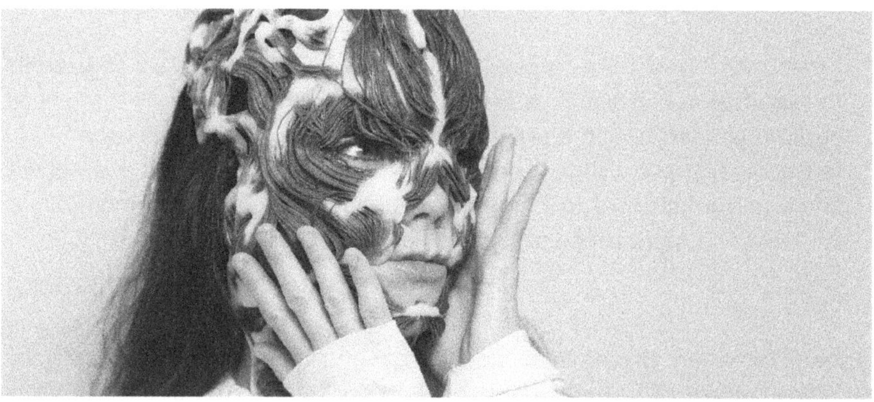

FIGURE 4.3 Rottlace 3D Mask, *2016, designed by the Mediated Matter Group in collaboration with Stratasys for Björk. Photo: Santiago Felipe / Mediated Matter Group. Image courtesy of Oxman New York.*

> This process enables the production of elaborate combinations of graded properties distributed over geometrically complex structures within a single object. The project implements Stratasys' Connex3 technology using three materials with pre-set mechanical combinations varying in rigidity, opacity, and colour as a function of geometrical, structural, and physiological constraints.
>
> (MIT MEDIA LAB)

The mask Björk selected for her Tokyo appearance showed human and animal features at the same time. The human's facial structure and the animal's fur-covered face evoked an uncanny creature that resembled both but belonged to neither. The dualism of hiding and revealing that the physical mask offered became ever more fluid in the virtual field where Gremmler's distinct and highly theatrical style focused on continuous processes of unfolding and transformation of body and face, often playing with two Björk faces at the beginning of a sequence that underwent complete transmutations that may or may not be completed with the end of a sequence or at the end of a song. The playful transitions between an outer face and an inner or hidden or other face were even more pronounced, and the vocabulary of transformations was enriched when entirely in the virtual realm. Björk's music videos and the concert stage projections show an abundance of the performative gestures of metamorphoses where plant, animal, human, not quite human and nonhuman features are depicted as powerful and fragile simultaneously in their in-between or liminal states. The digital worlds they inhabit comprise what Björk and Morton may call a fundamental 'animism' whose harmony, however, is profoundly threatened by the destruction of the earth.

Embodied experiences – Olafur Eliasson

Challenging human perception and proposing new ways of seeing, sensing and experiencing through an ecology of care, Icelandic-Danish artist Olafur Eliasson's (born 1967) analogue works, AR and VR installations and applications seek to disrupt the social-technological divide. Eliasson's work is as much about creating communal experiences as it is about affording individual ones. His Berlin studio presents as an artistic, scientific and social research hub with around eighty researchers working in disciplinary and interdisciplinary teams from ideation to iteration to the production of prototypes. The artist came to prominence with *The Weather Project* (2003), a large-scale installation created for the Turbine Hall of the Tate Modern in London. Eliasson's technical description shows his meticulous research into how atmosphere, in this case, the experience of a glowing sun in an interior space, is constructed:

> This site-specific installation employed a semi-circular screen, a ceiling of mirrors, and artificial mist to create the illusion of a sun. Aluminum frames lined with mirror foil were suspended from the ceiling to create a giant mirror that visually doubled the hall's volume – along with the semi-circular screen mounted on the far wall, its long edge abutting the mirrored ceiling. Backlit by approximately 200 mono-frequency lights, the semicircle and its reflection created the image of a massive, indoor sunset seen through the artificial mist emitted into the room. By walking to the far end of the hall, visitors could see how the sun was constructed, and the reverse of the mirror structure was visible from the top floor of the museum.
>
> (ELIASSON 2003)

Scrolling through the thirteen photographic stills of the installation on Eliasson's project website, the viewer finds associative words and phrases

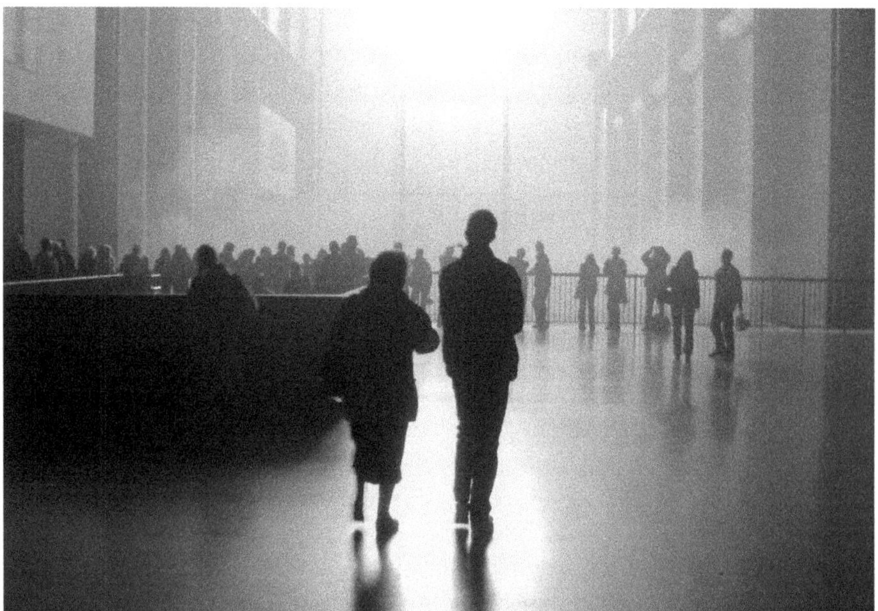

FIGURE 4.4 The weather project, *2003 Monofrequency lights, projection foil, haze machines, mirror foil, aluminium, scaffolding 26.7 × 22.3 × 155.44 m. Installation view: Tate Modern, London, 2003. Photo: Olafur Eliasson Courtesy of the artist / neugerriemschneider, Berlin / Tanya Bonakdar Gallery, New York & Los Angeles. © 2003 Olafur Eliasson.*

superimposed on and between the stills. These are 'looking up, looking down/being with/democracy/constructed nature/rethinking the institution/luminous/fog/sun/and spending time'. The keywords appear in no particular order, yet they articulate both Eliasson's conceptual thinking and the viewer's intended actions and perceptions when in the space together with others.

Embodied experience and embodied cognition are thus linked in the immediate sensual atmosphere of *The Weather Project,* which speaks to the senses to the point where viewers spend many hours in the space, even reporting (erroneously) heat arising from the object. In a catalogue essay for the project from 2003 titled 'atmosphère', sociologist and philosopher Bruno Latour, himself a relentless critic of the modernist Cartesian body-mind and nature-culture dualism, relates Eliasson's artistic position to that of philosopher Peter Sloterdijk who posited in the third volume of his trilogy *Sphären* (Spheres) that 'the real conditions of possibility are spheres, air, envelopes and ambiences' (Sloterdijk 2004: 127). Sloterdijk as a 'meteorological philosopher' and Eliasson as a 'meteorological artist', so Latour (2003: 8), ask questions not so much concerned with objects and subjects but with human survival, asking specifically, 'How are we going to survive?' (Latour 2003). In this sense, Eliasson's work presents as a laboratorium where the artist creates experimental testing grounds of material appearances and manipulations. These, as does Sloterdijk's philosophy, depart from the narrow confines of modernism and question the contemporary conditions of life in a time of an ongoing ecological catastrophe. To Latour, both artist and philosopher represent a new form of idealism that does not privilege mind over matter but contends that

> interesting things happen inside not outside. Because of the simultaneous extension of science and the ever-increasing entanglement of human activities with things, there is no longer any outside.
>
> (LATOUR 2023: 9)

Eliasson's interior exploration of a climatic condition, sunshine in the postindustrial Turbine Hall of Tate Modern, pointed to the entanglement between humans and things that Latour and others (see Haraway 1997) identify as a possibility for transformation. Thus, Eliasson's contention that his reading journey had taken him away from (classical) phenomenology (Eliasson 2002: 14) as a philosophical school concerned with the study of individual experience with the experience of the lived body (see Husserl, *Ideas II*, 1989) and of embodied perception (see Merleau-Ponty 2012) from a subjective or first-person perspective can be understood as the artist opening up towards the concept of *entanglement* as a mode of thinking about the world from a non-anthropocentric viewpoint. Eliasson cites Latour's mode of '*getting down to Earth* and being earthbound' (see Latour 2018) and

Haraway's influential term *naturec-ulture* (see Haraway 2003), which posits the symbiosis of nature and culture as inspirational for his thinking and work. However, with the mentioning of Evan Thompson's 2007 publication, *Mind in Life: Biology, Phenomenology, and the Sciences of Mind*', Eliasson's engagement with notions of consciousness and embodiment continues with an extension towards a kind of new phenomenology that Evans calls the 'enactive approach' (2007: 15). Thus titled, the enactive approach is a way to naturalize phenomenology, meaning that 'phenomenology needs to be able to understand and interpret its investigations in relation to those of biology and mind science' (2007: 14). Eliasson's exploration of the virtual model as one of his recent areas of practice comes as a direct result of his expansion of research and manipulation of material and immaterial elements with technologies of light, materials and time, yet always with a view on the viewer's individual and communal experience and perception.

Eliasson's first VR piece, *Rainbow* (2016), a collaboration with Acute Art, which is now hosted on their app, was the re-imagining of an environmental piece of the construction and perception of the natural phenomenon of a rainbow, first shown at the Leeum, Samsung Museum of Art in Seoul, as part of a solo exhibition titled, *The Parliament of Possibilities* in an analogue version. In an article on the show published by *Domusweb,* Eliasson outlines the concept behind his selection of twenty-two artworks from throughout his career,

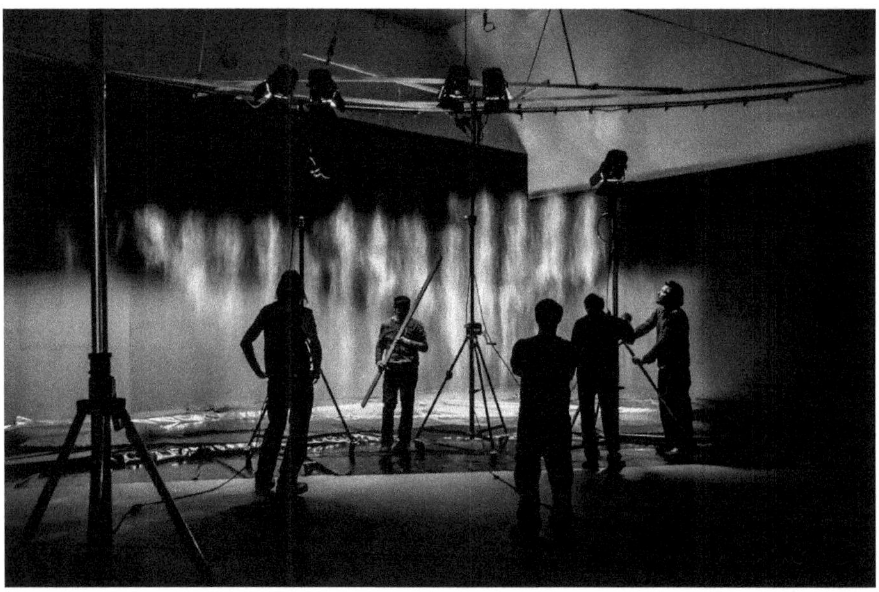

FIGURE 4.5 *Testing technical components of* Rainbow Assembly *at the Studio Olafur Eliasson, Berlin 2016. Photo: María del Pilar García Ayensa / Studio Olafur Eliasson. © 2016 Olafur Eliasson.*

> The Parliament of Possibilities celebrates the fact that the world and our feelings about it are constantly changing. when we see things as a continuous process of production and relation, we may also see their potential. we then have the opportunity to negotiate reality, to decide together what world to build. I would like to think that my works encourage people's engagement and experience of being present with and in the world. the artworks function as mirrors, reflecting a not-yet-verbalized emotional need that we carry inside ourselves.
>
> (DOMUS 2016)

In a play on words, the title of Eliasson's show adapts Latour's theory of the 'Parliament of Things' that articulated a new phase after humanism, 'posthumanism', where binary oppositions between human and nature, active and passive, subject and object are questioned and rearticulated towards new 'possibilities' (Latour 2020). *Rainbow Assembly* was presented as an installation made of water droplets and light that created a rainbow in an artificial atmospheric condition in the interior space of an exhibition hall with keywords and associative terms such as darkness/destabilization/disappearance/emergence/ephemeral/feel yourself seeing/heightened awareness/lightbending/natural phenomenon/prismatic/serenity/time (Eliasson 2016). The colours forming the rainbow emerged from the light refracted and reflected by the water droplets. However, to see the rainbow emanating from above the circular organization of lights directed towards a circle of mist, the viewer had to find a bodily position that allowed the piece to be fully realized. The work disappeared when the body moved to a position where the angle of the body and eye did not cooperate to co-produce the work. *Rainbow Assembly* is discussed here as the antecedent to Eliasson's first VR work, *Rainbow* from 2017, a collaboration with Acute Art, an innovative VR production company headed by Swedish curator Daniel Birnbaum, former curator of the 53rd Venice Biennale and Director of the Moderna Museet in Stockholm that commissions and collaborates exclusively with artists and curators to develop VR artworks. Acute Art's VR exhibition space titled *A museum without walls* was launched with nine artist projects, including LuYang's *Giant Doku* (for an extended discussion of LuYang's work, see Chapter 3). *Rainbow VR* translated the analogue and live experience of *Rainbow Assembly* to the virtual assembly of a rainbow. Conceived as a multi-user experience where several participants with VR headsets and handheld controls to manipulate the falling droplets of water could meet in the virtual space and together construct the rainbow, dependent on their bodily and eye movements, the piece highlights not only Eliasson's preoccupation with atmosphere but also his ethos of creating communal experiences.

> Virtual reality has the potential to become a platform for new ways of experiencing if we include the body in our virtual work – I don't believe in leaving the body behind,' says the artist. For this reason, I've been particularly interested in developing *Rainbow* so that it hosts many people at the same time. To me, this social aspect is crucial; it emerges through recognizing the presence of others, by experiencing others' impact on a space.
>
> (ELIASSON IN GOULD 2017)

In *Rainbow VR,* one may detect traces of what Husserl described as the experience of the lived body, here made complex through the technical apparatuses of the VR headset and handheld controls. It is the individual and subjective experience or the embodied kinaesthetic of bodily movement and cognition, and, in multi-player configurations, in addition, the individual experience of proprioception, that is, of one's body's physical extension, that Eliasson brought to the fore in this piece. From collaborating on his first app for VR with Acute Art, Eliasson moved on to expand his artistic and technical vocabulary into Augmented Reality with the 2020 project *Wunderkammer*. Like the historic baroque cabinets of curiosity, Eliasson's project comprised objects chosen by him in the role of the collector and curated to form a personal collection of virtual models. In line with his engagement with the natural world, Eliasson chose natural objects and specimens to come to life in the AR environment, from clouds that produced rain to a small rainbow, a handheld sun and many others.

Ephemeral natural phenomena produced in one's everyday environments that were meant to evoke wonder and a smile from the participant formed part of Acute Art's so-called 'collectables'; the concept of *Wunderkammer* was simply to carry nature in your pocket and to create natural phenomena with just your phone, foregoing the cumbersome VR headset. In keeping with his conviction not to leave the body behind, Eliasson created in 2022 the XR work, *You View Matter*, as part of a large solo exhibition at Palazzo Strozzi, Florence. Conceived as a physical journey within the Renaissance palazzo and augmented with virtual geometrical objects, the viewer participated in both, navigating the physical architecture and entering and exploring abstract mathematical configurations from the inside. The geometrical objects Eliasson chose for this work were the five Platonic solids, polyeders that possess maximum symmetries and a non-Platonic body as a sixth object, a sphere. The five Platonic solids are the regular tetrahedron, whose four sides are equilateral triangles; the cube, with six square sides; the octahedron, with eight sides of equilateral triangles; the dodecahedron, with twelve sides of pentagons; and the icosahedron, with twenty sides that are equilateral triangles. Euclid later proved that only five Platonic solids fulfil the requirement to be regular convex polyhedra. Thus, Eliasson's sixth object comprises a sphere. Located in the Strozzina, the inner courtyard of the Palazzo that specializes in contemporary art exhibitions, Eliasson describes the project with the keywords and associative terms of 'AR/VR/journey/ moiré effect/ collaboration/ geometry/ walking through/ you only see things when you move'. Plato first mentions the geometrical bodies constructed by Eliasson in his cosmological dialogue, *Timaeus*. Relating the four solids to the four elements, water (icosahedron), fire (tetrahedron), earth (cube) and air (octahedron), Plato develops the concept of the cosmos as comprising geometrical objects in perfect harmony.

> Now of the four elements the construction of the Cosmos had taken up the whole of everyone. For its Constructor had constructed it of all the fire, water, air, and earth that existed, leaving over, outside it, no single particle or potency of any one of these elements.
>
> (PLATO, TIMAEUS 32C)

Together, the four elements comprise the cosmos, created by the Demiurge, so Plato, from chaos. Plato then understands the world as a *paradeigma* (model) or copy of an eternal original cosmos designed by a divine creator (see Plato, *Timaeus* 28A) who creates a unified cosmos from chaos after an eternal model. The cosmos, or the world, thus constructed, comprises a model (for a detailed discussion of Plato's cosmology and his concept of the model in terms of its cosmopoietic capacity see Brejzek and Wallen 2018). Eliasson articulated the reality-producing or performative capacity of the model in the short text 'Models are Real' (2008). He describes models as 'co-producers of reality' in that they create their own reality.

> What we are witnessing is a shift in the traditional relationship between reality and representation. We no longer progress from model to reality, but from model to model while acknowledging that both models are, in fact, real. As a result, we may work in a very productive manner with reality experienced as a conglomeration of models. Rather than seeing model and reality as polarized modes, they now function on the same level. Models have become co-producers of reality.
>
> (ELIASSON 2008: 18)

This statement from 2008 becomes even more poignant when seen ten years later regarding the virtual model that can now be defined as a co-producer and even a producer of reality. The six virtual models of *Your View Matter* invited the participant on a journey into unfamiliar perspectives and geometries inside the models. Entering the models and being able to explore the complex bodies made up of triangles, their walls, corners and ceilings, some colourful, some black and white, transported notions of Plato's cosmology into contemporary virtual reality and made those elements that to Plato make up the world, tangible. Built into the models and in addition to their complex inner structures was an optical distortion, a moiré effect that was in constant flux dependent on the viewers' movement, the resolution of the VR headset and animation (see Eliasson 2022). In *Your View Matter*, the virtual model acted both as a navigation device and a journey of exploration into a theoretical geometry brought to life through XR.

In parallel to his artistic research and practice through Studio Olafur Eliasson in Berlin, the artist founded, together with social anthropologist and clinical medical scientist Andreas Roepsdorff, an interdisciplinary network of artists and researchers called *Experimenting Experiencing Reflecting* (EER) that draws on 'somatic, scientific and artistic approaches' in an 'exploration of experience, perspective-taking, uncertainty, and cultural learning' (eer.info /about). Funded by the Carlsberg Foundation from 2019 to 2025, participants meet in workshops, publish, and perform artistic research based on exploring or even attempting the application of critical posthumanism in group settings, performative exercises and digital strategies. Eliasson's research appears to be at the centre of the network's activities through his unique method of the exploration and practice of *nature-culture* in both physical and virtual settings. Contextualized within EER's non-hierarchical structure, the central phenomenological questions related to embodied knowledge, consciousness and perception come to the fore again in a distinct exchange with social practices in the environment. The virtual model, thus, operates in Eliasson's and EER's work not as an escape fantasy, a departure from Earth, but as a deep exploration into human and nonhuman agency.

Duality and transformation – Apitchong Weerasethakul

In Thai filmmaker Apichatpong Weerasethakul's VR work from 2022, the virtual model acts as a performative and worldmaking vehicle that transports the participant into interior spaces, inner states, memories and dreams where nature, human and nonhuman coexist in fields of difference rather than identity. His creative works in film, performance and installation engage with time, light and the body and are set in the luminous jungles of Thailand and Cambodia, enmeshed in the animistic worlds of mystery, ghost tales and transformations. Weerasethakul's unique way of developing narrative and storytelling through the atmospheric capacity of the moving image is discussed in relation to his artistic journey from film to cinematic installation, performance and, most recently, virtual reality performance. Born in 1970 in Bangkok, Weerasethakul was brought up in Khon Kaen in the remote Northern region of Isan, Thailand, by his medical doctor parents and his early cinematic influences were B-grade Hollywood movies, horror and science fiction films. In contrast, his cultural influences were the hospital setting of his childhood, surrounded by illness and healing in a rural setting. In his hometown, he first studied architecture at a time when Deconstructivism, with its primary form finding method of fragmentation, was at its height, followed by film studies at the Art Institute of Chicago, where Weerasethakul first encountered American experimental films such as Stan Brakhage and Andy Warhol, who sought to enter and redefine the structure of film itself. As in architecture, where the user enters a structure in time, in cinema, so Weerasethakul in a conversation with curator Hans Ulrich Obrist from 2020 (refer to the Lorcano Film Festival website), the viewer enters the structure or architecture of a film that occurs in time.

The element of time is central in his films and installations, characterized by a non-representational aesthetics of stillness, emptiness and dreamlike states, such as the liminal state between waking and sleeping. Weerasethakul's works belong to the genre of *trance* films linked to filmmakers of the expressionist avant-garde such as Maya Deren, whose intention for her influential, dreamlike and symbolist 1943 film *Meshes in the Afternoon* was 'to put on film the

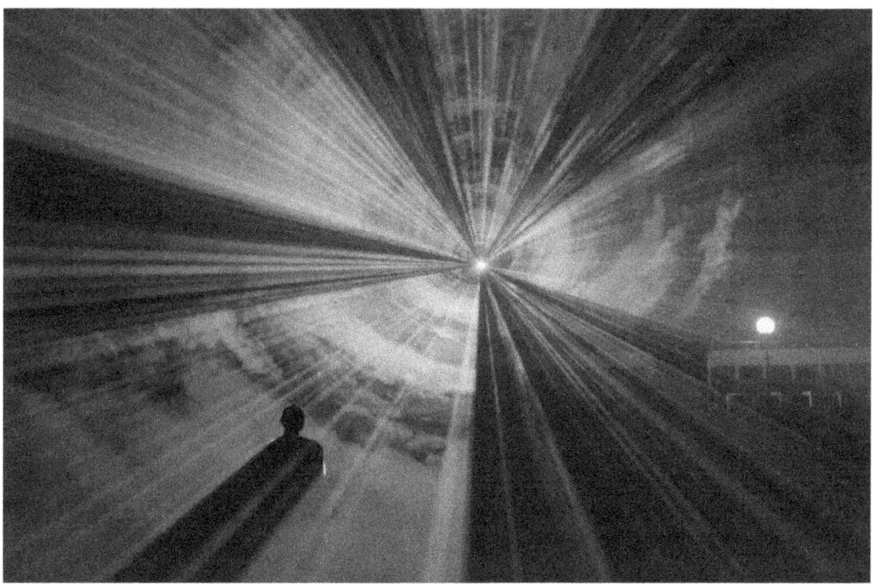

FIGURE 4.6 *Installation view of Apichatpong Weerasethakul's performance work* Fever Room *from 2022. Courtesy of Kick the Machine Films.*

feeling which a human being experiences about an incident, rather than to record the incident accurately' (Deren in MoMA 2024d (Museum of Modern Art 2019). Deren's aim for a cinematic portrayal of subjective experience and the experience of a transformation of the self—made possible through a transgressive sleep-like state that transcends and negates cultural and social norms and conventions aligns with Weerasethakul's strategy of exploring the in-between state where dreams and memories converge productively. Influenced by the popular culture that surrounded him as a child, such as 'Thai soap operas, local horror films, ghost stories, love songs, talk shows, tales for children, Buddhist fables and, more generally, a kitschy local culture' (Quandt as cited in Blümlinger 2022: 121), Weerasethakul's films emerge from the filmmakers' personal memories that range from his eclectic cinematic influences and spatial autobiography to sensory memories, dreams, colours, light and darkness. Deeply rooted in the cultural and natural landscapes of his home country, Thailand, Weerasethakul's narratives and cinematic qualities hover between wakefulness and sleep, with tropical landscapes and jungles acting as protagonists in the often feverish tales. Tales of transformation, or 'animism', that, with May Adadol Ingawanji, 'makes real the permeability of human and nonhuman worlds' (2021: 91) are central in Weerasethakul's work and often appear connected to the forest as the zone of 'wild nature and malignant spirits, but it is also a zone in which *anima* takes shelter' (2021: 94). In an interview with curator Gridthiya Gaweewong from 2010, he outlines how

> In my works the themes of duality and transformation variously appear in both content and structure. For example, I might explore the dualities of darkness and light, man and animal, or even the idea of a film with a split personality. In terms of transformation, the characters in my works might undergo a change from one identity to another. This could happen on a metaphoric, social level, but sometimes it is also a physical change – like a man becoming a monk, or a tiger, or a kick-ass heroine, or a Monkey Ghost, and so on.
>
> (GAWEEGONG 2010)

Tropical Malady (2004) is such a film that is formally split into two parts, with the first part showing a gentle romance between a soldier and a young man from the country, and the second part, the soldier's real or hallucinatory encounter with a shamanic man-tiger, a figure inspired by a popular Thai myth, when searching for the young man who had disappeared into the depths of the jungle. While *Tropical Malady* was widely received as a queer romance, and Weerasethakul was labelled a queer filmmaker, the term has a specific meaning to him that is independent (yet not excluding) from engaging with LGBTQ+ themes and issues. 'To me, queer means anything can happen. It's about openness to possibilities' (Weerasethakul in

Williams 2021). Already his first feature film, acclaimed by audiences, critics and scholars alike, the documentary *Mysterious Object at Noon* from 2000 explored such an openness with its narrative entirely authored by the film's lay actors. Unscripted and following the surrealist method of the *exquisite corpse*, the collective development of a story or image, Weerasethakul and his crew and actors travelled across rural Thailand to Bangkok, asking people of all ages and backgrounds to expand on a simple story of a disabled boy and a teacher in front of the camera. Non-professional actors later played out the story, interspersed with documentary sequences in the eighty-minute film's construction, which, due to funding issues, took three years to complete.

Shot in black and white with a dreamlike atmosphere that wove the fictional and documentary aspects of the film into a hypnotic fabric, *Mysterious Object at Noon* was followed by explorations in colour films, among them *Uncle Boonmee Remembers His Former Lives* which was awarded the Golden Palm at Cannes (2010) and numerous other awards since then, as well as installations and performances, shown at Sharjah Art Biennale and Documenta, MoMA, as well as significant galleries and theatre festivals worldwide. The move into art installation and performance, now a central

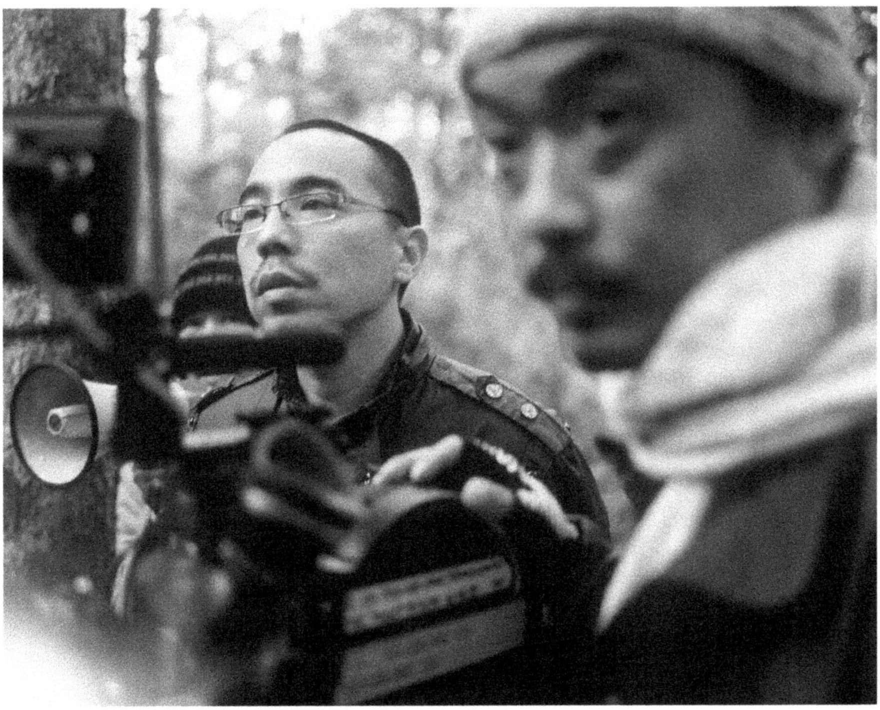

FIGURE 4.7 *Apichatpong Weerasethakul, on-location filming* Uncle Boonmee remembers his former Lives. *Photo: Nontawat Numbenchapol. Courtesy of Kick the Machine Films.*

part of his practice in parallel to filmmaking, has not altered Weerasethakul's desire to create from his personal memories but rather continues to be explored in different spatial settings, configurations and techniques while his central themes of the duality but more so the in-between states of light and darkness, reality and dreams, wakefulness and sleep, and transformation remain. In *Fever Room*, his first performance piece, commissioned *by* Kim Seong-Hee, the Artistic Director of the Asian Arts Theatre in Gwangju, in conjunction with funding for his latest film, *Cemetery of Splendour* (2015) and first performed in June 2015 at the Asian Arts Theatre (Gwangju, South Korea) followed by performances at festivals in Europe and Asia, transformation happens on two levels, firstly, a spatial transformation of the physical space and, within the film, the protagonists' experience of several transitions from wake to sleep, from health to illness. With no performers in the actual space, the piece might better be called 'live cinema' as to Weerasethakul, the piece 'does not qualify as theatre, but rather as film' (Weerasethakul in Sasaki 2017). The filmmaker explains how he did not 'think of the audience' during the production process but rather 'tried to become the audience and feel the images, the sound and the light form the observer's experience' (Sasaki 2017). What emerged through Weerasethakul's introspective method was a liminal space where dreams and reality may not be different from each other and where humans and nature breathe in similar ways. Performed in a cinema or theatre, the performance's spatial situation differs depending on the space. At the theatre festival in Styria 2016, *Fever Room* was set in a cinema, and the audience was seated on the stage facing several projections on a screen. Two-thirds of the way through the performance, the screen was raised, and the audience was confronted with the empty theatre auditorium. The light of a video projector at its far end shone through the fog, blinding the audience with constantly flickering light constellations making their way through the fog. In the last twenty minutes of the performance, shadows of humans were projected onto the fog. *Fever Room* was presented as a 'projection performance' (*kickthemachine* 2015) as the cinema itself came to life; its apparatuses were in movement, creating atmospheres through cinema-intrinsic transformations. The cinema space acted as a memory machine that was activated and made tangible through light, darkness, fog, reality and fantasy. Kickthemachine, Weerasethakul's production company, published a text (abridged here) on *Fever Room* that elucidates how the personal and the political came together through the notion of the dream as plot and metaphor.

> Apichatpong fuses his memories with the actors' and fictionalizes the narrative. Here the people take refuge in dreams while their land is on a

brink of collapse echoing Thailand's present state of military dictatorship. [. . .] In *Fever Room*, Apichatpong documents personal and regional history as if they will soon disappear.

(*KICKTHEMACHINE* 2015)

Fever Room worked with the ephemerality of the fog and the cinematic image, reversing the audience's gaze from the screen towards the light of a video projector projecting human shadows as if citing Plato's (epistemological) cave allegory that speaks of human incapacity for knowledge and their fate to live in a world of sheer shadows. Structured into two parts, both dramaturgically and spatially, *Fever Room* explored the audience's relationship with the narrative first in a traditional cinema set-up and then through the confrontation with the empty auditorium and thus the destruction of the fiction that was then replaced by the confronting yet sensual light and shadow sequence. Weerasethakul's second performance piece, *A Conversation with the Sun (VR)* from 2022 was first staged at Bangkok City Gallery, May to July 2022 with music by Japanese composer Ryochi Sakamoto (see Chapter 2 for Dumb Type's work with Sakamoto) in collaboration with the Bangkok scenography group DuckUnit and media technologist Pat Pataranutaporn from MIT's Media Lab. Weerasethakul used his personal film archive, which documented his life and texts, to create conversations that oscillated between memories and fiction in both the image and text. Using the Generative Pre-trained Transformer 3 (GPT3), an AI autoregressive language model (that uses the previous word to predict the following word) to create conversations between published texts by himself and (AI information on) well-known individuals such as the surrealist artist Salvador Dali and the Indian spiritual philosopher Jiddu Krishnamurti (1895–1986) but that also created conversations between Weerasethakul's texts and the sun. Spatially, he continued to play with the organization of a cinema, as in *Fever Room*, by liberating the cinematic projection screen from its traditionally fixed position.

In *Conversations*, a mechanized fabric curtain could obscure and reveal space and image in a two-part dramaturgical structure, allowing the audience to move freely in the space and around the hung screen. Limited to thirty audience members at a time, the first group explored the space wearing VR headsets for the first half of the performance but took these off for the second part while the second group entered the space performing the same sequence. With the VR headsets indicating nearby participants, audience members could sense each other's presence yet avoid bumping into each other. This introspective performance used the virtual model to invite participants into joining a dream and to walk as if dreaming through a shared memory space with others. To Weerasethakul, 'putting on a headset equates to learning to see with your eyes closed and enables us, as in meditation or dreaming, to reach new depths of consciousness' (Weerasethakul 2024). Then, taking off the headset for the performance's second half released the participant from the dream into the physical yet equally meditative space filled with memories, ghosted images and constructed texts. With *Conversations*, Weerasethakul created a participative VR journey that drew on the Buddhist mental practice of meditation to focus one's body and mind to be present in the moment and to attain self-awareness. The influence of his practice and experience of meditation is reflected strongly in his treatment of narrative, image and time, comprising even associative flows of memories, present time, dreams and fantasies rather than an action-driven plot. Weerasethakul's themes of transformation and transition stem from Thailand's traditional animistic beliefs that do not privilege the real over the virtual but portray all living and non-living entities as coexisting in a spiritual, tropical world. The artists' practice of personalizing technology, such as the video projector's focused light looking back at the audience and the headset acting as a navigator into a dreamlike state, speak of a techno-animism that is also infused with the ghostly presence of the ephemeral qualities of fog and light. The popular old ghost stories from Thai cinema and the B-grade horror and science fiction films and comics Weerasethakul consumed growing up have left atmospheric and formal traces in his work. Yet, it is the all-encompassing sensuality or queer desire, an openness and unfolding that uniquely permeates his work.

Memory, iconoclasm, animism

The artists and collectives examined in this chapter exploit virtual and augmented reality technologies as one medium among many, signifying that their technological choices do not exclusively define them or their oeuvre. Instead, these choices reflect an expansion in their practice and highlight specific conceptual decisions. Romeo Castellucci's use of a machine or mechanistic device with its origin in the medieval *ars combinatoria* that is regarded today as the antecedent to computing and artificial intelligence served to deconstruct language rather than find truth in an inversion of its historical purpose. The computer-controlled feeding machines that poured bone ash onto the stage in a ritual reflecting the theme of sacrifice in this interpretation of Stravinsky's *Rite of Spring* embodied Castellucci's notion of technology as a metaphor, as a symbol and understood as an animistic concept. Techno-animism is central to the singer and performer Björk's metamorphoses between human, nonhuman and not quite human. 3D-printed masks allow for physical transformation on stage, and projections of the virtual open her fluid persona to a dangerous, living nature. Björk's move into AR allows participants to experience their own planetary travel and transformations at wildly different scales on their mobile devices. Likewise, Olafur Eliasson's AR works are conceived to be a work of portable art, a collectable event and a new and different way to experience and explore his scientifically inspired constructions and configurations, from unknown geometries to handheld little suns and rainbows. Filmmaker Apichatpong Weerasethakul's practice expanded from film to cinematic installations in which the screen became a scenographic actor and the cinema a stage and auditorium. His adoption of virtual technologies positioned the space and participants as protagonists within tropical landscapes, between desire and death, ghosts and shamans, tigers and humans. In this context, binary distinctions dissolve, giving rise to a dreamlike dramaturgy of transformation and transition. In the works discussed, animism and techno-animism are a testament to that porous border between the virtual and the real this project aims to articulate.

5

Researching the virtual

The art and science lab

In the twenty-first century, the structure and nomenclature of the research lab have been co-opted by the cultural and educational sectors. Artists and creative researchers have established their labs based on models of the twentieth-century scientific, technology and engineering research labs. Scrutinizing the emergence of these interdisciplinary labs and institutions, this chapter reflects on the Western division of disciplines during the Industrial Revolution and revisits the figure of the automata as a mechanical construction, artistic creation and scientific advancement in the Arab-Islamic Renaissance.[1] The evolution of interactive and immersive digital visual media leading to the technical realization of virtual environments has a far shorter history, with the English term *virtual reality*, referring to a digitally constructed world, only coined in 1987 by Jaron Lanier of the American company *VPL Research* (Virtual Programming Languages Research) in conjunction with producing the first commercially available VR equipment leading to an uptake of VR artworks by institutionally supported artists shortly after that. Several institutions focusing on artistic production utilizing emerging digital technologies, including VR, were established, including the Centre of Art and Media (ZKM) in Germany in 1989 which will remain a primary example across this chapter, the Inter-Society for the Electronic Arts (ISEA) established in 1990, the NTT InterCommunication Center (ICC) in Tokyo established in 1997 and earlier the Ars Electronica Linz in 1979 and the V2 – lab for unstable media in 1981. The artworks of several pioneering virtual reality artists discussed in this chapter provide an artistic context for the later implementation of VR technology in theatre, art and architecture. Well-equipped interdisciplinary XR labs embedded in universities, dedicated centres and established performing arts companies, often collaborating with corporate labs, play a critical role in developing technologies and strategies for generating virtual worlds.

Interdisciplinary teams embedded in corporate labs, including Google, Apple and Meta labs, joined by university research hubs and international artists such as Japan's prolific art collective teamLab or performing art companies like London's Royal Opera House all research new ways of storytelling and the condition of being in the digital society. New Media centres such as the ZKM shifted their focus as their role in the culture evolved, exemplified by artist and media theorist Peter Weibel's first curated exhibition after assuming the directorship of the ZKM in 1999 entitled *Net_condition* away from the material artefact to the internet. At the start of the new millennium, the technology required to construct virtual environments, interactive artworks and digital video became increasingly available on laptops and non-specialized computers, critically removing artist's necessity to work (technically and politically) within these institutions and ushering in a new democratization of access to the medium that significantly shifted the culture. This availability, ease of use and relative affordability of computers and audiovisual equipment led to a proliferation of smaller new media and extended reality labs (XR labs) that operate within art collectives, architecture studios, theatre companies and the university sector. These small interdisciplinary labs have significantly contributed to digital cultural production, diverse storytelling methods and new approaches to architecture, performance and the visual arts. Attached

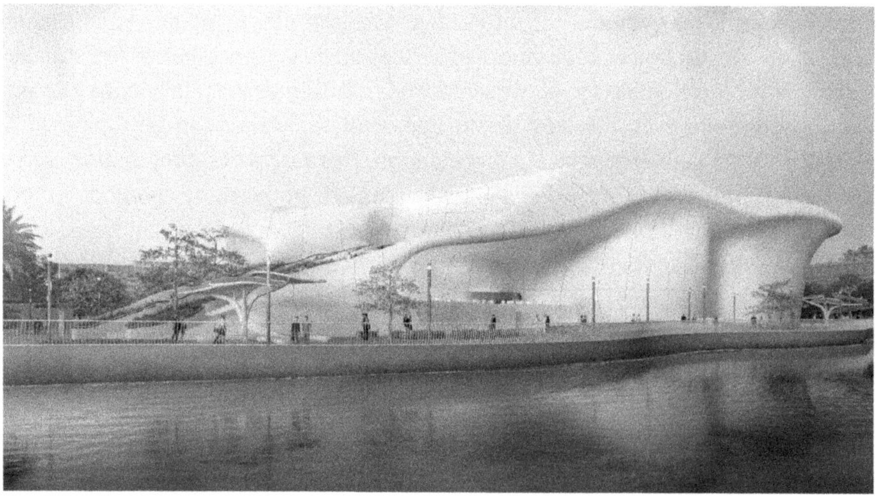

FIGURE 5.1 teamLab Phenomena Abu Dhabi *is a museum where both the architecture and the immersive content have been designed by international art collective teamLab for the Saadiyat Cultural District in Abu Dhabi. The architecture creates a structure that wraps around the experience rather than forcibly compressing it inside. Image courtesy of teamLab. © DCT Abu Dhabi, 2025.*

to theatre academies or independent performance companies, small experimental XR labs lever their non-native status in the digital world with their innate and specialized knowledge of the theatrical interaction of bodies, objects and spaces in physical staged environments as an edge for small-step experimentation in XR settings, novel perceptions of space, time and body on stage and new dramaturgy that blend virtual and physical storytelling. Funded interdisciplinary workshops within performing arts companies invite visual artists and programmers to expand analogue working and representation methods towards virtual worlds and networks that broadly propose future strategies across all areas of spatial design. However, innovative, project-based collaborations such as these are rarely sustainable due to funding shortfalls, and their findings often remain *one-offs*, rarely making it into the repertoire of the host theatre. Counteracting the limitations of one-off productions, federally based labs housed within and in the context of performing arts companies on a European level are currently being established and introduced here as examples of long-term alternatives. These make it possible to conduct training, develop productions and articulate best-practice guidelines for integrating digital media and the virtual into live performances and include specialized workshops for scenographers and dramaturgs that aim to foster the development of new theatrical forms by incorporating technology into the overall dramatic construction. This chapter brings forward case studies, firstly by introducing media art projects realized at the dawn of accessibility and goes on to focus on XR performance and performance-related labs while building a typology and theoretical frame around the discipline while simultaneously acknowledging the complexities, limitations and possibilities of XR for theatre practitioners and institutions and concurs with Peter Weibel's contention of the future of theatre as a *Theatre of Things* that requires a complete and unprecedented rethinking of all theatrical parameters, body, voice, gesture and space.

The emergence of the immaterial

Over the past decades, XR labs have emerged as pivotal institutions at the intersection of technology, arts and architecture, reviving a symbiosis that can be traced back to antiquity, with significant examples in the Italian Renaissance, Baroque and Islamic Renaissance (800–1200 CE) including the ninth-century *Bayt al-ḥikma* (House of Wisdom) in Bagdad initiated by Caliph *Al-Ma'mūn* (786–833) and the studio of Italian polymath *Leonardo de Vinci (1452–1519).* This tradition of cross-disciplinary research studios or labs, often associated with education and knowledge, reaches back to the third and second centuries BCE with the Library of Alexandria and later the Imperial Library of Constantinople, representing institutions devoted to pursuing knowledge through scientific and artistic means. Distinct disciplines became more defined and rigid during the Industrial Revolution in the mid-eighteenth century. By the mid-twentieth century, the extreme siloization of research engineers and scientists in the information age was the default. The engravings, paintings, automata, mechanical theatres and dioramas of the sixteenth, seventeenth and eighteenth centuries that promised awe and wonder and accompanied the romantic project in its dramatization of natural phenomena and imaginations of hybrid creatures between humans and non-humans are a testament to the desire to transcend the material world.

Anthropomorphic fusions between humans, virtual and nonhuman, as illustrated by sixteenth-century Italian Baroque artist Giovanni Battista Bracelli, who represented the human body through repetitive geometric forms, illustrates this desire. Titled fittingly, *Bizzarie di Varie Figure,*[2] many of Bracelli's engravings show two bodies rendered as mechanical with their bones and muscles drawn as squares, circles and triangles in a mechanistic play reminiscent of later cubist figures. In the illustration above, the body comprises material whisps that appear to envelop an immaterial body.

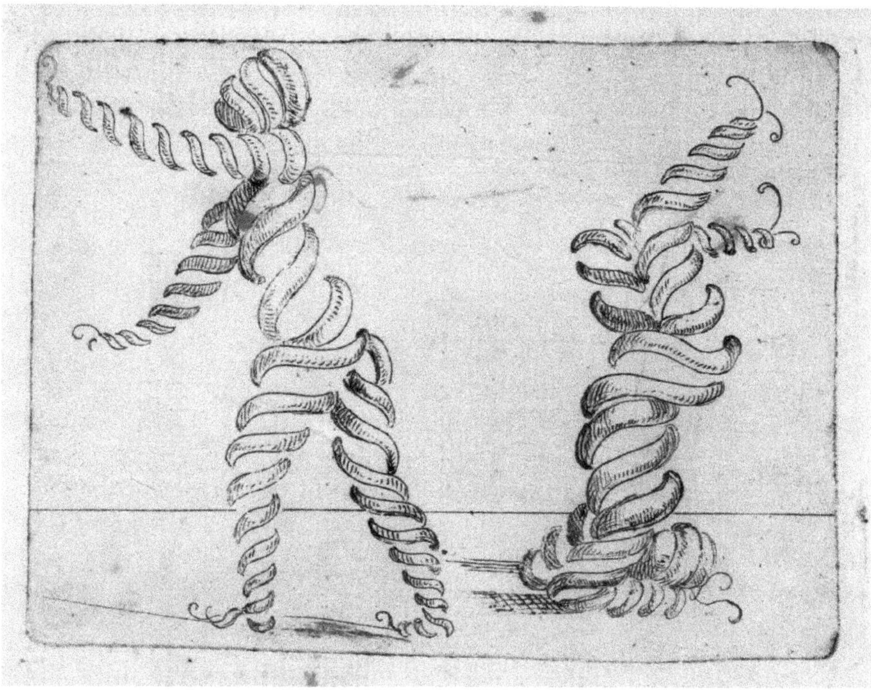

FIGURE 5.2 *Engraving by Giovanni Battista Bracelli in 1624 from a series of forty-seven etchings entitled* Bizzarie di Varie Figure. *Image courtesy of the British Museum.*

Bracelli's representation of a partial human form portrays the dissolution of the body into immaterial realms, placing the two human-like figures on the border between two worlds, the real and the virtual, with others featuring mechanistic-like qualities of the android. An engraving from *Bizzarie di Varie Figure* served as a key image, and the first plate in the catalogue of the 1968 MoMA exhibition entitled *The Machine as Seen at the End of the Mechanical Age*, curated by Pontus Hultén, whose influential role in the Art and Technology movement is discussed in Chapter 2. Hultén argues in the catalogue that the engravings of *Bizzarie di Varie Figure* evoked the conception of the Arab automata, a manifestation of technology through scholarship developed during the Arab-Islamic Renaissance from the ninth to the thirteenth century and made evident in Europe in the Middle Ages through spectacular performances in the European courts and festivals. Hultén's reference was intriguing in its inference of the role of the Arab-Islamic Renaissance in early scholarship and innovation in art and science through the figure of the automata. Four extant Arabic treatises documenting the automata and other devices were the foundation for the exhibition *Allah's Automata: Artifacts of the Arab-Islamic Renaissance*, produced and shown at the ZKM in 2015–16. Curated by eminent media theorists Peter Weibel and Siegfried Zielinski, Zielinski argues that media can be seen as the 'spaces of action for constructed attempts to connect what is separated' (Zielinski 20096: 7) manifested in the exhibition as two fully functional reconstructions of automata highlighting the period's advanced technological capabilities. The first was Ismail al-Jazari's (1136–1206) elephant water clock. This complex mechanical and cultural artefact assembled the knowledge of time into an extraordinary object that combined, according to Zielinski, hydraulic systems from Alexandria together with Greek and Mesopotamian mechanized clockwork components adorned with cultural references to Arabia (falcons), Persia (carpet), China (dragons), Ancient Egypt (phoenix) and India (the elephant and mahout). The reconstruction commissioned by the ZKM was realized in Bursa, present-day western Turkey.

The second reconstruction on display at the ZKM was a universal programmable music machine described by the Banū Mūsā brothers in the 850 CE treatise *Kitāb al-urghanun (The Instrument Which Plays by Itself)*. This treatise followed their notable treatise *Kitāb al-ḥiyal* (The Book of Knowledge of Ingenious Mechanical Devices), an exact facsimile displayed on loan from the Vatican Library that outlined one hundred mechanical devices ranging from 'kinetic sculptures, and automata – the latter being literally "devices that move of their own accord"' (Zielinski 2019: 384). The music machine used a drum and removable pin system to be programmed and utilized mechanical, hydraulics and pneumatics systems in its construction. Zielinski's intentions in mounting an exhibition that 'explores the rich and fascinating world of the automated mechanical devices' (Zielinski 2019: 382) are evident. In the exhibition and associated essays, technological inventions often attributed to the European Renaissance or Enlightenment were 'now in the process of being rediscovered and researched for a materialist history of arts and the media, which can be developed within the context of the arts, sciences, and technology' (Zielinski 2019). Reframing the history of cross-disciplinary knowledge into a more inclusive narrative has led to a re-examination of the origins of art and technology labs and their host institutions and placed their original formulation back into antiquity.

In producing *Allah's Automata: Artifacts of the Arab-Islamic Renaissance,* the ZKM, as an institution, critically reflected on its historic origins beyond its European roots. Reinforcing this line of inquiry, the 2023 exhibition *Renaissance 3.0: A Base Camp for New Alliances of Art and Science in the 21st Century,* curated by Peter Weibel and Anett Holzheid evoked a previous ZKM exhibition, identifying the Arab-Islamic Renaissance as the first Renaissance, the Italian Renaissance (fifteenth to early seventeenth centuries) as the second and, proposed through the exhibition and associated texts, a third Renaissance formed through a twenty-first-century accord between art and science. The exhibition presented contemporary artistic lines of research into the first two Renaissances and opened new research fields in the alliance between science and art. In justifying its claim, the exhibition argued that

> with the rise of technical media, a turning point had come: artists began to take an interest in the use of 'scientific' tools. Today, both disciplines increasingly work with the same tools, methods, and programs. This common 'pool of tools' points to the beginning of a new renaissance.
>
> (ZKM 2024C)

With both exhibitions, ZKM remains a curatorially driven platform for theoretical and praxis discourse on art and technology. It has also amassed an extensive media art collection depicting the evolution of media arts in the twentieth and twenty-first centuries. Since its founding in 1989, ZKM has hosted many of the best-known new media artists, curators and theoreticians, becoming a vocal advocate for the emergence of the new media art and visual arts contribution to science, technology, climate and contemporary socio-technical theoretical positions. As an institution with associated labs, institutes, exhibitions and performance spaces, it exemplifies the rise of art institutions focused on the relationships between art and technology in the late-twentieth century. Supported by the ZKM and similar institutes, internationally practising digital artists gained access to advanced technologies and graphic supercomputers from the 1980s and 1990s onwards, enabling the exploration of physical and virtual construction at the intersections of physicality, virtuality, presence and memory. These works expanded the virtual world's technological construction and aesthetic languages. Embracing the historical shift from concepts of universality to post-modern strategies of deconstruction, artists deployed

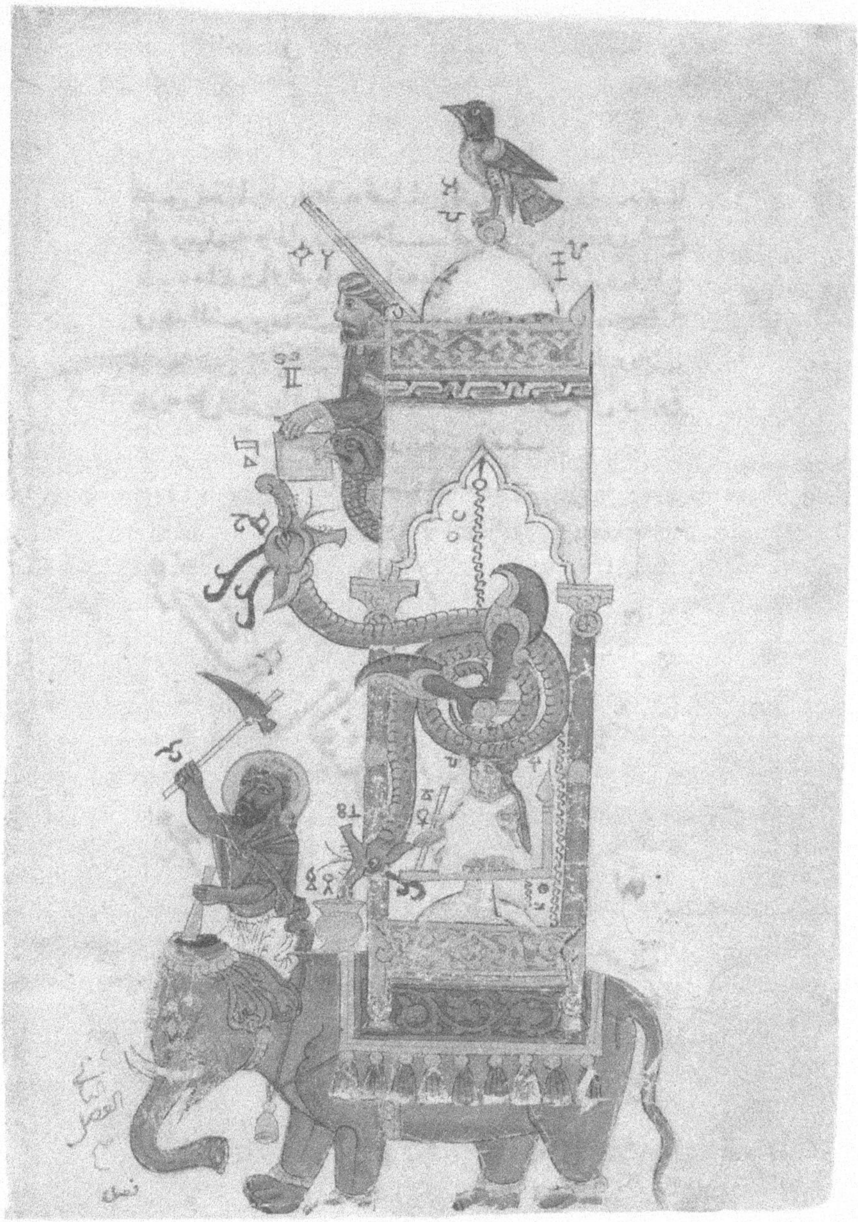

FIGURE 5.3 *Drawing of the elephant clock in a manuscript by Al-Jazari (1206 AD) from* The Book of Knowledge of Ingenious Mechanical Devices. *Public Domain Mark 1.0 Universal Creative Commons. Image Courtesy Wikimedia Commons.*

nonlinear narratives that appeared as visual fragments and that, overall, can be classified as kaleidoscopic transhistorical visual assemblages. In their visual and narrative dramaturgy and structure, early virtual reality artworks simulated the interlinked cognitive activities of forgetting and remembering, thus provoking and empowering the viewer and participant to activate, curate and edit memories that lie dormant in the code and make visible the invisible through navigational systems that explicitly utilize the participant's bodily and spatial interaction. In the late 1980s, the technologies to create and access computer-based virtual worlds became publicly available, albeit only through institutional or corporate-sponsored facilities due to their high cost. Artists became engaged in exploring these technologies, building the virtual worlds and the interfaces for navigation and display in conceptually and artistically coherent ways. They employed digital technologies and explored virtual reality in informally affiliated institutions such as the MIT Media Lab, the ICC and the ZKM. VPL research in Palo Alto was the first company to produce commercially available Datagloves (for navigation through VR environments), a head mounted display (HMD) in the form of VR goggles, presciently named the *Eyephone* and a stereo audio system for creating spatialized sound called the *AudioSphere*. VPL research also developed some of the first widely available software for rendering, producing and displaying VR. The software components included *Body-Electric*, a visual programming language used to program and control the experience, and *Isaac*, a real-time 3D visual rendering engine. Together with technologies developed by companies such as Silicon Graphics (graphic supercomputing), Discreet Logic (compositing) and Softimage (3D modelling and particles), this suite of technologies allowed artists to develop works in the virtual world. Aiming to provide an in-depth context for the emergence of extended reality labs, a look at the works and propositions of three pioneering artists working with VR is warranted: Canadian artist and founding director/head of visual research at Softimage Char Davis (born 1954), Hungarian-born artist Agnes Hegedues (born 1964) and Australian artist Jeffrey Shaw (born 1944) both associated with the ZKM where Shaw was Head of the Institute for Visual Media from 1991 to 2002. Their artworks, three discussed in the following, examine early and divergent approaches to VR made possible within corporate and institutional frameworks. They remain foundational examples of virtual reality in an artistic context.

Virtual reality typologies

Char Davies and her team developed two conceptually similar immersive and interactive seminal installations creating an embodied experience of space entitled *Osmose* (1996) and *Ephémère* (1998) that transported the user 'into a visually powerful simulation of a lush mineral-vegetable sphere which we can explore via an intimate interface' (Grau 2007: 3).

In an intensely physical interface, Davies utilized the user's breathing as the navigational control, allowing one to float through the virtual world, inspired by her deep-sea diving experiences that also informed the way of

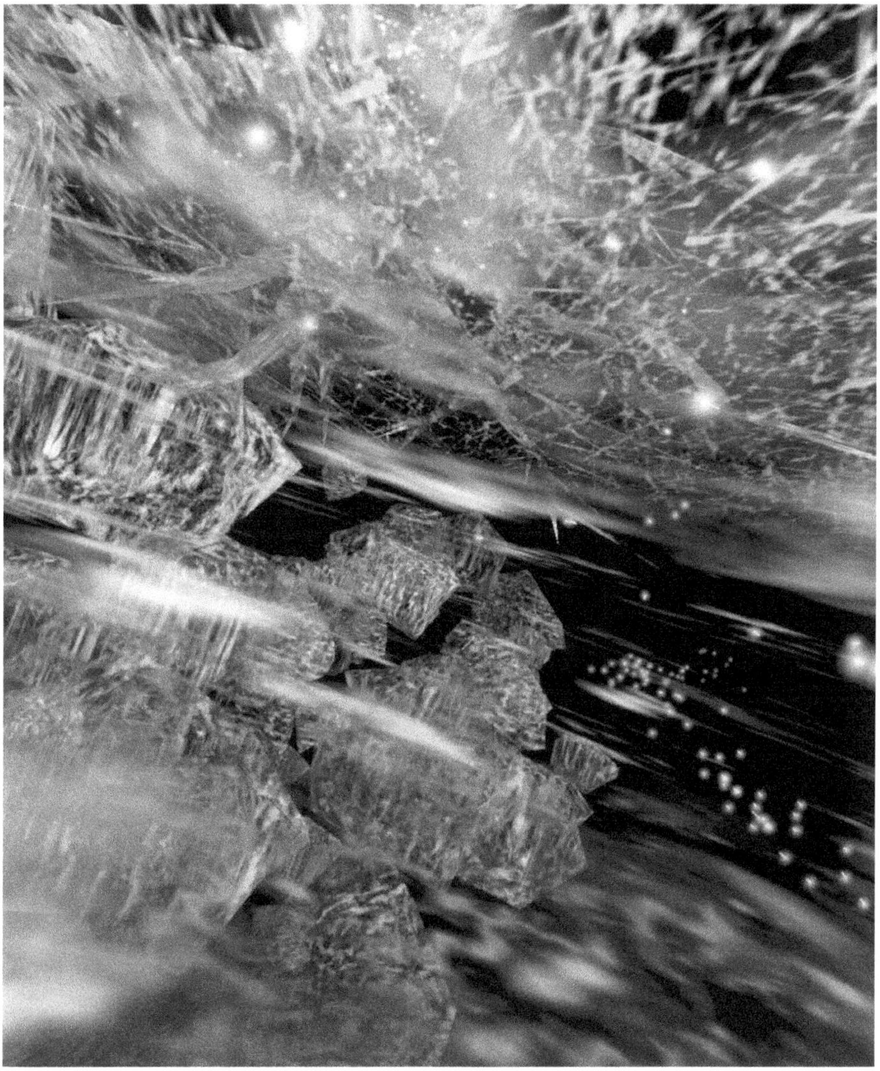

FIGURE 5.4 *Char Davies.* Roots, Rocks and Particle flow in the Underearth, Osmose. *Digital still captured in realtime through HMD (Head Mounted Display) during live performance of immersence virtual environment* Osmose *1995. Image Courtesy of Immersence.*

being within her virtual worlds (Davis 1996). *Osmose*[3] comprised distinct world spaces metaphorically named *the Clearing, Forest, Leaf, Cloud, Pond, Subterranean Earth, Tree, Abyss, Code* and *Text.* Immersants (Char's term for users) navigate past a Cartesian grid (as a transitional space) and into an abstracted, translucent, semi-representational, particle-streamed immersive environment for fifteen minutes before the worlds recede, and one returns to the reality of the museum or gallery. Some literary influences underpinning the work could be glimpsed in the text space, with quotes from Rilke and Thoreau becoming visible. *Ephémère* realized three years later, developed a related nature metaphor focusing on themes of landscape, earth, body and time 'where the earth and the body dissolve into each other' (McDonagh 1998) first shown at the National Gallery of Canada in Ottawa in June 1998. Ultimately, Davies' claim that the work is not about representing nature but is imagined provoking 'another sensibility, a different quality of being' (Davis 1996) is borne out of the 'deep emotional responses' (Davis 1996) of the immersants. Over time, however, in searching for ever-new user experiences, the conceptual and technical relationship between the physical interface and the virtual world's contents in early VR artworks became critical for artists. It led to exploring new interfaces that could form an integrated physical component of the artwork's intent.

In Shaw's pioneering bicycle interface *Legible City* (1989–91),[4] the user navigated a virtual urban landscape (based on maps of New York, Karlsruhe and Amsterdam) that comprised rendered texts relating to the individual cities arranged in the city blocks that the user cycled through to read. A small monitor on the handlebars allowed the user to see where they were in the city as you attempted to read quotes from Donald Trump, Frank Lloyd Wright, Ed Koch and others. In contrast to Char Davies' work, where the user was

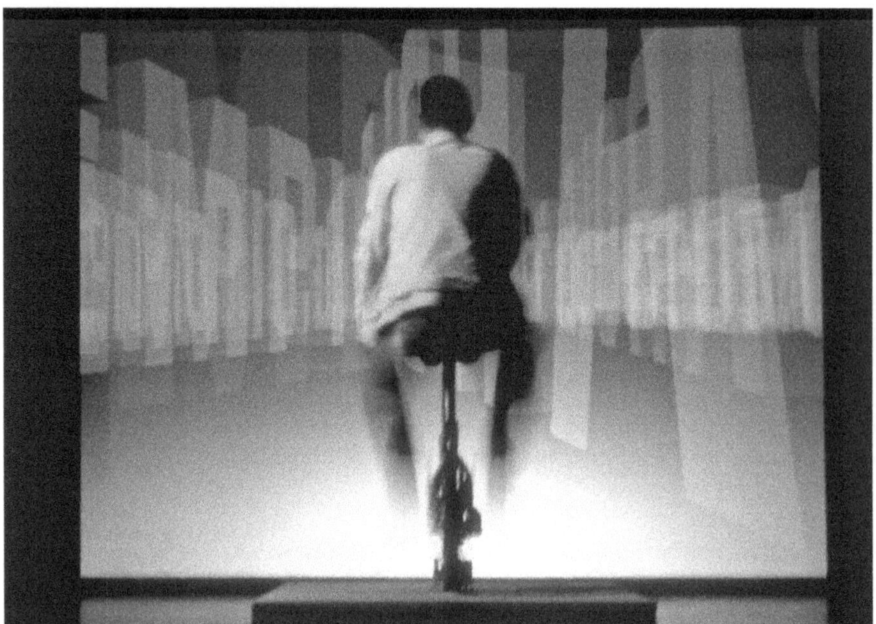

FIGURE 5.5 *Jeffrey Shaw, Dirk Groeneveld.* Legible City, *L'Immagine Elettronica, Chiesa di San Romano, Ferrara, Italy, 1990. Image courtesy of Jeffrey Shaw Compendium.*

fully immersed in the experience reinforced by the intimacy of a navigational device controlled by breath, Shaw's mechanical interface allowed for a critical distance from the work and retention of awareness of one's surroundings. Davies' work, by comparison, used the interfaces to immerse the viewer visually and emotionally in a world without a traditional sense of gravity or collision avoidance. If Shaw and Davies operated at opposite ends of the VR artistic spectrum of 1990s VR experimentation, Agnes Hegedues' highly referential VR artwork *Memory Theatre VR*[5] from 1997 searched middle ground through its reflection on artistic VR experimentation and its historical context with a direct physical and conceptual reference to Camillo's memory theatre (refer Chapter 1).

Hegedues' installation, articulated as a virtual museum, was set inside a cylindrical space with a diameter of eight metres, resembling an amphitheatre. The user could enter one of four virtual spaces through a compass indicating South, North, West and East by moving a spatial tracking device. Each space comprised, to Hegedues, 'a specific scenography of images and objects arranged inside this shared architectural environment and the projection screen in the virtual space, becomes a surface for showing film clips' (Hegedues 1997). The distinct thematic worlds showed the artist as a curator of the history of Virtual Reality, with images and artefacts that ranged from, as Hegedues writes, 'modern pioneers of virtual reality research (South)' to the Wunderkammer's early models of knowledge and collections of curiosities (West)' to a 'child's room: imagination as virtuality (East)' and finally to recent models of knowledge and the theme of deconstruction: 'analysis and disassembling (North)' (Hegedues 1997). Hegedues' four virtual worlds were constructed from subjectively collated historical and contemporary sources that prefigured, defined or expanded concepts of virtuality in film, literature and art, contextualized and brought into the present with media art of the time and research sources in each of the worlds. The viewer was invited to explore Jeffrey Shaw's early VR installation, *Virtual Museum* (1991) in her memory theatre.

In the world that represented modern pioneers of VR research among many other works and texts or to revisit the iconic liquid mirror scene of the passing into the underworld from Jean Cocteau's 1950 film *Orphée* in the world that related to the child's room, the user was further invited to move on to navigate through James Joyce's metaphoric labyrinths as a case study in the world dedicated to deconstruction. Striking in its conceptual clarity and textual and visual richness, *Memory Theatre VR* was realized with direct reference to Camillo's memory theatre, both architecturally and formally, through its separation into different knowledge items or worlds. Camillo's contemporary virtual reality counterpart enticed the participant to actively and seamlessly

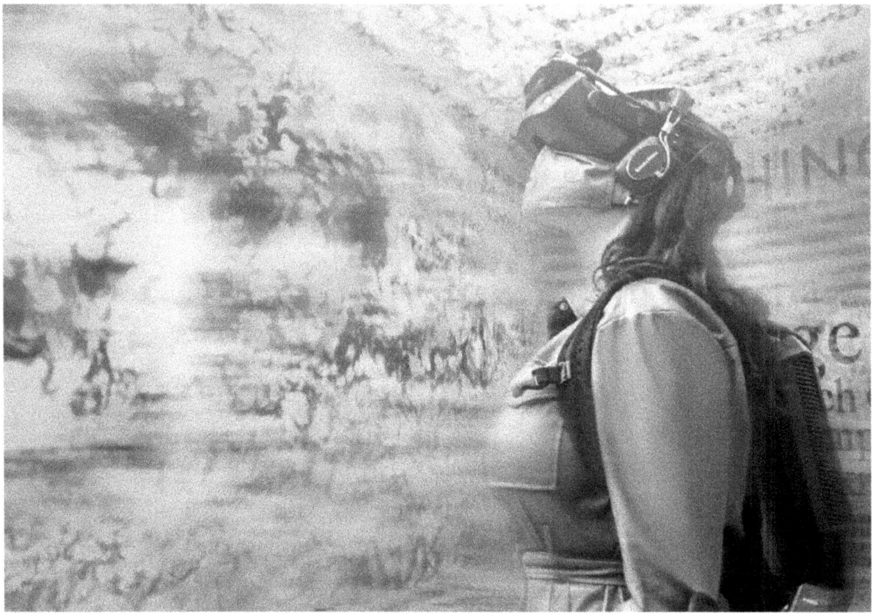

FIGURE 5.6 Current, Rising, *Royal Opera House, Linbury Theatre. Photo: Figment Productions and Joanna Scotcher 2020. Image courtesy of the Royal Opera House.*

transverse diverse landscapes of knowledge by tapping into subjective and fictitious virtual worlds and finally constructing one's inner virtual world as an overall result of the experience. The real and the virtual existed in parallel in this installation. The viewer/participant remained aware of their bodily presence and decision-making when navigating the device and turning their body towards the chosen world. The viewer's physical and spatial experience was intimate, while their virtual experience took them into infinite yet thematically linked worlds. Hegedues' *Memory Theatre VR* presented an enterable model as epistemic in that the installation produced endless combinations from four virtual worlds into new and different knowledge sets for the viewer and was performative in its spatial layout and usability.

Further works, realized in the 1990s by artists associated with the ZKM include artworks from artists Maurice Benayoun with *le Tunnel sous l'Atlantique (*1995), Rafael Lozano-Hemmer's *The Able Skin* (1997) *and* Simon Penny's *Traces* (1999) or Bill Seaman's *The World Generator / The Engine of Desire* (1996). While fragmentary in intent and construction, these works proposed new worlds and new ways of looking at the existing world, supporting American scientist Flavia Sparacino's argument that the World Wide Web has become today's memory theatre (Sparacino, Davenport and Pentland 1999).

Ontologies of the virtual

Virtual worlds have come to be understood as products of strategies that construct loci autonomous from the actual or real, but they possess distinct reality or realness. Philosopher Olaf Wallenstein and visual artist Koo Jeong confirm in a discussion on Koo's augmented reality works, titled *Ontologies of the Virtual*, that 'the virtual does not make place and physical location irrelevant' but asks for it to be 'conceived [. . .] differently' (Wallenstein and Koo Jeong A 2019). Unique to the virtual realm is that a virtual locus carries infinite numbers of further or other loci within itself. Thus, it presents as unstable and rhizomatic rather than as a stable and linear body (entity), and any single virtual model is to be understood as one of innumerable worlds perpetually in a fluid motion. The process of worldmaking through the virtual model remains forever unfinished and forever marked by potentiality, regardless of the expansion of artificial intelligence's remarkable speed and ability to synthesize virtual worlds. In performance design, immersive and interactive environments are created in XR labs, allowing artists to explore new dimensions of storytelling and audience engagement. By leveraging technologies such as XR, these labs have expanded the boundaries of traditional performance spaces, offering audiences unique, multisensory experiences. However, the audience experience is not the only focus of XR labs engaged with performance. Focused on the virtual model's potential capacity to enhance scenographic design and communication practices, *iCinema (Centre for Interactive Cinema Research)* is a cross-faculty Visualization Research Centre at the University of New South Wales in Australia operating at the forefront of AI-driven immersive Virtual reality research. Among a wide range of industry and cultural projects *iCinema* pioneered 'applying an XR environment to the theatre and performance design sector to explore ways of unlocking the full potential of dialogical aesthetics and 1:1-scale visualization' (Del Favero, Thurow and Wallen 2021) with projects focused on production and design processes, developed as collaborative tools for stage design, lighting and other dynamic technical aspects. The projects employed *iCinema*'s 360-degree AVIE visualization platform, a drum-shaped projection screen scalable from 7 to 10 metres in diameter and around 3.5 metres high with 3D projections, audio and motion tracking, allowing for a fully immersive experience. Virtual models of a specific theatre's interior were modelled, and the stage, seating and lighting were added, allowing the production team to start building up the stage as a virtual *Bauprobe* (1:1 prototype of the stage) and define the choreography with stage elements and lighting. *iCinema* has led two cross-institutional research projects to develop an immersive and interactive stage design toolkit. The project *iModel* focused on the opera stage, collaborating with renowned Australian Designer Michael Scott-Mitchell and Opera Australia. The second project, *iDesign*, involved collaborating with the National Institute of Dramatic Arts (NIDA), the University of Technology Sydney (UTS) and the Sydney Theatre Company to 'reformulate set design aesthetics through a dialogical model of interactivity' (Del Favero, Thurow and Wallen 2021). The project investigated 'full-body immersive visualization systems' capabilities to extend digital aesthetics' benefits to the entire design pipeline' (Del Favero, Thurow and Wallen 2021) through implementing interactive networked virtual environments that facilitate real-time, collaborative development of digital scenographic models in design and rehearsal settings (Del Favero, Thurow and Wallen 2021). Both *iModel* and *iDesign* utilize an experimental immersive system to reconceptualize spatial paradigms that simultaneously engage with the director, designer, lighting designer and technical director. The system provides stage designers with a toolkit to develop digital sketches and collages during preproduction and rehearsal while allowing for real-time alterations informed by easily accessible databases of relevant objects, materials, actors, props and historical precedents. One of the outstanding qualities of the system is its ability to deliver and manipulate lighting and render atmosphere in a highly realistic manner.

A second approach to XR performance research is characterized by established performing arts companies collaborating with advanced technology corporations or universities to develop staged productions rather than the process-driven research in the case of *iCinema*. These projects serve the research agenda of both universities and corporations while fulfilling the performing arts companies' desire to engage new audiences through new technologies. Two projects that exemplify this type of institutional Extended Reality research collaboration are *Project AR-ia* (2018), a research partnership between Google Creative Labs and Opera Queensland in Australia and *Current, Rising*, a mixed reality performance produced by London's Royal Opera House, production company Figment Productions and Royal Holloway University. *Project AR-ia* was an augmented reality, AI-powered prototype app with an Android smartphone interface promising to bring opera into the home. The app composited virtual opera singers and scenographic elements, including virtual holes in the physical walls of an actual apartment. *Project AR-ia* merged a specially devised studio-produced opera performance with a viewer's domestic environment through the screen and camera of a standard Android mobile phone.

The world experienced by the viewer was co-produced between artificial intelligence and the viewer's choices as to where they position themselves, in which direction they pointed the phone and which narrative strand of the performance they chose to follow. This process resulted in a fifteen-minute musical and scenic montage that transported Mozart's *The Magic Flute* from the opera stage into a domestic environment. Technically, this work was made possible by Google's ARCore (augmented reality platform for androids), the phone's built-in motion tracking ability, and an AI spatial-based system to calculate lighting developed by Google named *Relightable*. The avatars of the opera singers were modelled using photogrammetry,[6] which allowed for a highly realistic, dynamic re-creation of the singers and their costumes.

The alluring promise of an opera performance in one's living room was only thwarted by the technical limitations of read/write times on commercially available computers. However, perhaps it pointed towards a possible future domestication of the genre. This collaboration between an opera company and a high-tech creative lab remained tentative, with its value lying in the conceptual realization of a tailor-made individual AI performance experience and new ways of storytelling that transgress the borders between the actual and the virtual. *Project Ar-ia* succeeded as a prototype and has informed other projects, including the Immersive Storytelling Studio's cross-platform production of *All Kinds of Limbo,* directed by Toby Coffey National Theatre London in 2022, which was broadcast as an augmented performance and leading immersive theatre proponent Punchdrunk's unrealized gamified theatrical experience codenamed *Hamlet* in collaboration with *Pokémon Go* creators Niantic. The conceptual starting point of *Project AR-ia* was positioned on the border of the real and the virtual, and when activated, the performance blended both realms into the new realm of augmented reality. The cosmopoietic act occurred continuously throughout the opera's performance, whose narrative structure and scenography were fleeting, dynamic and liquid. It follows that the virtual models in AR, like all models, typically constitute both object and idea; however, both object and idea are continuously evolving and, in many respects, impossible to grasp. Circling back to Bergson and Deleuze's concepts of the virtual and its temporalities outlined in Chapter 1, this project affirms that the virtual model has its own reality – the reality of the virtual. Similar in its configuration of institutional collaboration was the short Virtual Reality Opera *Current, Rising*[7] (2020), created by the Royal Opera House through its experimental tech hub Audience Labs, production company Figment Productions and Royal Holloway University. This highly immersive production ushered the participant into a VR dreamlike expanding universe and, unlike *Project AR-ia,* did not allow immediate critical distance. The differing audience perception of the two opera projects echoes the differences between Shaw's VR bicycle and Char's immersive VR worlds explored earlier in this chapter; Shaw's bicycle and *Project AR-ia's* mobile phone mediated the experience, allowing for a critical distance while the highly immersive nature of Char's work and *Current, Rising* demanded from the user a dissolution into the virtual world. Inspired by Ariel's emancipation at the conclusion of Shakespeare's *The Tempest, Current, Rising* began with the projection of text associations and concluded with a cityscape rising out of the water and exploding into the air. The production was a sophisticated merging of a physical enterable white box and a virtual space with multisensory characteristics, including wind, touch and fragrance, that allowed four participants to engage with the VR aspects of the work at any given time.

Each participant encountered an enterable VR model world that expanded the traditional opera experience towards a fully immersive, spectacular and dramatically convincing environment. Funded by UK Research and Innovation and produced by Annette Mees, Head of Audience Labs at the Royal Opera House (ROH), Mees described the experience as a 'sequence of liminalities' (Mees 2021). Touted as the world's first opera in hyperreality, the physical set was built on the ROH's second stage, the Linbury Theatre. Its technology included VR goggles and a backpack-type computer for the participant to don before entering the first of several virtual worlds. The director, Netia Jones, explained that

> With *Current, Rising,* we have been exploring the possibilities of VR to expand the idea of what an opera can be, both in the process of creation and in the audience experience. VR challenges all the traditional hierarchies of opera and classical music and allows a completely different approach [. . .] Here, the audience are the protagonists; they are inside the work, and their physical experience is a part of the work itself.
>
> (JONES IN ROH PRESS RELEASE 2020)

In merging VR with multisensory features such as wind, touch and scent, *Current, Rising* demonstrated the persistence of an artistic aesthetic and scenographic thinking and a directorial rigour that ensured to avoid what can be experienced as technology's dominance over a creative team. Aided by the pandemic's enforced distance communication, both Jones, Mees and the composer Samantha Fernando stressed the collaborative nature of this piece, developed in many video conferencing sessions and with an emphasis on workshopping every aspect of the opera, be it the built set, the virtual experience, lighting, sound, voice and movement (ROH 2024). The four participants entered the VR environment through the theatre's auditorium and onto the actual stage, where they first encountered the physical set. The white cube with the opera's title sculpted into its form presented a physical entrance into a 'real' scenography built on an actual stage. Once on the stage, the participants became actors or agents in the VR opera while still physically being led further into the cube, from the entrance situation into the dressing room with goggles and a VR computer backpack. Now costumed, the actor-participants entered the first text-based virtual world. Named the 'insomnia' room by the creators, this world comprised literary citations from and around Shakespeare's *Tempest*, bylines, headlines and excerpts of documentary information about weather, climate change and society in diverse large black-and-white fonts, resulting for the viewer-actor to be immersed in a semantic text cloud. From the concrete world of the insomnia room, participants left the Euclidian geometry of the white cube and 'rose', as the title succinctly describes, into cosmic worlds of atmospheres from day into night and from night into day, into rivers of colour and shapes, and towards unstable and stunning horizons. A city structure seemed to rise high from the river and finally exploded, thus closing an overall metaphorical arch between creation and destruction. While the worlds unfolded and immersed the viewer during the fifteen-minute experience, they did so according to a linear, classical Aristotelian dramaturgy of introduction, conflict or drama, rising, resolution and catharsis. Mees explained that the experiential journey for the audience was mapped out as a linear narrative that took the group from the material (entrance into the auditorium, onto the stage and into the physical set) into the immaterial (virtual worlds) and back into the material world, exiting through the cube and from the stage through the auditorium to the theatre's exit (Mees 2021). In contrast to the blurring of borders between the real and the virtual in Opera Queensland's augmented reality opera project, *Current, Rising* employed traditional narrative and dramaturgical structures and a strict separation between the two realms. Nevertheless, both projects were immersive to a high degree, and both relied on the virtual model as its centrepiece and core. The modelling of space inhabited by avatars, as in *The Magic Flute*, or the modelling of uninhabited cosmic worlds, as in *Current Rising,* relied on the viewer's activity to realize the intended experience. Worldmaking, in *Current, Rising,* was thus a collaborative, performative and epistemic project. As shown in the virtual and augmented reality artworks and performances introduced in this project, worldmaking encompasses construction and reconstruction, invention and assemblage, fact and fiction and manifests translated into nonverbal symbolic systems of representation. Never restaged, however, due to funding and logistical restraints, *Current, Rising* remained a single project that highlighted the precariousness of project-based funding in the fostering and development of the integration of new technologies into live environments.

An understanding of the necessity of long-term funding at the intersection of the arts and technology is exemplified in numerous government and state-funded initiatives internationally. Based within the State Theatre Dortmund, Germany's Society of Scenographers initiated in 2022 a series of federally funded embedded labs and artistic research nodes that experimented with a wide range of digital technologies on and behind the stage, accompanied by lectures and symposia in cooperation with the Akademie for Theatre and Digitality (see theater.digital). While much of its current work retraces existing technologies, methods and effects from the early days of new media art, the collaboration between scenography students, programmers, dramaturgs and artists is promising in that the hybrid performance arts of the 1980s and 1990s that examined the relationship between the performer's physical body and digital technology (e.g. Troika Ranch, Blast Theory) is now challenged by a new generation of digital natives that rally behind LuYang's (see Chapter 3) provocation that on the web 'you can abandon your identity, nationality, gender and even your existence as a human being' (LuYang in Qin 2015: 2) resulting in an artistic examination of the relationship between immaterial technologies and immaterial bodies, and like the performance artists and theatre makers of 1960, contemporary artists and collectives artists are questioning the future of the physical theatre as the exclusive location for performance, now through a virtual lens.

From a sense of proximity to a sense of distance

Peter Weibel, an astute thought leader in digital innovation and its historical, cultural, technological and symbolic emergence and significance for the digital society and its future, has argued that theatre traditionally is engaged with proximity. He has posited that digital technologies and, in particular, artificial intelligence will enhance and expand theatre from the 'sense of proximity to a sense of distance' (Weibel 2017) and will extend the closed theatre space towards the city through digital platforms and networks, resulting in participation and an equal alliance between body, text and AI. The theatre as a whole will become a 'theatre of things' (Weibel 2017) and an intelligent and possibly autonomous system. Extrapolating from Weibel's vision, such an intelligent system will connect performers and audience, text, bodies and speaking objects, sensors and artificial intelligence into a radically new form of the theatrical encounter where, significantly, a division between analogue and digital, live and recorded, singular and networked will cease to exist. The performative space that emerges in a 'theatre of things' is analogous to the 'Internet of Things' (IoT), which refers to a network of 'physical devices, vehicles, appliances and other objects embedded with sensors, software, and network connectivity' (Hung-Chi and Yu-Jhe 2023: 13) allowing them to collect and share data. This space is vibrant due to its multiple temporalities, spatialities, real and imagined situations and the presence of both near and distant bodies, voices and objects. Complex relations exist between the elements of the ensemble and each element is required to be part of the communal task of the futuring of the live experience, yet with different histories and conventions of representation, materialities, meaning-making and modalities. Body, text, voice, sound, gesture, time, media, scenography, as well as body, voice and gesture of the audience, must be sought to be redefined in the live moment. In the theatre of things, thus, the virtual model has its locus and its reality distinct from other loci and realities that exist simultaneously on the stage (see also Chapter 1). The virtual may possess liveness that neither negates, disputes nor competes with bodies' liveness on the stage but exists autonomously in that new composition, that new scenography of things. Haraway's 1985 thesis of the cyborg as both imagination and material reality comes to mind, and with it, the activist potential of the virtual. The cyborg, to Haraway, is 'a kind of disassembled and reassembled, post-modern collective and personal self' (Haraway [1985], 2016: 33) necessarily fragmented, a fragmentation that acts as a productive source. Understood in this way, the cyborg as an idea and possibility exists in a virtual and actual reality, and both contribute to and feed from the intelligent system called theatre. Weibel's future-oriented thesis of the 'Theatre of Things' is significant in its implicit call to rethink theatre's anthropocentrism and a traditional dominance of the dramatic text. In adding another dimension, the theatre of things will not differentiate between animate and inanimate objects, between human and artificial intelligence, but regard all these equally – as things.

ZKM's mandate in developing and staging new works for a new theatre and giving space and time to experimental configurations has contributed to the extension of the analogue stage to virtual worlds and the creation of numerous complex interrelationships between material and immaterial elements on the stage and the presence of the performer. ZKM's Institute of Electro-Acoustic Music (merged into the Hertzlab in 2017 to better meet the needs of the digital society) has attracted international artists for residencies and project-oriented stays as well as initiating focused research into new theatrical expressions, primarily in the development of music and dance theatre coupled with the use and application of virtual technologies and diverse sensor-supported environments. In addition, interactive configurations and mathematically generated electronic compositions are used to extend the sound space and connect voice and music in new ways.

The play between distance and closeness posited by Weibel as one of the fundamental topoi of the theatre experience is thus reimagined in live media events where technological possibilities may challenge the scenic composition and the traditional segregation of performer and audience. ZKM's 2008–2010 three-part production, *Amazonas*, discussed here as an exploration into a new articulation of contemporary music theatre, can today be regarded as a technically historical yet significant project. Co-produced by the indigenous tribe of the Yanonami in the Amazonas and written by composers Klaus Schedl (part one), Tato Taborda (part two) and Ludger Brümmer (part three) and conceptualized by Weibel, *Amazonas* departed from a conventionalized dramaturgy to a seemingly epic format, namely a staged conference on an

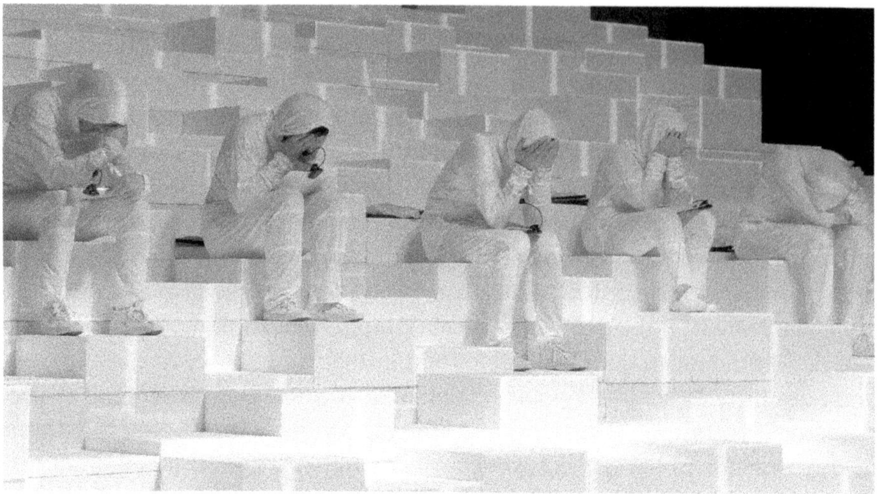

FIGURE 5.7 *Excerpt from* Amazonas. Music Theatre in Three Parts, *8 May 2010. Photo: © ZKM | Zentrum für Kunst und Medien Karlsruhe. Image courtesy of the ZKM | Center for Art and Media Karlsruhe.*

interactive, tiered and oversized platform with software developed by ZKM-based programmer and artist Bernd Lintermann. Different stakeholders, indigenous and non-indigenous experts on the state of the world, lamented the destruction of the Amazon. Networked music and imagery rendered the chorus and protagonists equally integral parts of an immersive yet strangely hermetic world. The world created in *Amazonas* or, in other words, its cosmopoietic faculty remained fragmentary and theoretical in that the intention to create a new theatre was demonstrated in parallel by the composer, director and cast, yet their contributions were not convincingly integrated. Nevertheless, as an uncompromisingly technology-driven piece, it pointed to many future formats where virtual reality as a significant scenographic agent challenges all other theatrical elements towards a new definition of liveness.

Similarly, at a smaller scale, institutions such as the Zurich University of the Arts (ZHdK) are pushing the boundaries of interdisciplinary exploration. At ZHdK, media artist Chris Salter heads the Immersive Arts Space (IASpace), conducting practice-based research between art, design and digital technology. Salter's work investigates the future of performative practices, with a current focus on tracking-based projection mapping through research, teaching and production. The IA Space research team engages in technologically supported artistic inquiry, examining digital immersion, mixed realities and the convergence of media-based and performative practices through innovative and multidisciplinary projects. These activities are aligned with practice-based research approaches to contemporary aesthetic and methodological trends in international design and art. Presentations of their work at Prague Quadrennial

2023, Kunstfest Weimar and festivals in Canada, Japan, Tasmania and Italy (all 2023 and 2024) show a focus on the integration of AI and Virtual Reality into live and participative formats to make visible social concerns such as (Switzerland's role in) colonialism and global climate change. In the live performance event *Animate* (2023), Salter uses the virtual model to evoke and communicate highly emotive states through AR, sound and haptic sensor technologies. In contrast to Weibel's Brechtian understanding of catharsis through distant critique and analysis, *Animate* aimed at producing an Aristotelian catharsis through *fear and horror* in the audience by participating directly in the desperate journey of two climate refugees through Canadian landscapes. Salter's project, conceptualized for a small audience of up to ten people, was shown in non-theatre spaces and abandoned industrial warehouses and began as a live, analogue performance, with the audience seated on wooden tree stumps, listening to two actors reading the story of the climate refugee couple then burst into virtual reality when the audience was invited to don VR headsets. Isolated from each other through the technical apparatus, each experienced their own dramatic action and, once leaving their seats and wandering through the bare space, found themselves in the middle of a myriad of falling rocks. Participants could feel a sonic vibration emanating from the rocks they were standing on. Salter asked for the audience's emotional involvement and identification with the actors, storyline and overall topic. To bring the reality of the impending climate catastrophe close to the audience, he employed a phenomenological method to experience virtual reality through visual and auditory senses and direct bodily sensations. *Animate* was presented as a theatrical experiment on a small scale that aimed to dissolve the traditional stage-auditorium segregation yet separated its small audience into individually perceiving subjects through the VR headsets. VR enabled the introduction of the simulation of nature as an actor into the performing space immediately and terrifyingly, where the audience was granted no distance and was participating, albeit, in this scenario, without agency, in a simulation of a natural catastrophe framed through essentially traditional theatrical devices. Similar to ZKM in its inquisitiveness and openness to embrace, test and develop new interrelationships in and between the analogue and the virtual, but framed within the mandate of education and practice-based research, IA Space is entirely focused on the question of immersion, both within a technological framework, human-computer interaction and the confrontation with a live event where the central question of structuring the encounter between humans and non-humans and between humans and other elements remains ever-present. There can, of course, be no dramaturgical blueprint for a new theatre, a new scenography and a new mode of audience reception; however, as the two examples, *Amazonas* and *Animate*, have demonstrated, they both aimed to achieve engagement in the audience as a call for action, be it through the Brechtian technique of distance and non-identification, or the Aristotelian experiential cleansing of emotions as fundamental drivers. The introduction of many more examples of live performance with digital technologies would prove the point that technological innovation and experiment in theatre do not necessarily go hand in hand with a redefinition of the theatrical experience and, indeed, a leaning on tradition is more often than not employed to frame the event. Nevertheless, new technologies that promise new bodily and sensory experiences for audiences even while seated for an event defined in time and space are also able to explode traditional dramaturgy, expand traditional aesthetic expectations and redefine the central theatrical parameters of body, sound, gesture, voice, space and time as postdramatic, non-hierarchical assemblages. In these, the virtual offers agency towards expanding time and space and, in conjunction with sensor technologies, can be mapped onto a moving body, creating an essentially volatile space. Without wishing to inscribe the term *virtual theatre* entirely to Artaud's vision of the *Theatre of Cruelty* (1938/1958: 49), his concept of the theatre as a machine resounds in networked performances that emerge from the virtual and that spill into the liveness of the physical stage of a theatre that is not body-centric but body-electric, that pulses and breathes as part of a network of autonomous systems and that has no centre. Artaud's 'bizarre project' (Weber 2004: 278) that understood theatre as the double of life, advocated, while distinctly anti-psychological, a theatre that comprises a dissonant and violent attack on the senses and that achieves virtualization through a process of dehumanization, of transgressing language, transgressing meaning. The writer Anaïs Nin seemed to have comprehended Artaud's desire for a dangerous, infectious theatre beyond his self-contradictory positions, acclamations and accusations in its essence. After witnessing his emphatic performance-lecture on the plague that severely alienated his academic audience at the Sorbonne in 1933, Nin wrote in her diary, 'It seems to me that all he is asking for is intensity, a more heightened form of feeling and living' (Nin 1966 as cited in Moe 2013: 6). This lecture was to become a chapter in *The Theater and Its Double* (1997), a collection of essays published in 1938, where Artaud identified both alchemy and the theatre as transformative arts, or 'virtual arts'. In a much-quoted passage from the essay, *The Alchemical Theatre*, he wrote, 'It is that alchemy and the theatre are so to speak virtual arts, and do not carry their end – or their reality within themselves' (Artaud 1997: 48). 'Theatre', Artaud wrote in what was to be his last letter to Paule Thévenin in 1948, 'is in reality the genesis of creation: It will come about' (2004: 233). Extrapolating on Artaud's equation between theatre and alchemy, the virtuality of his envisaged theatre stems from its utter negation of representation; it comprises not creation but the origin of creation itself, not dissimilar to the *prima materia* (first matter) of alchemy, the ur-substance used to begin the creation of the philosopher's stone. If the virtual arts that theatre is to Artaud does not carry its reality or its 'goal' within itself, its virtuality presents as autonomous, independent of life, yet simultaneously as the epitome of life, forever becoming. Equally, the virtual can exist in a continuous process of creation, independent of representation.

To be a machine

It is fitting that the Dublin-based performance collective Dead Centre around artistic directors Bush Moukarzel and Ben Kidd should have taken their cue from Artaud's notion of the virtual reality of theatre and its visceral effects on the bodies performing and perceiving for three of their VR and live performances between 2020 and 2022. In the latest iteration of their project, *To Be A Machine* (Version 2.0) from 2022, they stated,

> The phrase 'virtual reality' was first used by a playwright, Antonin Artaud, to describe the nature of theatre: a technology which allows us, for one night only, to get out of our heads. But what happens if theatre stops working? Where do we go next?
>
> (DEAD CENTRE 202 4)

Dead Centre had asked a similar question in their German language premiere at Burgtheatre Vienna 2020 concerning the second iteration of *To be A Machine* (Version 1.0), a VR and live performance based on Mark O'Connell's book with the same title (2018). Artaud's desire to transgress the confines of (theatrical) convention, evoked by the angular movements of the Balinese dancers and their collective out-of-body-like trance that shaped his thinking and writing throughout, seemed to shadow O'Connell's travels into the production sites and laboratories of transhumanism and cyber hacking.

> Wasn't technology itself, I thought, a strategy for disembodiment: Wasn't it all – internet, air travel, the invention of the wheel – an ancient yearning to be out of ourselves, out of our bodies, our location in space and time?
>
> (DEAD CENTRE AND O'CONNEL 2023)

Initially collaborating with Trinity College Dublin's Science Gallery, Dead Centre explored in this triad of projects how VR technology on the stage reimagines Artaud's negation of psychological realism in favour of a different body and a different voice, both live and mediated. In the encounter between live performer, live audience and their uploaded portraits, three temporalities and locations converged for the time of the performance. Both embodied and disembodied, audience and performer took on virtuality comprised of the confrontation of the live audience with its disembodied images as the main scenographic body, the confrontation of the live performer with their mediated image, and, thirdly, the confrontation of a live performer and a live audience in an immersive environment. What *To Be a Machine* explored is what happens if virtual reality appears more real than reality – will we never physically enter a theatre again? The following quote by Mark Zuckerberg that stood motto-like over the productions, 'The defining quality of the metaverse will be a feeling of presence – like you are right there with another person', promises a ubiquitous presence whose dark side – complete surveillance – unfolded in the three versions of *To Be a Machine*.

Exploring notions of presence and virtuality from a dramaturgical perspective, theatre and media scholars Peter Eckersall, Helena Grehan and Edward Scheer examine soundscapes, atmospheric stages and experience design through case studies by artists and groups such as Blast Theory, dumb type, Riyoshi Ikeda, Romeo Castellucci and Kris Verdonck in *New Media Dramaturgy: Performance, Media and New Materialism* (2017). They offer succinct analyses of the different kinds of dramaturgy that emerge in performances integrating new technologies, further elucidating the intricate relationships between live and mediated experiences in contemporary theatre. The authors posit a constant, relentless negotiation of the relationships between subjects and objects, humans and machines (2017: 119–21). However, the virtual performance transgresses even this negotiation and relies solely on the nonhuman. The robot, the cyborg and the avatar become not substitutes for the actor's body but constitute the body of the virtual in the same way in which the scenography of the virtual model constitutes its location, temporality and expanse. If storytelling can be thought of as the centre or the seed of performance and dramaturgy as its basic structural device to enable diverse modes of communication, spatiality must be considered as inextricably linked to both the desire for narrative and the need for its anchoring in real or imaginary space. The ability of networked systems to shift seamlessly through spaces while simultaneously creating them enables innumerable or infinite dramaturgical patterns of virtual storytelling that depart from conventional notions of plot, action, development and meaning. Rather, the gesture of immersion that both holds and disconnects participant(s) with their physical persona inevitably individualizes any narrative unfolding between interface, virtual reality and subject. Where the virtual experience is deliberately merged with a physical experience, virtual space and physical space work together to create a single combined reality activated through the participants' movements and actions.

Designing experiences through participants' immersion into XR environments lies at the centre of MIT's virtualXdesign experience design lab.

The lab is engaged in integrating virtual reality into research and education, and it conducts and facilitates interdisciplinary and applied research into immersive visualization in arts, science and technology. A recent virtualXdesign project, for example, *September 1955,* created an immersive experience of virtual (augmented) and physical reality. The single participant could move around in the simplified physical reconstruction of a photographer's studio in Istanbul in 1955. Demarcations of the floor indicated the studio's dimensions. On a single wall facing the participant, historical photographs presented the historical and thematic point of departure, namely the state-organized pogrom on ethnic minorities in Istanbul on two days in September 1955. Far from being distant historical documentation, the installation immersed the participant through physical and virtual exhibits from a time ago, and a role-play was initiated where the participant viewed the events from the perspective of a local shop owner. While not unique in the terrain of interactive, immersive artworks, the intended merging of both spaces and dramatization of the situation, namely *September 1955*'s dramaturgical structure and storytelling character, achieved a sense of immersion that to the participant appeared to transgress physical-virtual limits towards the experience – as if in the present – of a complete historical world. Overall, *September 1955* was conceptualized as an exemplary project that was easily adaptable for diverse contexts and contents rather than a unique artwork. The lab's aim to develop and disseminate basic research to a wider audience is also evident in its 2022 collaboration with MIT's Transmedia Storytelling Initiative for the project *Latent Archive: Immersive Storytelling Platform for Examining Spatial History.* The ongoing project performs forensic 3D spatial reconstructions of existing and historical moving image documents such as films, newsreels and documentaries. The team aims to 'combine and develop technologies to produce a single prototype platform for translating moving image archives into spatial formats that can be examined in immersive media and XR' (transmedia.mit.edu). The project's innovation and significance lie in the potential for future humanities, film and media research utilizing the single platform prototype for spatial analysis through XR media rather than the examples the lab uses for development. The MIT labs, ZKM and ZHdK's IA space are equally invested in software development and new visualization technologies and in producing seminal individual projects staged for the public. The emphasis on authored artistic projects continues to be paramount in institutions directly linked to art schools and art and technology centres with diverse possibilities for dissemination to the general public and specialized users. In contrast, institutions linked to architecture and technology universities like MIT tend to focus on technical invention and visualization technologies.

But what happens if the theatre stops working?

Parallel to the established and emerging publicly funded university labs and art and culture centres and largely financially independent from commercial activities or box office income, federal funding initiatives for immersive and digital arts have emerged in Europe and the UK. These initiatives stem from a political understanding of the significance of the contemporary cultural shift towards a digital society that exists increasingly in and between the physical and the virtual in work, daily life, entertainment and education. There, cultural policies understand, support and expand investment into the digital and immersive arts as an investment into the community-building aspect of the arts, into people's well-being and the fostering of a new generation of arts practitioners and audiences who are not only digitally literate but expect the arts to relate to contemporary culture. Organizationally, these grants, while essentially centrally funded, are administered by several art funding bodies and realized by networks of universities and theatres accompanied by advisory boards of experts. It has come to be understood by the funding bodies that knowledge-sharing, prototyping and structured long-term programmes support and enable digital innovation and are a valuable long-term investment compared with short-term project-based support in closing the knowledge gap of many theatre practitioners concerning the digital tools already widely accessible, let alone the conceptual possibilities of innovative interdisciplinary projects. Governmental funding to specifically support new immersive technologies has most recently been awarded to arts organizations linked with universities and research labs in the UK (2024–27), while European-wide funding enabled, among others, the foundation of a digital theatre initiative in the framework of the European Theatre Convention (ETC). Considering the rapidly changing social and cultural landscape towards everyday cohabitation and even immersion into all aspects of the digital, the ETC received two-year funding (2016–2018) for the establishment of the European Theatre Lab (ETL), to be solely engaged with the specific role of European state theatres in this new digital environment. Experimental research, conferences, publications and co-productions were at the centre of the project and were directed towards its forty member theatres in twenty-four European countries as well as universities, artists from the field and an advisory board of experts. Among the members of the Advisory Board were Gerfried Stocker, long-time artistic director of Linz' Ars Electronica, the groundbreaking digital arts festival founded in 1979, and Simon Mellor, the Deputy Chief Executive of the Arts Council England, both highly experienced in harnessing the future for contemporary art projects beyond a single genre. Seven European state theatres participated directly in the ETL through direct cooperation and open labs, resulting in four productions and two publications. One of which comprises a case book with statements from the advisory board and participating artists, while the other publication, *Drama Goes Digital vs Theatre Invades Digital* (2023), is a summary of 'suggestions and recommendations for publicly funded theatres, policymakers and funders at the local, national and European level', both published at the close of the project with the overall aim of a reflection on the projects realized and to provide a forward-looking path towards the integration of digitality into the workings of state theatre companies. Directly participating theatres were Badisches Staatstheater Karlsruhe (DE), Kote Marjanishvili State Drama Theatre (GE), CDN Nancy Lorraine La Manufacture (FR), Theatre de Liege (BE), Teatrul National Craiova (RO), Det Norske Teatret Oslo (NO) and Croatian National Theatre Zagreb (HR). Among the four realized productions, the participative citywalk *Stage your City* (2018) with media artists Chris Ziegler and Bernt Lintermann from ZKM exemplifies the need for theatre practitioners to collaborate with digital artists to comprehend the possibilities and limitations of digitality in the live context and begin, on a small scale, to experiment with several digital formats to achieve, what Jan Linders. leading dramaturg of Badisches Staatstheater Karlsruhe emphatically calls 'the digital empowerment of the audience to participate' (2023, 29). Reminiscent of Gob Squad's 2003 *Super Night Shot*, a city performance through the night full of unexpected encounters with strangers, its duration limited by the length of the DV tape (180 minutes) and their live and digital experiences shared with the audience on the performers return to the theatre after 60 minutes, Rimini Protokoll's *The Walks* (since 2021), an app-based individual urban walk with staged situations, or Janet Cardiff and George Buren's audio walks (since 1991) and, more recently, video walks, all point to a desire to explore and augment urban reality with a fictional, atmospheric, subjective component that in many ways originated in Walter Benjamin's modernist concept of the flaneur and, in the 1950s, the dérives of the Situationists that meant to disrupt the capitalist society of the spectacle. *Stage Your City*, in comparison, appears strangely devoid of a concept beyond the general involvement of a small audience and the use of several technologies, such as an augmented reality app accessed via smartphones and iPads and a 360-degree film. Linders explains, 'Many projects rely on a single technique and use it to its full potential. We preferred to experiment with many new technologies and test possible artistic applications. The focus is not on technology, but on the history of the common migration into the future of the cities' (2023, 28). One may disregard the naivety of the dramaturg as to their understanding of the level of digital literacy of their audience, yet this quote highlights the desire of the theorist to embrace technology in the theatre; yet, at the same time, it reveals the need for dialogical research between new technologies and theatrical formats with an eye for the use of new technologies used by a majority of potential audiences in their everyday life. Rather than simply affirming their use under the assumption of 'newness', new technologies must be pushed beyond commonplace aesthetics, use and handling, as did media artists in the 1970s and 1980s. On an ACuTe Art panel in Bilbao, Spain, around digitality in the theatre, Karla Maeder, Head Dramaturg at Deutsches Theater Berlin, posited that 'Theatre is a hungry medium' (Maeder in ACuTe Art Talks 2024). This statement is perhaps the simplest and, at the same time, most productive statement for the future of theatre in a contemporary world that increasingly blurs the lines between the real and the virtual. Theatre's relationship with technology throughout the twentieth century affirms the hunger Maeder speaks of, a hunger for the new, for a 'more' and a 'different' of expression, interpretation and representation, a hunger for new theatre buildings, new stages and new scenographies. Gropius' and Piscator's 1927 kinetic media theatre, the Total Theater, is just one example of a modernist programmatic vision of technology at the heart of theatre architecture and scenography. Theatre's inherent hunger continues with its adoption of television screens and live cameras on the stage such as Wolf Vostell's 1979 set design for *Hamlet* with a multimedia scenography comprising more than one hundred television screens, cameras and microports as an early European state theatre example staged at the State Theatre Hamburg and the State Theatre Stuttgart, while the work of the Wooster Group in New York around director Elizabeth LeCompte is an example for a free theatre ensemble intrinsically linking live performance and media in the exploration of dramatic representation from the mid-1970s onwards. Baudrillard's 1981 notion of the implosion of any differentiation between the virtual and the real found entry in the postdramatic theatre of the time with the adoption of hyperreal aesthetics that embraced popular culture and hyperconsumerist imagery via video screens (see Baudrillard 1981). Since then, the simultaneity of stage action, manipulation of time, the fragmentation or doubling of bodies, voices and gestures and the multiplication of locations have become ubiquitous and often deliberately overbearing, directly referencing and commenting on the media and social media saturation that defines contemporary daily life. The inclusion of media on the stage, while still predominantly digitally produced and displayed on video and LED screens, now increasingly extends to immersive and sometimes interactive virtual reality theatre. This development demonstrates the readiness of theatre to observe, name and define emerging social and cultural phenomena and to acquire both conceptual and technical expertise in their translation and adaption for the stage. The extension of the physical stage towards the virtual and their constant dialogue and exchange, however, demands that if technology is to become a fundamental and equal element in performance and performance design, a rethinking of the role of scenography must take place in light of the unfolding of time, space, narrative, voice and body that specifically virtual technologies afford to the theatrical whole.

Aiming to act as an incubator, research and production facility for such a rethinking through the integration of digital technologies into live performance, the German Academy for Theatre Digitality in Dortmund in 2019 was established as the sixth section of the State Theatre Dortmund (together with the five existing sections of theatre opera, ballet, orchestra, children and youth theatre). Since 2023, with its own building and dedicated team, in 2024, the Academy hosted the first so-called ACuTe Knowledge Transfer Days, an EU-financed large-scale four-year project engaged with research, development and presentation of new technologies in theatre (see ACuTe2024). Accompanied by a consortium of experts and universities, among them the Academy for Applied Sciences in Oulu, Finland, the Dortmund Academy acted as both host and artistic and scientific project partner. With the acronym ACuTE (not to be confused with XR platform Acute Art) that stands for 'Culture Testbeds for Interactivity, Performance and Technology', this partnership of several European theatres began in 2021 as a five-year interdisciplinary project with the explicit aim to research, develop and test new technologies, fostering professional competencies through co-creating processes in the digital field. In prototyping (the use of) new technologies in the live performing arts context, ACuTE focuses on three themes in their articulation of 'testbeds', namely, innovation in dramaturgy or storytelling, innovation in stage design both aesthetically and technically, and audience engagement and interaction. Between 2021 and 2025, nine experimental productions are envisaged. Training workshops, residencies and online and face-to-face networking activities support participating partner organizations and theatres across Europe. One of these residencies serves as an example where ACuTE acted as a mediator between the National Theatre Marin Sorescu (Craiova-Romania) and the Centre of Society and Contemporary Culture, Azkuna Zentroa. During the ten-day residency, an artist working with virtual spaces and the theatre's dramaturg worked together on the experimental development of mixed reality theatre and film performance involving live performers and a 'gamified multi-layered mediaturgy' that allowed the audience to participate and co-create a performance that engaged with the question of 'reenactment' between truth and fiction, in this case of an iconic Romanian film from 1968. Acting as an incubator, this residency, while short, enabled the theatre practitioners involved to leave behind pressing production schedules and traditional audience expectations and delve into experimental methods of theatrical space, its virtual construction and interactive presentation. The theatre's dramaturg, Catinka Draganescu, describes the new task of the stage designer to be the designer of experiences, analogous to the rise of the user experience designer in commercial creative agencies (Heikkinen 2024) in what designates a significant step away from conventionalized departmental silos in the practicality of the repertory theatre towards an understanding of co-creation and interactive processes between the creative team, performers and audiences. Several productions, both realized and in the making in the framework of ACuTE, demonstrate the energy with which theatre makers embrace the expansion and deliberate redefinition of all theatrical elements with the freedom of the central idea of 'testing' rather than presenting final and definite projects (Heikkinen 2024). The participants' understanding that the integration of digital technologies enables specific outreach possibilities to connect with new, in particular, younger, digitally literate audiences is central in their choices of technologies that initially tend to involve mobile phones due to familiarity and ease of use. A 2024 experimental production by the Nova Gorica Theatre, Slovenia, in cooperation with the Dortmund Academy, looks at the potentiality of location-based gaming in the public sphere to (digitally) connect inhabitants of the once-separated cities of Gorizia and Nova Gorica. Aiming to transcend political, cultural and language borders, the gaming character of the project that leads participants from both cities on an exploratory city tour may seem neither new nor original but reflects accurately the small steps that many theatre companies need and are eager to take – in their embrace of the digital. Focused on prototyping methodologies and technologies that can become an inherent part of a theatrical production, ACuTE's development of a 'Testbed Design Toolkit' demonstrates the consortium's engagement in a long-term and sustainable optimization of the complexity of team design processes in the performing arts that involve new technologies where different levels of knowledge and experience in the team may be counterproductive to finding innovative concepts, formats and solutions. The open-source interactive document presents a design thinking manual that 'supports a structured development process' (ACuTE 2023: 5) in the three target areas of new dramaturgy, stage design and audience engagement. ACuTE's 54-page document offers an introductory scenario workshop featuring a provocative scenario: 'It is the year 2030. Virtual theatre has become normalized. Actors and audiences meet in virtual spaces in digital bodies. The multi-player VR experience will be the default setting for a theatre visit' (ACuTE 2023: 8). Starting from this provocation that, in its absoluteness, offers countless ways to be unpacked, differentiated and rearticulated, the toolkit aims to support the theatre practitioners and creative media and technical teams to find a common language through the rigorous application of iterative design and communication methods that invite teams to critically reflect on a project's strengths, weaknesses, opportunities and threats. Having used the toolkit, Paulien Geerlings, Head Dramaturg at one of the partner theatres companies, De Toneelmakerij, a youth theatre located in Amsterdam, Netherlands, spoke to their production of *Rabbit Hole* from 2023 in an ACuTe interview (ACuTe 2023). *Rabbit Hole* comprised a chatroom via mobile phones for both audiences and the protagonist throughout the show. Geerlings points to the user-centric quality of design thinking and its emphasis on research, testing and audience feedback, which ACuTe's toolkit enables. Introduced to Geerlings by a cooperating university, the basics of an iterative, nonlinear, yet structured design process supported the team-based structured development of the production with the interactive technology presented as a central dramaturgical, dramatic and scenographic element well-suited to the theatre's young audience. The examples provided above highlight the immediate and enduring benefits stemming from ACuTe's directive, which, by the design of its mission and funding framework, eschews a direct return on investment but rather stems from the understanding of the fluidity of contemporary culture and is grounded in long-term thinking. This perspective recognizes the imperative for the arts to function as proactive entities, integrating seamlessly into, critically engaging with, and adhering to ethical principles in the contemporary digital age while also being able to shape its present and forthcoming development. Equally, the UK's 2024–2027 substantial investment of six million UKP from the Xartists grant scheme through a funding collaboration between the Arts and Humanities Research Council (AHRC), the Arts Council England, Arts Council Northern Ireland, Arts Council Wales and Creative Scotland is directed towards consortia of artists and supporting institutions with the explicit aim to foster research activities, training and dissemination in what is widely termed 'immersive arts' and led by the University of the West of England (UWE) Bristol, this grant initiative will be watched closely as to its current and future impact on creative practitioners, academics, industry and the general public. As Darren Henley, CEO of Arts Council England, states

> Creative producers and cultural organizations have always been vital in unlocking the potential of new technology, as we are seeing in the innovative experiences artists and cultural organizations are creating for immersive platforms.
>
> (HENLEY 2024)

At the time of writing, applications for this initiative have yet to open; however, with storytelling at its centre, these are expected to emphasize innovative approaches to all art forms, modes of communication and modes of reception. The National Theatre's Immersive Storytelling Studio, founded by Coffey in 2016, has already developed several projects that overall utilize Virtual, Mixed and Augmented Reality technologies in conjunction with live performance to explore, test and present new methods of dramatic production and presentation through a continuous funding model which appears to have been reversed in early 2024.

Until now, however, the role of the virtual as a spatial and scenographic potentiality has rarely been explored and emphasis instead given to the visualization and presentation of the actor's body and communication of the narrative. A '(nascent) grammar' of digital scenography comprising of 'political agency, singularity, (in)determinism, innovative repurposing, digital specificity, noetic reactivation, and increasing technological performativity' as proposed by Trinity College Dublin academic Neill O'Dwyer (O'Dwyer 2021: 169) while focusing on the spatial aspects of the virtual presents a valuable contribution to the theoretical discourse on the complex practices of the linking, juxtaposition and dialogical relationship between physical and virtual spaces for performance. O'Dwyer acknowledges the need for any framework that may categorize digital scenographies to be ever-expanding and ever-reflective in the same way that current self-learning algorithms force notions of knowledge, originality, innovation and aesthetics to be continuously rethought and newly articulated. In addition, where virtual spaces can be designed using text prompts rather than programming, traditional categories of originality, authorship, precedent and process become obsolete. The re-articulation of the central parameters of scenography's primary role as the spatial framework for theatre, media and exhibition in XR configurations and their integration into live presentation remains the major challenge for the cross-disciplinary art form. Secure funding with a long-term perspective that does not require instant box office and critical success but is open to authentic experimentation that allows 'failure' as a productive artistic category is needed, as the case studies in this chapter demonstrate.

While producing highly innovative future prototypes, the uptake of extended reality technologies for performance projects in the research lab environment has often proved unsustainable in the long-term due to organizational restraints and limitations regarding audience size and real-world implementation. Notable federally funded labs and projects, such as the European Theatre Lab, the ACuTE initiative and the UK's Xartistis grant scheme, recognize the potential for digital technologies to transform theatrical practices. These projects highlight the necessity of rethinking traditional theatrical roles and scenography in light of digital possibilities, storytelling, immersion and audience engagement. The structured, long-term programmes and collaborative networks facilitated by these grants enable substantial knowledge-sharing and experimentation, looking to close the gap in digital competencies among theatre practitioners but also, with Dead Centre's recourse to Artaud's assignation of *la réalité virtuelle* to theatre, ask, where do we go if we stop going to the theatre as a physical location?

Notes

Introduction

1 In the authors' earlier monograph, *The Model as Performance. Staging Space in Theatre, Art and Architecture* (2018), the authors established that the physical model was not a second-order object awaiting realization but a performative, epistemic and cosmopoietic active agent in the making of space. Tested against a multitude of case studies, from Alberti's notion of the mute model that needs to be performed to the Venetian temporary Teatri del Mondo to the urban models used by the National Socialists' propaganda machine or Norman Bel Geddes' enterable *Futurama* for General Motors at the 1939 New York World Fair to interactive and participative models in contemporary visual and performing arts, a further type of model emerged. Beyond the two established manifestations of the model, the iterative and the representational, a third type of model was identified. Referred to as an autonomous model, it constitutes an end-product unto itself with no further artefact anticipated. Such models are highly referential and are 'neither process-driven nor representational but conceptualized and built to be autonomous' (Brejzek and Wallen 2018: 4). Beyond the *Model as Performance,* recent publications, including the articles 'Worldmaking through the Virtual Model' in the journal *Theatre and Performance Design*, 'Model & Fragment: On the Performance of Incomplete Architectures' in *AD: Architectural Design Journal* and 'On Models – Architecture, Model, Performance' published by e-flux, have contributed passages, structure and thinking primarily to Chapters 1 and 5 of this monograph. The history of the virtual and research into the model, worldmaking, the fragment and the spatial *Doppelgänger* have been developed over many years and reached a point of timely convergence in this volume.

Brejzek, T. and L. Wallen (2018). *The Model as Performance: Staging Space in Theatre and Architecture*. London: Bloomsbury Methuen Drama.

Brejzek, T. and L. Wallen (2022), 'On Models- Architecture, Model, Performance', www.e-flux.com, Available online: https://www.e-flux.com/architecture/on-models/489648/architecture-model-performance/

Brejzek, T. and L. Wallen (2021). 'Model & Fragment: On the Performance of Incomplete Architectures', *Architectural Design*, 91 (3): 74–81. https://doi.org/10.1002/ad.2695

Brejzek, T. and L. Wallen (2021). 'Worldmaking through the Virtual Model', *Theatre and Performance Design*, 7 (1–2): 116–33. https://doi-org.ezproxy.lib.uts.edu.au/10.1080/23322551.2021.1925470

Chapter 1

1 Foucault defines the dispositif/apparatus as follows: 'What I'm trying to pick out with this term is, firstly, a thoroughly heterogeneous ensemble consisting of discourses, institutions, architectural forms, regulatory decisions, laws, administrative measures, scientific statements, philosophical, moral and philanthropic propositions – in short, the said as much as the unsaid. Such are the elements of the apparatus. The apparatus itself is the system of relations that can be established between these elements'. Foucault in 'The Confession of the Flesh' (1977) in *Power/Knowledge Selected Interviews and Other Writings* (ed Colin Gordon) (1980: 151–2).

2 The term Digital Twin (DT) came into common usage via the original NASA technology roadmaps (2010–2012), in which fourteen space technology areas were defined, including NASA principal technologist John Vickers's characterization of the process by which virtual models of spacecraft allowed NASA engineers to design and test prior to construction and deployment. The NASA roadmaps continue to evolve, adapting to new technologies and production techniques. The original digital twin's simultaneous conception and implementation is also attributed to NASA and their dramatic impromptu conversion of flight simulators into a real-time computer model of the crippled Apollo 13 module after an explosion in the oxygen tank rendered it partially inoperable (see Allen 2021). In this case, the ad-hoc invention of the digital twin was critical in successfully retrieving the astronauts and capsule from space in 1970 by first mirroring the real-life situation in a virtual computer simulation and then proposing a solution to be applied in the real world. The critical capacity of the digital twin has given rise to ambitious projects such as the European Commission's Initiative Destination Earth (DestinE), which seeks 'to develop a highly accurate digital model of the Earth on a global scale' (DigitalEU 2024), slated for completion in 2030 and the European Space Agency (ESA) Digital Twin Earth Programme.

The European Space Agency (ESA) initiated the ESA Digital Twin Earth Programme (ESA DTE) based on its critical role in Earth Observation (EO). Working in partnership with the European Centre for Medium-Range Weather Forecasts (ECMWF) and the European Organisation for the Exploitation of Meteorological Satellites (EUMETSAT), the three organizations are collaborating on the European Commission initiative *Destination Earth* (DestinE) that seeks 'to develop a highly accurate digital model of the Earth on a global scale' (DigitalEU 2024). The first two *DestinE* digital twins were launched in June 2024, focusing on extreme events and climate change adaptation. Slated to be launched in 2030, the completed *DestinE* project will deliver 'a complete digital replica of the Earth with very high-resolution modelling that can be accessed on demand' (Puschmann 2024). As the Programme Manager for *DestinE*, Lothar Wolf explains, 'We're looking at replicating what's actually happening across the globe, including in relation to the atmosphere, land, ocean, people, cities, and agriculture. Destination Earth will allow us to ask, "what if"? questions in a more meaningful and more complete way' (Lothar in Puschmann 2024). Similar and eventually integrable European projects funded by the EU scientific research initiative, *Horizon Europe*, include Digital Twins for Biodiversity (BioDT), Geophysical Extremes (GEO DT), Digital Twin of the Ocean (DTO) and ESA's Digital Twin of the Antarctic. In Japan, the DT project PLATEAU is developing precise 3D models of cities across Japan, China is developing DTs for water governance and conservancy, and TwinGrid Labs is developing DTs for India's vast power grid.

Chapter 2

1 Pontus Hultén (1924–2006) is regarded as one of the most influential museum directors of the twentieth century. From 1960, as director of the Museum of Modern Art in Stockholm (Moderna Musee), he bridged the American and European art world through exhibitions and a presence in New York. He went on to direct the Musée National d'Art Moderne at the Centre Georges Pompidou in Paris (1974–1981), established the Museum of Contemporary Art in Los Angeles (MOCA) and was the founding director of the Palazzo Grassi in Venice (1984–1990). He took up the position of artistic director of the Art and Exhibition Hall of the Federal Republic of Germany in Bonn (1991–1995) and, in 1996, was appointed the founding director of the Jean Tinguely Museum in Basel.

2 The international style of modernist architecture 'emerged in Europe (principally Germany and France) in the 1920s and 1930s. Historian Henry-Russell Hitchcock and architect Philip Johnson coined the term International Style to describe this plain, unadorned architecture of rectilinear forms built of steel, reinforced concrete, and glass. The style transformed the skylines of many major cities around the world' (MoMA 2024a). International modernism was the predominant architectural reference in the post-war period, coming into question in the 1960s as new forms and experimental strategies rose to prominence.

3 Starchitect is a term used to describe an architect (mainly white European males except for Iraqi-born Zaha Hadid) who has achieved a rock star-like status through buildings that focus on innovative form-making and highly conceptual and theoretical design strategies leading to object-focused approaches. Notable Stararchitects include Frank Gehry, Zaha Hadid, Renzo Piano, Bjarke Ingels, Jean Nouvel, Norman Foster, Steven Holl and Rem Koolhaas. Jeremey White, in his chapter entitled *Starchitecture* in *The Routledge Companion to Critical Approaches to Contemporary Architecture,* from 2019, lays down the four rules that govern the guild of the Starchitects: 'First, that a starchitect is prohibited from copying the work of another. Think of this as the first bylaw of the starchitect's guild. Their work is their signature and forgery is a crime punishable by ejection from the guild. This first idea is as old as the hills, derived from art history, and is predicated on the rather peculiar and impractical definition of a building as an art object. Second, are the hidden actors who make the starchitect possible. Third, the starchitect's work must express relevance of the now, which is to say, it may not copy work from the vault of the past. The guilded starchitect must embrace the now, and like the avant-garde artist, their work must be reflexively relevant. And fourth, perhaps the most obvious point to make, the starchitect's work must be visually striking. Glam is everything, measured by its photogenic promise, trumping even space. There is no conceptual or techno-logical limit on what an aspiring starchitect may resort to in the service of the visual' (White 2019: 405).

Chapter 3

1 In expanding the definition of XR performance and installation to include the systems of production and capture, such as spatial and geospatial technologies and postproduction environments and data-driven modelling tools that are ultimately played back via projection or monitors within a performance or exhibition, this project embraces a wide range of artists that point or have pointed to the future of expanded reality performance and installation. Extended reality (XR) is a term covering virtual reality (VR), augmented reality (AR), mixed reality (MR) and, increasingly, artificial intelligence (AI) as technical, visual and conceptual devices. By extension, extended reality performance (EXP) or extended reality installation (ERI) is defined as a performance that utilizes one or more of these technologies in its realization. Code, Data and linear time-based media such as video or animation are associated media that support the implementation and display of extended realities in the performance and installation context. They are critical adjunct forms included in the broader definition proposed by this project that expand the definition to include the technology directly used in the performance and the technology in the production and postproduction of visual and audio elements. Thus, we include in this definition the visual material generated in immersive and three-dimensional virtual postproduction environments that use parametric or other data-driven modelling tools that are ultimately played back via projection or monitors within a performance or exhibition context. In coalescence, this suite of technologies in the hands of the highlighted artists has a cosmopoietic capacity (worldmaking) realized both in purely virtual environments and in highly mediatized 'real' performance spaces that combine material with immaterial elements and form the focus of this project.

2 Allahyari's work has been shown at the Venice Architecture Biennale, Centre Pompidou Paris, Tate Modern, Queens and Dallas Museums of Art, The Whitney Museum of Modern Art and San Francisco Museum of Modern Art, which also have artworks by Morehshin in their permanent collections. Among numerous other grants and fellowships, Morehshin is the recipient of the University of California Chancellor's Postdoctoral Fellowship Award (2024). Her artistic work and activist engagement take her to galleries, labs and universities, and she has, since 2022, been actively involved in the online event WOMXN, LIFE FREEDOM sparked by the murder of twenty-two-year-old Kurdish Jina (Mahsa) Amini by the religious morality police of Iran's government. The project is described as follows on Allahyari's website: 'WOMXN, LIFE, FREEDOM is an online event series for co-learning, co-growing, solidarity, and kinship with our Iranian siblings. We come together as artists, thinkers, and organizers, mainly in the diaspora, to share, amplify, and weave together a refusal of long-lasting cultural and political gender/sexual oppression in Iran' (Allahyari 2023).

3 By example, *The Book of Wonders*. The *Kitab al-Bulhan*, or *Book of Wonders*, is an Arabic manuscript dating mainly from the late fourteenth century CE and probably bound together in Baghdad during the reign of Jalayirid Sultan Ahmad (1382–1410). The manuscript is made up of astrological, astronomical and geomantic texts compiled by Abd al-Hasan Al-Isfahani, as well as a dedicated section of full-page illustrations, with each plate titled '"A discourse on. . ..," followed by the subject of the discourse (a folktale, a sign of the zodiac, a prophet, etc.' See Al-Isfahani, Abd-al-Hasan (2022), h *Kitab Al-Bulhan or Book of Wonders* (1390).

4 Austro-Hungarian dancer and choreographer Rudolf Laban (1879–1958) was one of the founders of European Modern Dance, collaborating with dancers such as Kurt Jooss and Mary Wigman. Laban established a method and system, choreology, to notate and analyse dance movements and advocated a feeling and free body to express itself and was associated with the Monte Verità life reform movement, a meeting place of the counterculture between 1900 and the 1920s. Expressive or expressionist dance emerged out of the life reform movement against classical ballet forms with bodily movements and clothing freed from restrictive tradition and close to nature.

Chapter 4

1 A VR music video is created using a 360-degree camera (either physical or virtual or both) combined with spatial audio, allowing the viewer to choose and change the position from which they view and hear the music, thus adding interactivity and an illusion of immersion to the viewer's experience.

Chapter 5

1 The history of programmable machines predates the computer, spanning from the ninth-century programmable music automata developed in the *Bayt al-ḥikma* (House of Wisdom) by the Persian Banū Mūsā brothers to composers Karl Heinz Stockhausen (1928–2007) and György Ligeti (1923–2006) pioneering electro-acoustic work from the 1950's in the electronic music studio of German broadcaster Westdeutscher Rundfunk (WDR) through to the founding of labs dedicated to electro-acoustic music in the seventies, including the Studio for Electro Instrumental Music (STEIM) founded in 1971 in Amsterdam and the Institut de Recherche et coordination acoustique (IRCAM) founded by Pierre Boulez and opened in 1997 in Paris.

2 Two intact volumes of *Bizzarie di Varie Figure* by Italian Baroque artist Giovanni Battista Bracelli etchings are known to exist, one in the Library of Congress in Washington, DC, and the other in the Bibliothèque Nationale de France in Paris.

3 *Osmose* and *Ephémère*, 1995 and 1998. Concept, direction, art direction: Char Davies. Custom VR software: John Harrison. Computer graphics: Georges Mauro. Sonic architecture/programming: Dorota Blaszczak. Sound composition/programming: Rick Bidlack. Initial development: SOFTIMAGE® 3|D. Environment: Silicon Graphics Onyx2 Infinite Reality.

4 *The Legible City*, 1988–1991, bicycle interface, computer (SGI Indigo II Maximum Impact), operating system (IRIX), custom software, computer (PC), operating system (Linux), custom software, custom-made electronics, TFT monitor, projector, concave projection surface, installation dimensions variable. Co-authors: Jeffrey Shaw, Dirk Groeneveld. Custom Software: Gideon May, Lothar Schmitt, Bernd Lintermann. Hardware: Charly Jungbauer, Huib Nelissen.

5 *Memory Theatre VR*, 1997, interactive computer-based installation; polygonal wooden room with interior painting, concave projection screen, a sculpture (pyramid stump) and an acrylic glass model of the room; technical equipment: computer: SGI Indigo II Maximum Impact, operating system: IRIX, software: custom software, other devices: projector, 3-D tracking system Polhemus, height 360 cm, Ø 790 cm, ZKM | Center for Art and Media. Author: Agnes Hegedues. Custom Software: Gideon May. Video: Christina Zartmann.

6 Photogrammetry is a technique for creating virtual objects using precise measurements and models based on two-dimensional images that, in this case, were captured in a dome-like structure equipped with cameras at Google's *Lightstage Studio* in Los Angeles. The photogrammetry software analysed the visual data to calculate distances and reconstruct the singer's shape, size, position and movement by capturing multiple overlapping images from different angles. Photogrammetry leveraged principles of geometry and computer rendering to transform images into an accurate spatial representation, resulting in a highly realistic animated virtual model of the opera singer, including costumes, facial expressions and movement that is then composited into the AR environment.

7 Audience Labs at the Royal Opera House is an artist-led innovation program that combines pioneering artists and next-generation technology to create boundary-breaking contemporary opera and ballet experiences. Rooted in the Royal Opera House's tradition of stagecraft and open to the possibilities of immersive technologies, Audience Labs invites new and diverse audiences to experience ambitious and innovative work – wherever they are. Audience Labs works through partnerships and a diverse range of collaborators, from artists to major international technology companies to government departments, museums, festivals and more. Committed to sharing learnings and insight from R&D and projects and serving as a resource for the UK arts sector, Audience Labs aims to spark a dialogue around collaboration and innovation, enabling connections between cultural organizations and the technology sector by bringing together diverse creative talent, reducing barriers to entry and improving opportunity for digital adoption.

References

ACuTe (2023), 'ACuTe Interview W/ Paulien Geerlings, de Toneelmakerij', *YouTube*, Available online: https://www.youtube.com/watch?v=-f2zTb1Yl64 (accessed 15 September 2024).

ACuTe (2024a), 'ACuTe Talks – Session 1: A Confluence of Innovation and the Performing Arts – ACUTE', *Oamk.fi*, Available online: https://vanha.oamk.fi/acute/acute-talks-session-1-a-confluence-of-innovat (accessed 15 September 2024).

ACuTe (2024b), 'ACuTe–Culture Testbeds for Performing Arts and New Technology', *Oamk.fi*, Available online: https://vanha.oamk.fi/acute (accessed 15 September 2024).

Agamben, G. (2009), *What Is an Apparatus?: And Other Essays*, Stanford, CA: Stanford University Press.

Akademie for_Theatre_and_Digitality (2023), 'Academy: Akademie For_Theatre_and_Digitality', *Theater.digital*, Available online: https://theater.digital/en (accessed 15 September 2024).

Allahyari, M. and Ransom, B. (2022), 'Censorship and Creative (Re) Production: A Conversation', in C. Paquette, K. Kleinfelder and C. Mile (eds), *In And Out of View. Art and the Dynamics of Circulation, Suppression, and Censorship*, 247–55, New York: Bloomsbury.

Alemani, C., ed. (2022), *The Milk of Dreams Biennale Arte 2022*, 1st edn, Venice: La Biennale di Venezia.

Al-Isfahani, A.-H. (2022), 'Kitab Al-Bulhan or Book of Wonders (1390)', *https://archive.org/details/KitabAlBulhan/page/n11/mode/2up*, Available online: https://publicdomainreview.org/collection/kitab-al-bulhan-or-book-of-wonders-late-14thc/ (accessed 16 September 2024).

Allahyari, M. (2017), 'Morehshin Allahyari: On Digital Colonialism, Re-Figuring, and Monstrosity', *www.youtube.com*. Available online: https://www.youtube.com/watch?v=HcK9K4Yty74 (accessed 24 January 2023).

Allahyari, M. (2020), 'Digital Colonialism (2016–2019)', *Morehshin Allahyari*, Available online: https://morehshin.com/digital-colonialism- (accessed 15 September 2024).

Allahyari, M. (2021), 'She Who Sees the Unknown', Available online: https://shewhoseestheunknown.com (accessed 15 September 2024).

Allahyari, M. (2022), 'ماه تعلط / Moon-Faced (2022)', *Morehshin Allahyari*, Available online: https://morehshin.com/moonfaced (accessed 15 September 2024).

Allahyari, M. (2023), 'WOMXN, LIFE, FREEDOM, Pt. III: Transnational Feminism: Womxn, Life, Freedom Is a Daily Practice', *Morehshin Allahyari*, Available online: https://morehshin.com/womxn-life-freedom-pt-iii-transnational-feminism-womxn-life-freedom-is-a-daily-practice (accessed 15 September 2024).

Allen, B. D. (2021), 'Digital Twins and Living Models at NASA', *ntrs.nasa.gov*, Available online: https://ntrs.nasa.gov/citations/20210023699 (accessed 15 September 2024).

Ambasz, E. (1972), *Italy: The New Domestic Landscape: Achievements and Problems of Italian Design: (Exhibition; Museum of Modern Art, New York, May 26-September 11, 1972)*, Greenwich, CT: New York Graphic Society; Florence: Centro Di.

Anon. (1954), *Rhetorica ad Herennium*, trans. Harry Caplan. Cambridge, MA: Harvard University Press.

Ansell-Pearson, K. (2005), 'The Reality of the Virtual: Bergson and Deleuze', *MLN*, 120 (5): 1112–27.

Aquinas, T. (n.d.), 'Summa Theologiae, by St Thomas Aquinas, Doctor of the Church', *Summa-theologiae.org*, Available online: http://summa-theologiae.org (accessed 15 September 2024).

Aristotle (2024), 'Metaphysics Perseus Catalog', *Perseus.org*, Available online: https://catalog.perseus.org/catalog/urn:cts:greekLit:tlg0086.tlg025.perseus-eng1 (accessed 19 September 2024).

Ars (2018), 'Ars Electronica', *Ars Electronica*, Available online: https://ars.electronica.art/news/en (accessed 15 September 2024).

Artaud, A. (1997), *The Theater and Its Double*, trans. M. C. Richards, New York: Grove Press.

Artaud, A. C. Schumacher and B. Singleton (2004), *Artaud on Theatre*, Chicago: Ivan R. Dee.

Artribune (2014), *'Romeo Castellucci. Uso umano di esseri humani'*, Available online: https://www.artribune.com/mostre-evento-arte/romeo-castellucci-uso-umano-di-esseri-umani/2014 (accessed 15 September 2024).

Bardiot, C. (2006), '9 Evenings: Theatre and Engineering diagrams', Available online: https://www.fondation-langlois.org/html/e/page.php?NumPage=572https://www.fondation-langlois.org/html/e/page.php?NumPage=572 (accessed 10 May 2025).

Bartana, Y. (2024), 'Yael Bartana', *Yaelbartana.com*, Available online: https://www.yaelbartana.com/essay/deflections-anti-mirrors-2 (accessed 15 September 2024).

Baudrillard, J. (1981), *Simulacra and Simulation*, Ann Arbor: The University of Michigan Press.

Bennett, J. (2010), *Vibrant Matter a Political Ecology of Things*, Durham: Duke University Press.

Bergson, H. (1975), *Mind-Energy*, Westport,London: Greenwood Press.

Bergson, H. (1991), *Matter and Memory*, trans. N. M. Paul and W. S. Palmer, New York: Zone Books.

Bird, G. (2018), 'Dwelling in the Proper. May 168, Political Economy, and Identity Politics', *Shift. International Journal of Philosophical Studies*, 1: 31–43.

Bird, G. (2023), 'Problematizing Dispositifs', in G. Bird and G. Tusa (eds), *Dispositif: A Cartography*, 1–19, Cambridge MA: MIT Press.

Biro, M. (2022), 'The Cyborg as Producer, in Cecilia Alemani (Ed), Biennale Arte 2022: The Milk of Our Dreams, Milano: Silvana Editorials S.P.A. 500–505.', *The Milk of Our Dreams*, 2022.

Bishop, C. (2023), 'Information Overload', *Artforum*, 61 (8). Available online: https://www.artforum.com/features/claire-bishop-on-the-superabundance-of-research-based-art-252571/ (accessed 10 May 2025).
Björk (2011), *Biophilia*. app, <https://itunes.apple.com/us/app/bjork-biophilia/id434122935?mt=8> (accessed 15 September 2024).
Björk (2019), 'Björk Vulnicura Virtual Reality Album on Steam', *Steampowered.com*, Available online: https://store.steampowered.com/app/1095710/Bjrk_Vulnicura_Virtual_Reality_Album (accessed 15 September 2024).
'Björk's Cornucopia' (2019), *The Shed*, Available online: https://www.theshed.org/program/29-bjork-s-cornucopia (accessed 15 September 2024).
Blümlinger, C. (2022), 'Memory as a Motor of Images: The Essayistic Mode in Apichatpong Weerasethakul's Variations of Uncle Boonmee', in Brenda Hollweg, and Igor Krstic (eds), *World Cinema and the Essay Film*, 107–21, Edinburgh: Edinburgh University Press.
Bolzoni, L. (1999), 'The Play of Memory between Words and Images', *Springer eBooks*, 11–18.
Braidotti, R. (2017), 'Posthuman Critical Theory', *Journal of Posthuman Studies*, 1 (1): 9.
Braidotti, R. (2018), 'A Theoretical Framework for the Critical Posthumanities', *Theory, Culture & Society*, 36 (6): 31–61.
Brejzek, T. and L. Wallen (2018), *The Model as Performance: Staging Space in Theatre and Architecture*, ed. J. McKinney and S. Palmer, London: Bloomsbury Publishing PLC.
Brejzek, T. and L. Wallen (2021a), 'Model & Fragment: On the Performance of Incomplete Architectures', *Architectural Design*, 91 (3): 74–81.
Brejzek, T. and L. Wallen (2021b), 'Worldmaking through the Virtual Model', *Theatre and Performance Design*, 7 (1-2): 116–33.
Brejzek, T. and L. Wallen (2022), 'On Models- Architecture, Model, Performance', *www.e-flux.com*, Available online: https://www.e-flux.com/architecture/on-models/489648/architecture-model-performance/(accessed 15 September 2024).
Browne, C. and P. Diehl (2019), 'Conceptualising the Political Imaginary: An Introduction to the Special Issue', *Social Epistemology*, 33 (5): 393–97.
Capodivacca, S. (2022), 'Beyond Imagination: Deleuze and the Real Virtual', *Aesthetica*, 120: 35–51 (gennaio-aprile 2022).
Carson, J. (2012), 'Art of the Impossible- The Jewish Renaissance Movement in Poland (JRMiP)', Available online: https://www.yaelbartana.com/essay/deflections-anti-mirrors-2 (accessed 15 September 2024).
Castellucci, R., C. Guidi and C. Castellucci (2001), *Epopea Della Polvere*, Milan: Ubulibri.
Castellucci, R., S. R. Sanzio, V. Valentini, B. Marranca and J. House (2004), 'The Universal: The Simplest Place Possible', *PAJ: A Journal of Performance and Art*, 26 (2): 16–25.
Castoriadis, C. (1984), *Crossroads in the Labyrinth*, Brighton: Harvester.
Cateforis, D., S. Duval and Shepherd Steiner (2019), *Hybrid Practices: Art in Collaboration with Science and Technology in the Long 1960s*, Oakland: California University of California Press.
Centre, D. (2014), 'Die Maschine in Mir (Version 1.0)', *Dead Centre*, Available online: https://www.deadcentre.org/die-maschine-in-mir (accessed 15 September 2024).

Cesta Cursach, Y. (2002), *Voyage*. Program Notes, Chicago: Museum of Contemporary Art.
Chude Sokei, L. (2017), 'Race and Technology: A Creole History', Available online: https://www.technosphere-magazine.hkw.de/p/Race-and-Technology-A-Creole-History-fTkwqWGX4M24K2MixKVrUk (accessed 15 September 2024).
Chu, H.-C. and Y.-J. Lin (2023), 'Improving the IoT Attack Classification Mechanism with Data Augmentation for Generative Adversarial Networks', *Applied Sciences*, 13 (23): 12592–92.
Clarke, J. (2012), 'Iannis Xenakis and the Philips Pavilion', *The Journal of Architecture*, 17 (2): 213–29.
Cohen Ionannides, M. W. (2019), 'Judaism and Extraterrestrials:Theological Lessons from Science Fiction', *The Journal for Popular Culture*, 52 (5): 1200–1217.
Cottingham, J. (1988), *The Rationalists*, Oxford: Oxford University Press.
Coyne, R. (1994), 'Heidegger and Virtual Reality: The Implications of Heidegger's Thinking for Computer Representations', *Leonardo*, 27 (1): 65.
Čufer, E. and NSK (1992), 'NSK STATE IN TIME- Texts- Irwin-Nsk.org', *irwin-nsk.org*, Available online: https://irwin-nsk.org/texts/nsk-state-in-time/ (accessed 18 July 2024).
Cugurullo, F. (2019), 'The Origin of the Smart City Imaginary: From the Dawn of Modernity to the Eclipse of Reason', in C. Lindner and M. Meissner (eds), *The Routledge Companion to Urban Imaginaries*, 113–24, London: Routledge.
Davies, C. (2004), 'Virtual Space', in F. Penz, G. Radick and R. Howell (eds), *Science, Art and Society*, 69–104, Cambridge: Cambridge University Press.
Davis, E. (1996), 'Osmose', *Wired*, Available online: https://www.wired.com/1996/08/osmose (accessed 19 September 2024).
Davis, H. (2014), 'Stories from Wide Open, Wild Country: An Interview with Ursula K. Le Guin', *Hobo Magazine Paris*, 130–31.
Dazed (2015), 'Björk Shares a Series of Her Personal Emails', *Dazed*, Available online: http://www.dazeddigital.com/music/article/25630/1/bjork-searches-for-meaning-in-these-personal-emails (accessed 15 September 2024).
Dazed (2019a), 'How Björk Created Her Cornucopia', *Dazed*, Available online: https://www.dazeddigital.com/music/article/44409/1/bjork-cornucopia-the-shed-new-york-interview (accessed 19 September 2024).
Dazed (2019b), 'For Björk Visual Artist Tobias Gremmler, Nature Is the Source of All Beauty', *Dazed*, Available online: https://www.dazeddigital.com/beauty/article/46893/1/bjork-tobias-gremmler-nature-digital-art-artist-cornucopia-tour (accessed 19 September 2024).
Dead Centre and M. O'Connel (2023), 'To Be a Machine (Version 2.0)', Available online: https://www.deadcentre.org/tobeamachine-2 (accessed 14 May 2025).
Dead Centre (2024), 'Dead Centre', *Dead Centre*, Available online: https://www.deadcentre.org/tobeamachine-2 (accessed 15 September 2024).
Del Favero, D., S. Thurow and L. Wallen (2021), 'The IDesign Platform: Immersive Intelligent Aesthetics for Scenographic Modelling', *Theatre and Performance Design*, 7 (1–2): 82–95.
Deleuze, G. (1989), *Cinema / 2, the Time-Image / translated by Hugh Tomlinson and Robert Galeta*, London: Athlone Press.
Deleuze, G. (1991), *Bergsonism*, New York: Zone.
Deleuze, G. (2014), *Difference and Repetition*, trans. P. Patton, London: Bloomsbury.

Deleuze, G. (2023), 'What Is a Dispositif', in G. Bird and G. Tusa (eds), trans. T. Armstrong, *Dispositif: A Cartography*, 231–8, Cambridge: MIT.
Deleuze, G. and Félix Guattari (1987), *A Thousand Plateaus: Capitalism and Schizophrenia*, trans. B. Massumi, Minneapolis; London: University Of Minnesota Press.
Deleuze, G. and Charles T. Wolfe (1997), 'The Actual and the Virtual.' *Any: Architecture New York* (19/20): 19.6–19.7.
'Desert Rain' (1999), *Blast Theory*, Available online: https://www.blasttheory.co.uk/projects/desert-rain/ (accessed 19 September 2024).
DigitalEU (2024), 'Destination Earth | Shaping Europe's Digital Future', *digital-strategy.ec.europa.eu*, Available online: https://digital-strategy.ec.europa.eu/en/policies/destination-earth (accessed 5 July 2024).
Dixon, S. (2007), *Digital Performance: A History of New Media in Theater, Dance, Performance Art, and Installation*, Cambridge MA: MIT Press.
Domus (2016), 'Eliasson in Leeum', *Domus*, Available online: https://www.domusweb.it/en/art/2016/09/27/olafur_eliasson_the_parliament_of_possibilities.html (accessed 15 September 2024).
Dumb Type (2009), https://www.epidemic.net/en/videos/dumbtype/index.html (accessed 18 June 2024).
E.A.T. (2024), 'Experiments in Art and Technology', ed. H. Sorger, *EAT*, Available online: https://www.experimentsinartandtechnology.org/ (accessed 19 September 2024).
EC (2024), 'Green Digital | Shaping Europe's Digital Future', *digital-strategy.ec.europa.eu*, European Commission, Available online: https://digital-strategy.ec.europa.eu/en/policies/green-digital (accessed 19 September 2024).
Eckersall, P., H. Grehan and E. Scheer (2017), *New Media Dramaturgy: Performance, Media and New-Materialism*, London: Palgrave Macmillan.
EER (2024), *Eer.info*, Available online: https://www.eer.info/about (accessed 15 September 2024).
Eliasson, O. (2008), 'Models Are Real', in E. Abruzzo, E. E. Ellingsen and J. D. Salomon (eds), *Models*, 18–25, New York: 306090 Books.
Eliasson, O. (2022), 'A Space without Beginning and End', *Olafureliasson.net*, The Frick Collection, Available online: https://olafureliasson.net/read/a-space-without-beginning-and-end-2022.
ETC (2023), 'Drama Goes Digital vs Theatre Invades Digital. ETC 2023', *European Theatre Lab*, Available online: https://www.europeantheatrelab.eu (accessed 15 September 2024).
ETL (2023), 'Drama Goes Digital. Connecting Theatre and Audiences across Europe. European Theatre Lab', *European Theatre Lab*, Available online: https://www.europeantheatrelab.eu (accessed 15 September 2024).
FDL (2024), 'La Fondation Daniel Langlois- Accueil', *www.fondation-langlois.org*, Available online: https://www.fondation-langlois.org (accessed 23 July 2024).
Fierro, A. (2024), *Architectures of the Technopolis*, London: Lund Humphries.
Forensic Architecture (2024). Available online: https://forensic-architecture.org/ (accessed 10 May 2025).
Forensic Architecture and D. Wengrow (2023), *The Nebelivka Hypothesis*, Available online: https://content.forensic-architecture.org/wp-content/uploads/2023/04/The-Nebelivka-Hypothesis_FA-Wengrow_Book.pdf. (accessed 10 May 2025).

Foucault, M. (1980), *Power/Knowledge: Selected Interviews and Other Writings, 1972–1977*, ed. C. Gordon, 78–108, New York: Pantheon Books.
Gardner, W. O. (2020), *The Metabolist Imagination Visions of the City in Postwar Japanese Architecture and Science Fiction*, 1st edn, Minneapolis: Minneapolis London University of Minnesota Press.
Garmire, E. (2016), 'Pepsi Pavilion a Brief Walk-Through', *Experiments in Art and Technology*, EAT, Available online: https://www.experimentsinartandtechnology.org/garmire-walk-through (accessed 19 September 2024).
Garwood, D. (2007), 'The Future of an Idea: *9 Evenings* – Forty Years Later', *PAJ: A Journal of Performance and Art*, 29 (1): 36–48.
Georgescu, I. (2022), 'Bringing Back the Golden Days of Bell Labs', *Nature Reviews Physics*, 4 (2): 76–78.
Gaweegong, G. (2010), 'Apichatpong Weerasethakul – ART IT（アートイット）', *ART IT*（アートイット, Available online: https://www.art-it.asia/en/u/admin_ed_itv_e/ia0dz5obqpcessojlxj4 (accessed 15 September 2024).
Gezerlis, A. (2001), 'Castoriadis and the Project of Autonomy. A Review of the Imaginary Institution of Society', *Democracy & Nature*, 7 (3): 469–87.
Goodman, N. (1978), *Ways of Worldmaking*, Indianapolis, IN: Hackett.
Gould, R. (2017), 'A Virtual Reality Museum Launches with New Work by Olafur Eliasson', *Culture Trip*, The Culture Trip, Available online: https://theculturetrip.com/north-america/usa/california/articles/a-virtual-reality-museum-launches-with-new-work-by-olafur-eliasson#:~:text=Eliasson (accessed 15 September 2024).
Grau, O. (2007), *MediaArtHistories*, Cambridge, MA: MIT Press.
Hanlon, W. W. (2022), 'The Rise of the Engineer: Inventing the Professional Inventor during the Industrial Revolution', *NBER Working Paper No. 29751*,MA: Cambridge.
Haraway, D. (1997), *Modest_Witness@Second_Millennium.FemaleMan©_Meets_ Onco Mouse™*. London: Routledge.
Haraway, D. (2004), *The Haraway Reader*, New York: Routledge.
Haraway, D. (2015), 'Anthropocene, Capitalocene, Plantationocene, Chthulucene: Making Kin', *Environmental Humanities*, 6 (1): 159–65.
Haraway, D. (2019), *Introduction. The Carrier Bag Theory of Fiction*, 9–22, London: Ignota.
Haraway, D. J. (2003), *The Companion Species Manifesto: Dogs, People, and Significant Otherness*, vol. 1, Chicago: Prickly Paradigm Press.
Haraway, D. J. (2016), 'A Cyborg Manifesto: Science, Technology, and Socialist-Feminism in the Late Twentieth Century', in D. J. Haraway and C. Wolfe (eds), *Manifestly Haraway*, 64–107, Minneapolis: University of Minnesota Press.
Harris, C. (1999), *Art and Innovation: The Xerox PARC Artist-In-Residence Program*, Cambridge, MA: MIT Press.
Hegedues, A. (1997), 'Memory Theater VR', *ZKM*, Available online: https://zkm.de/de/werk/memory-theater-vr (accessed 15 September 2024).
Heikkinen, J. (2024), 'Prototyping Artist as Designer of Experiences – ACUTE', *ACuTe*, Available online: https://vanha.oamk.fi/acute/prototyping-artist-as-designer-of-experiences/ (accessed 23 June 2024).
Henley, D. (2024), 'New £6m Investment to Help Artists and Cultural Organisations Unlock Creative Potential of Immersive Technology', *Arts Council England*, Available online: https://www.artscouncil.org.uk/creative-

matters/news/new-ps6m-investment-help-artists-and-cultural-organisations-unlock-creative-potential-immersive-technology (accessed 19 September 2024).

Hobson, B. (2020), 'Dezeen Interview with Peter Cook', *Dezeen*, VDF, Available online: https://www.dezeen.com/2020/05/11/archigram-origins-peter-cook-video-interview-vdf/ (accessed 28 July 2024).

Holzer, D. (2023), 'Foster + Partners', *Foster and Partner- Plus Journal*, Foster+Partners, Available online: https://www.fosterandpartners.com/insights/plus-journal/design-technology-and-the-team-between (accessed 19 September 2024).

'Home | European Theatre Convention' (n.d.), *www.europeantheatre.eu*, Available online: https://www.europeantheatre.eu (accessed 19 September 2024).

Houtum, H. J. van (2010), 'Deterritorialization', in M. Bevir and P. Patton (eds), *Encyclopedia of Political Theory*, 377–8, London: Sage.

Hultén, P. (1966), *9 Evenings: Theater and Engineering. Catalogue*, ed. Pontus Hultén and Frank Königsberg, New York: E.A.T. + 1 loose addenda sheet.

Hultén, P. (1968), *The Machine, as Seen at the End of the Mechanical Age*, 1st edn, New York: The Museum of Modern Art.

Hulten, P. and H.-U. Obrist (1997), 'The Hang of It', *Artforum*, Available online: https://www.artforum.com/features/the-hang-of-it-201940/ (accessed 19 June 2024).

Hung-Chi, C., and Yu-Jhe, L. (2023). 'Improving the IoT Attack Classification Mechanism with Data Augmentation for Generative Adversarial Networks', *Applied Sciences*, 13 (23): 12592.

Husserl, E. (1989), *Studies in the Phenomenology of Constitution*, Dordrecht; Boston: Kluwer Academic.

IBM (2024), 'What Is the Internet of Things?', *IBM*, Available online: https://www.ibm.com/topics/internet-of-things (accessed 19 September 2024).

idesign (2018), 'IDesign- ICinema | UNSW Sydney', *UNSW Sites*, Available online: https://www.unsw.edu.au/research/icinema/our-research/projects/idesign (accessed 15 September 2024).

'Immersive Storytelling Studio | National Theatre' (2023), *Nationaltheatre.org.uk*, Available online: https://www.nationaltheatre.org.uk/about-us/theatre-makers/immersive (accessed 15 September 2024).

Ingawanji, M. A. (2021), 'Animism and the Performative Realist Cinema of Apichatpong Weerasethakul', in Pick,A. and Guinevere Narraway (eds), *Screening Nature*, Oxford/New York: Berghahn Books.

'Interview de LuYang Open Space # 14' (2024), *Video*. Available online: https://www.fondationlouisvuitton.fr/en/flv-play/lu-yang-interview-open-space-14 (accessed 18 June 2024).

ISEA (1996), 'PAIR: The Xerox PARC Artist in Residence Program – ISEA Symposium Archives', *isea-archives.siggraph.org*, Available online: https://isea-archives.siggraph.org/presentation/pair-the-xerox-parc-artist-in-residence-program/ (accessed 23 June 2024).

Jasanoff, S. (2015a), 'Future Imperfect: Science, Technology, and the Imaginations of Modernity', in S. Jasanoff and S.-H. Kim (eds), *The Dreamscapes of Modernity: Sociotechnical Imaginaries and the Fabrication of Power*, 07–43, Chicago: The University of Chicago Press.

Jasanoff, S. (2015b), 'Imagined and Invented Worlds', in S. Jasanoff and S.-H. Kim (eds), *The Dreamscapes of Modernity: Sociotechnical Imaginaries and the Fabrication of Power*, 346–68, Chicago: The University of Chicago Press.

Kane, A. (2015), 'Björk Shares a Series of Her Personal Emails', *Dazed*, Available online: http://www.dazeddigital.com/music/article/25630/1/bjork-searches-for-meaning-in-these-personal-emails (accessed 15 September 2024).

Kant, I. (2014), 'Kant's Inaugural Dissertation of 1770, translated into English, with an Introduction and Discussion: Kant, Immanuel, 1724–1804: Free Download, Borrow, and Streaming: Internet Archive', *Internet Archive*, Available online: https://archive.org/details/kantsinauguraldi00kant (accessed 19 September 2024).

Katzenbach, C. and T. C. Bächle (2019), 'Defining Concepts of the Digital Society', *Internet Policy Review*, 8 (4): 1–6.

Keats, J. (2018), 'From Superstudio to Archizoom, These Radical Italian Architects Will Change Your Ideas about Cities', *Forbes*, 11 January.

Khalili, B. (2008), 'The Mapping Journey Project. Video Installation. 2008-2011 – BOUCHRA KHALILI', Available online: https://www.bouchrakhalili.com/the-mapping-journey-project/ (accessed 19 September 2024).

Kickthemachine (2015), 'Fever Room', *Kick the Machine*, Available online: https://www.kickthemachine.com/page80/page34/page59/index.html (accessed 15 September 2024).

Klüver, B. (1966), *9 Evenings: Theater and Engineering.Program Book*, ed. P. Hultén and F. Königsberg, 12 pp + 1 loose addenda sheet., New York: The Foundation for Contemporary Performance Arts, Inc.and EAT.

Knight, C. (2024), 'Review: Was the 1964 Venice Biennale Rigged? The Documentary "Taking Venice" Looks at Conspiratorial Claims', *Los Angeles Times*, Available online: https://www.latimes.com/entertainment-arts/story/2024-05-20/taking-venice-documentary-biennale-robert-rauschenberg (accessed 30 June 2024).

Korzybski, A. (1948), *Science and Sanity: An Introduction to Non-Aristotelian Systems and General Semantics*, Lakeville, CT: The International non-Aristotelian library publishing company; Institute of general semantics, distributor.

Lab, D. (2014a), 'September 1955. MIT Virtual Experience Design Lab', *MIT Virtual Experience Design Lab*, Available online: https://virtualxdesign.mit.edu/projects#/storm (accessed 15 September 2024).

Lab, D. (2014b), 'Latent Archive. MIT Virtual Experience Design Lab', *MIT Virtual Experience Design Lab*, Available online: https://virtualxdesign.mit.edu/projects#/latent-archive (accessed 15 September 2024).

Latour, B. (2003), 'Atmosphère, Atmosphère', in *O. Eliasson's Exhibition the Weather Project*, London: New Tate Gallery.

Latour, B. (2006), 'Air', in Caroline A. Jones (ed.), *Sensorium: Embodied Experience, Technology, and Contemporary Art*, 105–7, Cambridge, MA: MIT Press.

Latour, B. (2018), *Down to Earth: Politics in the New Climatic Regime*, trans. Catherine Porter. Cambridge: Polity Press.

Latour, B. (2020), 'How to Understand the "Parliament of Things" Thirty Years Later, Spinozalens Lecture | Bruno-Latour.fr', *www.bruno-latour.fr*, Available online: http://www.bruno-latour.fr/node/891.html (accessed 19 September 2024).

Le Fleur, I. (2012), 'TEDxFortGreeneSalon- Ingrid LaFleur- Visual Aesthetics of Afrofuturism', *www.youtube.com*, Available online: https://www.youtube.com/watch?v=x7bCaSzk9Zc (accessed 19 September 2024).
Le Guin, U. K. (2019), *The Carrier Bag Theory of Fiction*, Brighton: Ignota Books.
Lentini, D. and S. Takatani (2022), *Dumb Type*, Wien: Verlag Fur Moderne Kunst.
Lunsing, W. (2017), 'The Creation of S/N and the Debate about Sexuality in 1990s Japan', in P. Eckersall, E. Scheer and S. Fujii (eds), *The Dumb Type Reader*, 97–109, Copenhagen: Museum Tusculanum Press.
Lyotard, J.-F. (1976), 'The Tooth, the Palm', *Substance*, 5 (15): 105–10.
Matussek, M. (2001), 'The Renaissance of the Theatre of Memory', *Janus*, 8 (2001): 4–8.
Mccray, P. (2020), *Making Art Work: How Cold War Engineers and Artists Forged a New Creative Culture*, Cambridge, MA: The MIT Press.
McDermott, E. (2024), 'I am a Stream of Consciousness', *Flash Art* 347 (Summer 2024), Available online: https://flash---art.com/article/lu-yang/https://flash---art.com/article/lu-yang/ (accessed 10 May 2025).
McDonagh, P. (1998), 'Char Davies' Éphémère', *Immersence.com*, Available online: https://www.immersence.com/publications/1998/1998-PMcDonagh.html (accessed 19 September 2024).
McEwan, C. (2021), 'An Opera Set in Your Home – Opera Queensland', *Opera Queensland*, Available online: https://www.oq.com.au/an-opera-set-in-your-home/# (accessed 18 September 2024).
Mcquaid, M., A. New, R. Academy, Schirn Kunsthalle Frankfurt and Museu Serralves (2002), *Envisioning Architecture: Drawings from the Museum of Modern Art*, New York: Museum Of Modern Art.
Mees, A. (2021), 'Current, Rising', *Zoom Interview with Thea Brejzek*.
Melton, A. W. (1963), 'Implications of Short-Term Memory for a General Theory of Memory', *Journal of Verbal Learning and Verbal Behavior*, 2 (1): 1–21.
Merleau-Ponty, M. (2012), *Phenomenology of Perception*, from the French Original of 1945, trans. C. Smith, London and New York: Routledge.
Mindrup, M. (2022), 'On Models- Matthew Mindrup- (In)Exactitude and the Digital Twin: Limitations and Possibilities in Re-Presenting the Built Environment', *www.e-flux.com*, Available online: https://www.e-flux.com/architecture/on-models/520002/in-exactitude-and-the-digital-twin-limitations-and-possibilities-in-re-presenting-the-built-environment/ (accessed 19 September 2024).
Miya, Y. (2017), 'Amateurism', in P. Eckersall, E. Scheer and F. Shintaro (eds), *The Dumb Type Reader*, 127–44, Copenhagen: Museum Tusculanum Press.
Moe, J. R. (2013), 'PRINCE of FOOLS? A Close Reading of Antonin Artaud's Le Théâtre et Son Double', University of Oslo.
Molinari, A. (2024), 'Cover #9 Björk in Noir Kei Ninomiya S/S 2024 – Purple MAGAZINE', *Purple*, Available online: https://purple.fr/magazine/the-essence-of-fashion-issue-41-s-s-2024/cover-9-bjork-in-noir-kei-ninomiya-s-s-2024 (accessed 15 September 2024).
MoMA (2024a), 'Jean Tinguely. Fragment from Homage to New York. 1960 | MoMA', *The Museum of Modern Art*, Available online: https://www.moma.org/collection/works/81174 (accessed 19 September 2024).
MoMA (2024b), 'International Style | MoMA', *The Museum of Modern Art*, Available online: https://www.moma.org/collection/terms/international-style (accessed 19 September 2024).

MoMA (2024c), 'In the Galleries | MoMA', *The Museum of Modern Art*, Available online: https://www.moma.org/calendar/exhibitions (accessed 19 June 2024).

MoMA (2024d) *Art and Artists, Deren M. and Alexander Hammid, Meshes of the Afternoon 1943*. Publication excerpt from *MoMA Highlights: 375 Works from The Museum of Modern Art, New York*, 2019, New York: The Museum of Modern Art.

Monteith, J. (2024), 'The Project Gutenberg EBook of First Lessons in Geography, by James Monteith', *Gutenberg.org*, Available online: https://www.gutenberg.org/files/11722/11722-h/11722-h.htm (accessed 15 September 2024).

Morton, T. (2013), *Realist Magic: Objects, Ontology, Causality*, Ann Arbor, MI: Open Humanities Press.

Morton, T. (2015a), 'Timothy Morton: What If Art Were a Kind of Magic?', *Artreview.com*, Available online: https://artreview.com/november-2015-feature-timothy-morton-charisma-causality (accessed 15 September 2024).

Morton, T. (2015b), 'We Were Never Displaced', Available online: https://olafureliasson.net/read/we-have-never-been-displaced-by-timothy-morton-2015/ (accessed 19 September 2024).

Najmabadi, A. (2005), *Women with Mustaches and Men without Beards Gender and Sexual Anxieties of Iranian Modernity*, Berkeley, CA: University Of California Press.

'News- Acute Art' (2023), *Acute Art*, Available online: https://acuteart.com/news (accessed 15 September 2024).

Nin, A. (1966), *The Diary of Anaïs Nin: 1931–1934*, New York: Harvest.

Ochanji, S. (2019), 'Opera Queensland Partners with Google Creative Lab to Bring the Opera Home with AR and AI – Virtual Reality Times – Metaverse & VR', *Virtualrealitytimes.com*, Available online: https://virtualrealitytimes.com/2019/11/30/opera-queensland-partners-with-google-creative-lab-to-bring-the-opera-home-with-ar-and-ai/ (accessed 18 September 2024).

O'Connell, M. (2018), *To Be a Machine*, London: Granta Publishing.

O'Dwyer, N. (2021), *Digital Scenography*, London: Bloomsbury Publishing.

Oliver, B. (2020), 'The Royal Opera House Presents Current, Rising, the World's First Opera in Hyper Reality', *Rbo.org.uk*, Available online: https://www.rbo.org.uk/news/the-royal-opera-house-presentscurrent-rising-the-worlds-first-opera-in-hyperreality (accessed 18 September 2024).

Olof-Ors, M., Moderna Museet and Verlag Der Buchhandlung Walther König Köln (2015), *Olafur Eliasson Reality Machines*, London: Koenig Books.

'Oremus Bible Browser: Isaiah 42:6' (2021), *Oremus.org*, Available online: https://bible.oremus.org/?ql=514886395 (accessed 15 September 2024).

Ovid (2014), 'Metamorphoses: Translated into English Prose with the Latin Text and Order of Construction on the Same Page, and Critical, Historical, Geographical, and Classical Notes in English: Ovid, 43 B.C.-17 or 18 A.D: Free Download, Borrow, and Streaming: Internet Archive', *Internet Archive*, Available online: https://archive.org/details/metamorphosestra00oviduoft/page/n27/mode/2up (accessed 15 September 2024).

Pavis, P. (2012), 'Semiology after Semiology', *Theatralia*, 15 (2): 37–49.

Pérez-Milans, M. (2021), 'Futures, Imagined Cities and Emerging Markets: The Semiotic Production of Professional Selves', *Social Semiotics*, 31 (1): 1–22.

Perlson, H. (2022), '"I Felt the Lightning Right next to Me": Artist Lu Yang on How a Harrowing Flight Experience Led to a Breakthrough Digital Artwork', *Artnet News*, Available online: https://news.artnet.com/art-world/lu-yang-artist-2124984 (accessed 19 September 2024).
Pownall, A. (2019), 'Designers of Björk's Cornucopia Show "Ignored the Concert Rule Book"', *Dezeen*, Available online: https://www.dezeen.com/2019/12/13/bjork-cornucopia-chiara-stephenson-set-design (accessed 15 September 2024).
Puschmann, S. (2024), 'A Virtual Earth | EUMETSAT', *www.eumetsat.int*, Available online: https://www.eumetsat.int/features/virtual-earth (accessed 5 July 2024).
Qin, A. (2015), 'Q. And A.: Lu Yang on Art, "Uterus Man" and Living Life on the Web (Published 2015)', *New York Times*, 27 November.
'Rainbow Assembly • Artwork • Studio Olafur Eliasson' (2016), *Olafureliasson.net*, Available online: https://olafureliasson.net/artwork/rainbow-assembly-2016 (accessed 15 September 2024).
'Reconstituirea '68- Un Proiect de Teatru Digital La Teatrul Național Din Craiova-Teatrul National "Marin Sorescu" Din Craiova' (2023), *Teatrul National 'Marin Sorescu' din Craiova*, Available online: https://tncms.ro/en/reconstitution-68-a-digital-theatre-project-at-the-national-theatre-in-craiova-2/ (accessed 15 September 2024).
Richardson, K. (2016), 'Technological Animism: The Uncanny Personhood of Humanoid Machines', *Social Analysis*, 60 (1): 110–28.
Reigart, E. M. (2021), 'Has Ryoji Ikeda Captured "the Sound of Data and the Data of Sound"?', *NAB Amplify*, Available online: https://amplify.nabshow.com/articles/ryoji-ikeda-sound-of-data-data-of-sound (accessed 15 September 2024).
ROH (2024), 'Audience Labs', *Audience Labs*, Available online: https://www.audiencelabs.org/roh-immersive-opera-lab (accessed 19 September 2024).
'Romeo Castellucci / Uso umano di esseri umani'/ *Kunstenfestivaldesarts* 2015. https://vimeo.com/128971506 (accessed 19 September 2024).
Rosenfeld, P. (1920), *Musical Portraits*, New York: Harcourt, Brace and Howe.
Rovner, L. (2022), '"Anatomy of an Artist: Ryoji Ikeda"', *Nowness.com*, Available online: https://www.nowness.com/series/anatomy-of-an-artist/ryoji-ikeda (accessed 15 September 2024).
Roy, M. and A. Roy (2021), 'The Rise of Interdisciplinarity in Engineering Education in the Era of Industry 4.0: Implications for Management Practice', *IEEE Engineering Management Review*, 49 (3): 56–70.
Saarinen, E. (2011), 'Great Big Mirror Dome Osake Expo 1970', *Vimeo*, Zakros InterArts, Available online: https://vimeo.com/24850126 (accessed 18 June 2024).
Sal, T. (2019), 'Ramon Llull: From the Ars Magna to Artificial Intelligence', in A. Fidora and C. Serra (eds), *Ramon Llull: From the Ars Magna to Artificial Intelligence*, 25–37, Barcelona: Artificial Intelligence Research Institute, IIIA Consejo Superior de Investigaciones Científicas.
Sasaki, A. (2017), 'APICHATPONG WEERASETHAKUL—Fever Room | Features | Japan Foundation-WA Project', *Japan Foundation-WA Project*, Available online: https://asiawa.jpf.go.jp/en/culture/features/f-ah-tpam-apichatpong-weerasethakul (accessed 15 September 2024).
Sloterdijk, P. (2004), *Sphären. III: Schäume, Plurale Sphärologie*, Frankfurt a.M.: Suhrkamp Verlag.

Smith, D. (2009), 'Deleuze's Concept of the Virtual and the Critique of the Possible', *Journal of Philosophy: A Cross-Disciplinary Inquiry*, 4: 34–43.

Solis, R. (2012), 'Romeo Castellucci "Tout Doit Disparaître"', *Libération*, Available online: https://www.liberation.fr/theatre/2012/07/05/romeo-castellucci-tout-doit-disparaitre_831406 (accessed 15 September 2024).

Sozzani (2007), 'Superarchitettura', *Fondazione Sozzani*, Available online: https://fondazionesozzani.org/exhibitions/2007/04/superarchitettura/ (accessed 25 July 2024).

Sparacino, F. G.Davenport and A.Pentland (1999), *City of News: Cataloguing the World Wide Web through Virtual Architecture*, SIGGRAPH '99, Visual Proceedings, Emerging Technologies, Los Angeles, CA.

Spatial Music Forum (2021), 'Le Corbusier / Varèse / Xenakis: Philips Pavilion', *YouTube*, Available online: https://www.youtube.com/watch?v=P-a5UUiyyWY (accessed 1 July 2024).

Stachowiak, H. (1973), *Allgemeine Modelltheorie*, Vienna: Wien Springer .

Stauffer, M. T. (2020), 'Learning from No-Stop City: Archizoom's Utopia Revisited', in D. Donetti (ed.), *Architecture and Dystopia*, 102–29, New York: Actar D.

Stewart, S. (2021), *Ruins Lesson: Meaning and Material in Western Culture*, Chicago: University of Chicago Press.

Stryker, C. and E. Kavlakoglu (2024), 'What Is Artificial Intelligence (AI)?', *IBM*, Available online: https://www.ibm.com/topics/artificial-intelligence (accessed 19 September 2024).

Sugiyama, R. (2008), 'Dumb Type S/N 1/2', *YouTube*, Available online: https://www.youtube.com/watch?v=8fpw6EYOEig (accessed 15 September 2024).

'Surah Al-Jinn- 1-28' (n.d.), *Quran.com*, Available online: https://quran.com/al-jinn (accessed 19 September 2024).

Tate (2024), '6 Artists Who Use Technology in Their Work – List', *Tate*, Available online: https://www.tate.org.uk/art/art-terms/e/experiments-art-and-technology-eat/6-artists-who-use-technology-their-work (accessed 18 June 2024).

Taylor, C. (2002), 'Modern Social Imaginaries', *Public Culture*, 14 (1): 91–124.

The Powers of Ten (1977), IBM Pyramid Films.

'The Relightables: Volumetric Performance Capture of Humans with Realistic Relighting' (2019), *Github.io*, Available online: https://augmentedperception.github.io/therelightables/ (accessed 19 September 2024).

'The Testbed Design Toolkit – ACUTE' (2024), *Oamk.fi*, Available online: https://vanha.oamk.fi/acute/the-testbed-design-toolkit/ (accessed 15 September 2024).

'The Weather Project • Artwork • Studio Olafur Eliasson' (2022), *olafureliasson.net*, Available online: https://olafureliasson.net/artwork/the-weather-project-2003 (accessed 19 September 2024).

Thompson, J.B. (1982). 'Ideology and the social imaginary', *Theor Soc* 11: 659–81.

Thompson, E. (2010), *Mind in Life*, Cambridge, MA: Harvard University Press.

Thresholds (2024), German Pavilion, 60th International Art Exhibition La Biennale of Venezia, Stuttgart: Institut für Auslandsbeziehungen.

TSI (2024), 'About TSI', *MIT*, MIT, Available online: http://transmedia.mit.edu/about (accessed 15 September 2024).

Tymieniecka, A.-T. (2011), *Gardens and the Passion for the Infinite*, Dordrecht; London: International Society For Phenomenology, Fine Arts, And Aesthetics. Conference- Springer.

UNESCO (2021), 'UNESCO Science Report the Race against Time for Smarter Development (Executive Report)', 42, Paris: UNESCO.

Universität, T. (2019), 'Der Digitale Grimm', *Uni-trier.de*, Available online: http://dwb.uni-trier.de/de/ (accessed 19 August 2019).

Valle (2016), 'Pad Italia '70 OSAKA | My Site', *Studio Valle*, Available online: https://www.studiovalle.com/padiglione-italia-oasaka-1970 (accessed 2 September 2024).

Vasarainen, M., S. Paavola and L. Vetoshkina (2021), 'A Systematic Literature Review on Extended Reality: Virtual, Augmented and Mixed Reality in Working Life', *International Journal of Virtual Reality*, 21 (2): 1–28.

Vaziri, A. (2021), 'Björk to Bring Theatrical "Cornucopia" Show to San Francisco', Datebook, San Francisco Arts & Entertainment Guide, Available online: https://datebook.sfchronicle.com/music/bjork-to-bring-first-theatrical-show-to-san-francisco (accessed 12 May 2025).

Wallen, L. (2020), 'On the Reconstruction of Landscape', *Leonardo*, 53 (1): 92–3.

Wallenstein, S. O. and K. Yeong A (2019), 'Ontologies of the Virtual', *www.e-flux.com*, Available online: https://www.e-flux.com/architecture/are-friends-electric/289162/ontologies-of-the-virtual/(accessed 19 September 2024).

Wartofsky, M. W. (1979), M*odels: Representation and the Scientific Understanding*, Dordrecht; Boston: D. Reidel Pub. Co.

Weber, S. (2004), *Theatricality as Medium*, New York: Fordham University Press.

Weerasethakul, A. (2024), 'Apichatpong Weerasethakul – a Conversation with the Sun (VR) | Festival D'Automne', *Festival-automne.com*, Available online: https://www.festival-automne.com/en/edition-2024/apichatpong-weerasethakul-a-conversation-with-the-sun-vr (accessed 15 September 2024).

Weibel, P. (2017), 'Digital Innovation in Theatre', *ZKM*, Available online: https://zkm.de/en/event/2017/04/digital-innovation-in-theatre (accessed 15 September 2024).

Weibel, P. (2024), 'Founding Director Heinrich Klotz | ZKM', *ZKM.de*, Available online: https://zkm.de/en/about-us/history/founder-heinrich-klotz (accessed 23 June 2024).

Welsch, W. 'Virtual to Begin With?', (2024), Available online: https://www.helsinki.fi/assets/drupal/s3fs-public/migrated-generic-group-long-pages/files/154920-welsch.pdf (accessed 19 September 2024).

White, J. (2019), 'Starchitecture', in S. Chattopadhyay and J. White (eds), *The Routledge Companion to Critical Approaches to Contemporary Architecture*, 405–23, London: Routledge.

Wiens, B. E. (2014), *Intermediale Szenographie*, Paderborn: Brill Fink.

Wiens, B. E. (2019), *Contemporary Scenography*, London: Bloomsbury Publishing.

Williams, C. (2021), '"Where the Filmmaker Apichatpong Weerasethakul Goes, Few Can Follow"- Interview Magazine', *Interview Magazine*, Available online: https://www.interviewmagazine.com/film/where- (accessed 15 September 2024).

Wright, L. and S. Davidson (2020), 'How to Tell the Difference between a Model and a Digital Twin', *Advanced Modeling and Simulation in Engineering Sciences*, 7 (1). https://doi.org/10.1186/s40323-020-00147-4

'Wunderkammer • Artwork • Studio Olafur Eliasson' (2020), *Olafureliasson.net*, Available online: https://olafureliasson.net/artwork/wunderkammer-2020 (accessed 15 September 2024).
XRLab (2024), 'About', *XR Lab- UC Berkeley*, Available online: https://berkeleyxrlab.org/about/ (accessed 22 June 2024).
Yalcinkaya, G. (2022), 'Lu Yang', *Metalmagazine.eu*, Available online: https://metalmagazine.eu/en/post/interview/lu-yang (accessed 19 September 2024).
Yates, F. A. (1966), *The Art of Memory*, London: Routledge & Kegan Paul.
'Your View Matter • Artwork • Studio Olafur Eliasson' (2022), *Olafureliasson.net*, Available online: https://olafureliasson.net/artwork/your-view-matter-2022 (accessed 15 September 2024).
Zielinski, S. (2009), *Deep Time of the Media: Toward an Archaeology of Hearing and Seeing by Technical Means*, Cambridge, MA: MIT Press.
Zielinski, S. (2015), 'GLOBALE: Allah's Automata', *ZKM*, ZKM Karlsruhe, Available online: https://zkm.de/en/exhibition/2015/10/globale-allahs-automata (accessed 19 September 2024).
Zielinski, S. (2019), *Variations on Media Thinking*, Minneapolis: University Of Minnesota Press.
Zielinski, S., P. Weibel and Zentrum Für Kunst Und Medientechnologie Karlsruhe (2015), *Allah's Automata: Artifacts of the Arab-Islamic Renaissance (800–1200)*, Ostfildern: Hatje Cantz.
ZKM (2024a), 'Amazonas. Music Theatre in 3 Parts', *ZKM*, Available online: https://zkm.de/en/project/amazonas (accessed 15 September 2024).
ZKM (2024b), 'Renaissance 3.0', *ZKM*, Available online: https://zkm.de/en/exhibition/2023/03/renaissance-30 (accessed 7 September 2024).
ZKM (2024c), 'Agnes Hegedüs', *ZKM*, Available online: https://zkm.de/en/person/agnes-hegedus (accessed 19 September 2024).
Zurich (2024), 'Immersive Arts Space | ZHdK.ch', *ZHdK*, Available online: https://www.zhdk.ch/en/immersive-arts-space-10984 (accessed 15 September 2024).

Index

www.ingramcontent.com/pod-product-compliance
Ingram Content Group UK Ltd.
Pitfield, Milton Keynes, MK11 3LW, UK
UKHW020818290926
15470UKWH00003B/1231

9 781350 449800